LINCOLN CHRISTIAN UNIVERSIT

LANGUAGE AND LITERACY SERIES

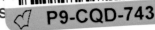

Dorothy S. Strickland, FOUNDING EDITOR
Celia Genishi and Donna E. Alvermann, SERIES EDITORS

ADVISORY BOARD: Richard Allington, Kathryn Au, Bernice Cullinan, Colette Daiute, Anne Haas Dyson, Carole Edelsky, Shirley Brice Heath, Connie Juel, Susan Lytle, Timothy Shanahan

For volumes in the NCRLL Collection (edited by JoBeth Allen and Donna E. Alvermann) and the Practitioners Bookshelf Series (edited by Celia Genishi and Donna E. Alvermann), please visit www.tcpress.com.

Educating Emergent Bilinguals

POLICIES, PROGRAMS, AND PRACTICES FOR ENGLISH LANGUAGE LEARNERS

Ofelia García
Jo Anne Kleifgen

FOREWORD BY

JIM CUMMINS

Teachers College
Columbia University
New York and London

Published by Teachers College Press, 1234 Amsterdam Avenue, New York, NY 10027

The authors wish to acknowledge that parts of this work were modified from "Equity Matters: From English Language Learners to Emergent Bilinguals," by Ofelia García, Jo Anne Kleifgen, and Lorraine Falchi, from *Research Review* #1. Copyright © 2008 by the Center for Education Equity. Used by permission.

Table 3.1 was adapted from *Educating English Learners: Language Diversity in the Classroom* (5th ed.) by James Crawford. Copyright © 2004 by James Crawford. Used by permission.

Library of Congress Cataloging-in-Publication Data

García, Ofelia.
  Educating emergent bilinguals : policies, programs, and practices for English language learners / Ofelia García, Jo Anne Kleifgen ; foreword by Jim Cummins.
    p. cm. — (Language and literacy series)
  Includes bibliographical references and index.
  ISBN 978-0-8077-5113-8 (pbk. : alk. paper) — ISBN 978-0-8077-5114-5 (hardcover : alk. paper) 1. Education, Bilingual. 2. English language—Study and teaching—Foreign speakers. 3. English language—Acquisition. 4. Second language acquisition. I. Kleifgen, Jo Anne. II. Title.
  LC3715.G37 2010
  370.117'5—dc22
                                                                                        2010022444

ISBN 978-0-8077-5113-8 (paperback)
ISBN 978-0-8077-5114-5 (hardcover)

Printed on acid-free paper

Manufactured in the United States of America

17 16 15 14 13 12 11 10   8 7 6 5 4 3 2 1

For all those bilingual students around the world who have come through our classroom doors and enriched our lives as educators.

Contents

Foreword

Perhaps once or twice a decade you read a book that is so lucid, convincing, and inspirational that you want to order copies for every teacher, administrator, and policymaker across the nation. Ofelia García and Jo Anne Kleifgen have written such a book. Their message is very simple: *If you want students to emerge from schooling after 12 years as intelligent, imaginative, and linguistically talented, then treat them as intelligent, imaginative, and linguistically talented from the first day they arrive in school.*

Woven throughout the pages of *Educating Emergent Bilinguals* is the reminder to educators and policymakers that effective schooling has much more to do with the quality of human relationships orchestrated between teachers and students than with the simple transmission of content. These relationships are obviously influenced by the conditions within which educators work—the curricula they are mandated to teach, the standardized tests that often operate as a proxy curriculum, the language(s) and varieties thereof that are considered legitimate within the ideological space of schooling. Yet, despite the myriad constraints within which educators (including administrators) operate, there are always degrees of freedom that permit and require them to make choices on a continuing basis.

Thus individual educators are never powerless; they always exercise agency, understood as the power to act. While they rarely have complete freedom, educators do have choices in the way they structure the interactions in their classrooms. They determine for themselves the social and educational goals they want to achieve with their students. There are always options with respect to educators' orientation to students' language and culture in the forms of parent and community participation they encourage and in the ways they implement pedagogy and assessment.

The choices we make in the classroom are infused with images: images of our students as we perceive them now and in the future; images of our own identities as educators. To what extent are we communicating to the students in our classrooms an image of themselves as: Capable of becoming bilingual and biliterate? Capable of higher-order thinking and intellectual accomplishments? Capable of creative and imaginative thinking? Capable of creating literature and art? Capable of generating new knowledge? Capable of thinking about and finding solutions to social issues?

As García and Kleifgen point out, when students see themselves (and know that their teachers see them) as *emergent bilinguals* rather than as *English language learners* (or some other label that defines students by what they lack), they are much more likely to take pride in their linguistic abilities and talents than if they are defined in deficit terms. Similarly, when students are given opportunities to engage in critical inquiry with their peers aimed at *generating knowledge*, they are likely to adopt what Patrick Manyak (2004) has called *identities of competence*. These identities of competence propel students into active engagement with literacy and learning.

Unfortunately, far too few low-income students in North American classrooms are given opportunities to engage in cognitively powerful and identity-affirming learning experiences in comparison to their higher-income peers. The No Child Left Behind legislation institutionalized high-stakes standardized testing as the simultaneous gauge of student learning and teacher effectiveness, thereby reinforcing the pedagogical divide between schools serving economically privileged communities and those serving the impoverished and dispossessed. Frequently, the dispossession continues within the school as emergent bilingual students are further stripped of their home language and culture. Defined by their limited English skills and their low standardized test scores, emergent bilingual students struggle, often unsuccessfully, to escape from the externally imposed identity cocoon within which they find themselves.

One of the most powerful messages woven into this book is that, as educators, we do have the power to push back against myopic and irresponsible policies that ignore the research evidence in relation to bilingual students' academic development. When we articulate our choices, individually and collectively, we will find ways of connecting academic content with our students' prior knowledge; we will identify ways of enabling students to engage in higher-order thinking through the translanguaging instructional strategies outlined in this book; we will explore how technological tools can be used creatively by students to generate knowledge; and we will infuse a sense of pride and affirmation of identity into the projects that our students undertake. In this process of articulating and acting on our choices, our own identities as educators will expand. The classroom interactions we orchestrate with our students will shape, rather than simply reflect, our society.

—Jim Cummins

Acknowledgments

The preparation of this book could never have happened without the help of Heidi Batchelder, a graduate student at Teachers College, Columbia University, who prepared the chapters for submission and collected missing references. We are very grateful to her for her attention to detail and for keeping up with our tight schedule. We also thank Meg Lemke from TC Press for her encouragement and support. Several doctoral students, who read and commented on different parts of the book, also deserve our heartfelt thanks—Laura Ascenzi-Moreno, Nelson Flores, Kristin Gorsky, Laura Kaplan, Briana Ronan, Karen Velasquez, and Heather Woodley—as does our colleague Ricardo Otheguy.

This book is an extension of a report we originally wrote for the Campaign for Educational Equity at Teachers College, Columbia University. We thank the campaign; its executive director, Michael Rebell; its deputy director, Amy Stuart Wells; and its policy director, Jessica Wolff, for giving us the opportunity to write the report and for offering excellent suggestions. In particular, we owe a special debt of gratitude to our coauthor in the report, Lori Falchi, who supported our original thinking and writing as the report took shape.

A number of people contributed significantly in the preparation of the review we conducted for the Campaign for Educational Equity. We are most grateful to Jim Crawford for his willingness to share his expertise from the very beginning and for continuing to support us as we updated the information for this book. Besides Crawford, a number of people read and commented on parts of the original review—Jamal Abedi, Bruce Baker, Luis Moll, and Terry Wiley. And others provided us with essential pieces of information—Lyle Bachman, Tim Boals, Ellen Forte, Margot Gottlieb, Luis Reyes, Roger Rice, Pedro Ruiz, and Mariano Viñas.

Gracias to all for contributing to the efforts to improve the education and lives of language minority students in the United States.

CHAPTER 1

Introduction

This introductory chapter:

- Discusses the labels used for students who are not yet proficient in English and advocates for using the term *emergent bilingual*
- Gives reasons why thinking of students as emergent bilinguals can result in a more equitable education for these students
- Provides an overview of the book

There is no equality of treatment merely by providing students with the same facilities, textbooks, teachers, and curriculum; for students who do not understand English are effectively foreclosed from any meaningful education.

—*Lau v. Nichols*, 1974

EMERGENT BILINGUALS

One of the most misunderstood issues in pre-K–12 education today is how to educate students who are not yet proficient in English. English language learners (ELLs) or limited English proficient students (LEPs) (as they are most often known throughout the U.S. school system) are those students who speak a language other than English and are acquiring English in school. Although local and state education agencies may use different definitions, the federal government defines them as students who are between the ages of 3 and 21 and are "enrolled in elementary or secondary education, often born outside the United States or speaking a language other than English in their homes, and not having sufficient mastery of English to meet state standards and excel in an English-language classroom" (as cited in Batalova, 2006). No Child Left Behind (NCLB) further describes them as students "whose difficulties in speaking, reading, writing, or understanding the English language may be sufficient to deny the individual the ability to meet the State's proficient level of achievement on State assessments" (2001, sec. 9101(37)).[1]

According to data from the National Assessment of Educational Progress (NAEP), only a very small percentage of these students in the eighth grade are proficient in reading (4%)[2] and in math (6%) (Batalova, Fix, & Murray, 2007). These students trail English proficient students by 39 points in reading and 36 points in math on a 500-point scale nationally (Batalova et al., 2007). They are also not graduating in proportionately the same numbers as those who are English proficient. A survey by Hopstock and Stephenson (2003a) revealed that 50% of students who are not yet proficient in English fail their graduation tests, compared with 24% of all English proficient students. Goldenberg (2008, p. 11) summarizes the gap in academic achievement of ELL in the NAEP, saying: "The gaps between ELLs and non-ELLs are 3 to 18 points larger than the gaps between students who are and are not eligible for free or reduced-price lunch."

Referring to these students as ELLs, as many school district officials and educators presently do, or as LEPs, as federal legislators did in the NCLB, signals the omission of an idea that is critical to the discussion of equity in the teaching of these children.

ELLs are in fact *emergent bilinguals*. That is, through school and through acquiring English, these children become *bilingual*, able to continue to function in their home language[3] as well as in English—their new language and that of school. When officials and educators ignore the bilingualism that these students can and must develop through schooling in the United States, they perpetuate inequities in the education of these children. That is, they discount the home languages and cultural understandings of these children and assume that their educational needs are the same as a monolingual child.

There is little agreement about what name best describes these students. In addition to the terms *limited English proficient* (LEP) and *English language learners* (ELL), students who are acquiring English in the nation's schools are also variously referred to in the literature as *English learners* (EL), *culturally and linguistically diverse* (CLD), children with *English language communication barriers* (ELCB), *English as a second language* (ESL), *language minority* (LM), and *bilingual*. Each label has different connotations and problems. Federal documents, agencies, and legislation (including NCLB) all use the term *limited English proficient* (LEP), but critics of this label argue that it focuses on the students' limitations rather than their potential. Students labeled as *culturally and linguistically diverse* and *language minority* can also include culturally and linguistically different minority students who are already bilingual, although the *language minority* label may better offer a legal basis for rights and accommodations. *English as a second language* refers to a subject and not to people; furthermore, this label does not encompass students for whom English is a third or fourth language. Thus, the term *English language learners* seems to be the label that is most inclusive, while still acknowledging the fact that all these students are learning English in school.[4] At the same time, this label has its own limitations—it devalues other languages and puts the English language in a sole position of legitimacy. It also focuses solely on the academic English-development part of the students' education.

We prefer, and use here, the term *emergent bilinguals* because it has become obvious to us that much educational inequity is derived from obliterating the fact that a meaningful education will turn these English language learners not only into English proficient students, but more significantly, also into bilingual students and adults. At times, however, we occasionally use the designations preferred by federal regulators and state policy makers—*limited English proficient* for the federal government and *English language learner* for states and other policy entities.

WHAT'S IN A NAME?

Thinking of these students as emergent bilinguals has important consequences not only for the children, but also for teachers, policy makers, parents, the language education profession, and U.S. society at large (García, 2009b).[5] The use of this term allows us to imagine a different scenario. Instead of being regarded as "limited" in some way or as mere "learners of English," as the terms *limited English proficient* and *English language learner* suggest, students are seen instead for their potential to become bilingual, and bilingualism begins to be recognized as a cognitive, social, and educational resource, which is consistent with research on this topic (see Chapter 4).

For teachers, working with these students as emergent bilinguals means holding higher expectations of these children and not simply remediating their limitations and focusing on their English learning. In recognizing the emergent bilingualism of students, educators are building on their strengths—their home languages and cultural practices. They are thereby making positive use of the students' home languages and bilingual practices, rather than suppressing or ignoring them.

In naming these students emergent bilinguals, policy makers begin to require a more rigorous curriculum and more challenging instructional material. Insisting that these children are emergent bilinguals, whose language development exists within a bilingual continuum, also calls for development of bilingual pedagogy for *all* children, not just those whom we are calling here emergent bilinguals. Educational policy makers thus become more patient, understanding that, as research has clearly shown, it takes children 5 to 7 years to develop complex academic skills in an additional language[6] (see Chapter 4). And it becomes easier to demand that assessment be valid for *all* bilinguals. A more flexible norm can then be adopted that includes all children along a bilingual continuum, instead of insisting on a rigid monolingual standard (see Chapter 8).

Giving these students a name that does not focus on their limitations means that the language practices in the home are seen as an educational resource. Instead of assigning blame to parents and communities for language practices that may not include English, the school begins to see the parents and communities as the experts in the children's language and cultural practices, which are the basis of all learning. As such, parents and community members are able to participate in the education of their children from a position of strength and not from a position of limitations.

The language education profession is presently compartmentalized in ways that do not support the holistic education of students. Focusing on the students' emergent bilingualism facilitates the integration of four aspects of language education that presently exist separately in the United States—the teaching of English to speakers of other languages (TESOL), bilingual education (BE), the teaching of the heritage language (HL) when available, and the teaching of a foreign language (FL). As a result, teaching begins to be centered on the students rather than on the profession. By focusing on the students' emergent bilingualism and making bilingualism the norm, the field of language education is able to move to the center of educational endeavors for *all* U.S. children.

Finally, we know that bilingual practices in the 21st century are more important than ever, and thus important for U.S. society. It is clear that having flexible language practices, being able to use language bilingually in ways described by García as *translanguaging* (2009a; see Chapter 4), can become an important resource for all in the future. The language resources of the United States have never been greater. Despite our insistence in identifying ourselves as a monolingual nation-state, the United States has perhaps the world's most complex bilingual practices. The benefits of harnessing these linguistic resources are more evident than ever for our country.

THIS BOOK

The central idea that we present in this book is that there is a growing dissonance between *research* on the education of emergent bilinguals, *policy* enacted to educate them, and the *practices* we observe in schools. Whereas research has consistently shown the importance of building on the children's home language as they develop English language proficiency whether in ESL instruction or bilingual education,[7] U.S. educational policy has often ignored these research findings. In fact, in recent years in the United States— as we explain below—educational policy toward emergent bilinguals has become more rigid, embodying a view of these children solely from a deficit perspective and increasingly demanding that English alone be used in their education. Educators, who are closer to the ground than many policy makers and researchers, are often caught in the middle of the dissonance between research, policy, and the immediacy of having to educate emergent bilinguals. As a result, educators' teaching practices sometimes suffer as they strive to find alternative ways of acting on top-down national and local educational policies that are plainly misguided for the education of these children. This frequent incompatibility between research, policy, and teaching practice is responsible for much of the miseducation of emergent bilinguals in the United States and their failure in school.

Chapter 2 in this book characterizes the students who are the subject of our attention: emergent bilinguals. We raise questions regarding the ways in which demographic data on these students are collected at state and national levels and used to identify them for educational purposes. Chapter 3 briefly reviews the policies and practices targeted toward this group of students that have developed over the past 40 years. We then turn to the main part of the book, which includes theoretical constructs, empirical evidence, and practices related to what we think are the four most important aspects of the education of emergent bilinguals—language considerations (Chapters 4 and 5), curriculum and pedagogy issues (Chapter 6), participation of parents and communities (Chapter 7), and assessment (Chapter 8). The objective of these chapters is to expose the educational inequities that directly affect the education of emergent bilinguals and to provide descriptions of alternative practices that alleviate these injustices. Most of the inequities stem from policy makers' and often educators' lack of understanding of bilingualism itself. Thus, we will discuss how misunderstandings of the nature of bilingualism have educational equity consequences for some of the most disadvantaged children. Finally, Chapter 9 offers recommendations for advocates, policy makers, educators, and researchers.

STUDY QUESTIONS

1. Discuss some of the issues that emerge from the different labels that have been assigned to students who are developing English proficiency in schools.
2. What are the reasons why García and Kleifgen name these students *emergent bilinguals*? Discuss the effect of this term on students, teachers, policy makers, parents, the language education profession, and U.S. society.
3. What is the central idea in this book?

CHAPTER 2

Who Are the Emergent Bilinguals?

This chapter provides background information on emergent bilinguals. Specifically, the chapter asks the following key questions:

- How do we know who they are?
- How many are there?
- How are they classified?
- How are they reclassified?
- Where do they live and go to school?
- What languages do they speak?
- What are their demographic characteristics with respect to:

    Ethnicity/race and socioeconomic status?
    Age distribution and access to pre-K programs?
    Nativity?

- Do they live in homes where English is spoken?
- How are their language skills in English and their home languages?
- Who are the Latinos?
- What do all emergent bilinguals have in common?

In this chapter, we address the issue of how students are identified, counted, and designated as limited English proficient or English language learners, as we elucidate their ethnolinguistic and social characteristics. But this chapter brings to the forefront the mismatch between the policies that dictates how data on their characteristics are collected and considered, the reality of the students themselves, and what research tells us about emergent bilingual students. In other words, the dissonance between the research and the policies and practices enacted, which is the central theme of this book, begins with descriptive data that has shaped the way these students are defined. As we consider the data, we will point out these contradictions.

HOW DO WE KNOW WHO THEY ARE?

Part of the difficulty in understanding the characteristics of emergent bilinguals results from the great inconsistency in the data that purport to describe them.[1] The federal government and most states do a poor job of collecting primary data on students needing services. Under NCLB (2001), each state reports its limited English proficiency (LEP) enrollments to the U.S. Department of Education's Office of English Language Acquisition, Language Enhancement, and Academic Achievement for Limited English Proficient Students (OELA). These data are then shared with the National Clearinghouse of English Language Acquisition (NCELA), which puts together summary reports (J. Crawford, personal communication, March 27, 2007). However, state definitions of English language learners vary. Reporting is inconsistent from state to state, and data collection procedures have changed over the years to adapt to new requirements. NCLB gives states the flexibility to define the subgroup LEP in one of two ways: 1) only those students who receive direct daily services or 2) students receiving services as well as those only being monitored based on their achievement on academic assessments. State reports also do not reveal the mechanisms by which districts have identified their LEP population or the characteristics of their students.

NCLB requires the U.S. Department of Education (DOE) to select the more accurate method of counting limited English proficient students: it may use either the state reports or the U.S. Census Bureau data on the population aged 5 to 17 who speak a language other than English (LOTE) at home and who speak English less than very well to distribute funds for the education of these students. Because of what are considered inconsistencies in state reporting, the DOE uses data from the census known as the American Community Survey (ACS, 2004) to make these federal funding allocations. The ACS figures, however, are based on estimates of the population. There are huge discrepancies between the numbers counted by the Census Bureau and those reported by states. As a result, many states are either unfairly penalized or rewarded in federal funding for the education of these students (Crawford, 2007). Capps et al. (2005) estimate that there is a 12% disparity between state-reported estimates of LEP students and census-based estimates. For example, in 2000, California reported 400,000 more English learners than were accounted for in the census. Seventeen other states, mostly located in the West, also showed large discrepancies (Capps et al., 2005).

The use of census data has another drawback. While state-reported data are based on the number of emergent bilinguals receiving services, the census numbers are not. Therefore, the use of census data gives districts no financial incentive to identify and serve these students. In the past, such funding formulas have led to widespread discrimination, as they did, for example, in Texas before the 1950s (Crawford, 1993).

In summary, both sets of data that the federal government has relied on for counts of these students—the census data and state-reported data—are limited as shown in summary form in Table 2.1.

TABLE 2.1. Comparison of U.S. Census and State-Report Data on English Language Learners

U.S. Census Data	State-Reported Data
Uniform procedures with standardized definition	Procedures and definition vary by state, district, and even school
Evaluates only ability to speak English	Evaluates ability to read and write, as well as speak and understand English
Reported by parents or whoever fills out the census form	Reported by teachers and professionals
ACS uses sampling strategies that can omit selected populations	Based on direct counts and more complete
Counts are taken for more general purposes, and are not directly tied to funding opportunities	Counts can be overstated because funding allocations depend on the numbers
Finds fewer students	Finds more students
Includes all 5 to 17 year olds, whether in school or not	Includes all students enrolled in grades K-12, regardless of age

HOW MANY ARE THERE?

However inaccurately we count these students, we do know that the numbers of emergent bilinguals are rapidly increasing. Between the 1989–90 and the 2004–05 school years, the number of students classified as limited English proficient by the U.S. Department of Education (USDOE) in Grades pre-K through 12 in the nation's schools more than doubled—from 2,030,451 to 5,119,561 (National Clearinghouse for English Language Acquisition [NCELA], 2006). According to NCELA (2006) this represents approximately 10.5% of the total public school student enrollment by 2005. The 2004–05 number, however, includes enrollments in U.S. protectorates outside the 50 states, including Puerto Rico and American Samoa.[2] If we consider the LEP population in the 50 U.S. states only, we see it has grown from 1,927,828 in 1989–90 (USDOE, 1991, p. 10) to 4,459,603 in 2004–05[3] to 4,985,120 in 2005–06 (OELA, 2008) meaning that this domestic emergent bilingual population has also more than doubled in the past 25 years.

Comparing census data from 1980 to 2000, Capps et al. (2005) found that the percentage of all pre-K to fifth-grade students who are emergent bilinguals increased from 4.7% to 7.4%, whereas the percentage of students in Grades 6 to 12 who are emergent bilinguals increased from 3.1 to 5.5%. Zehler et al. (2003) claim that overall, from 1991–92 to 2001–02 there has been a 72% increase in the emergent bilingual population.

No matter which data we use, it is also clear that nationally, the emergent bilingual population is growing much more rapidly than the English-speaking student population. Between 1995 and 2005, the enrollment of emergent bilinguals in public schools nationwide grew by 56%, whereas the entire student population grew by only 2.6% (Batalova et al., 2007). In fact, the emergent bilingual student population seems to be increasing at nearly seven times the rate of total student enrollment (NCELA, 2006). This means that, over time, the proportion of all students who are emergent bilinguals is growing as well. In 2001–02, an estimated 45,283 of the approximately 91,000 regular K–12 public schools nationwide—approximately one half of all schools—had English language learners (Zehler et al., 2003).

It appears that the rapid growth rate of emergent bilinguals is consistent despite the different methods of identifying these students. For instance, as we noted above, the census provides information about the number of students between the ages of 5 and 17 who speak a different language (LOTE) at home. The census also asks families who report that they speak a LOTE at home to indicate whether they spoke English "very well," "well," "not well," or "not at all." Children who live in households where English is spoken less than "very well" are considered limited English proficient according to the federal government. Table 2.2 indicates the number of 5- to 17-year-olds who speak LOTEs at home, as well as the number who live in families that speak English less than "very well."

According to the census, there were 2.8 million 5- to 17-year-old ELLs in 2004; in contrast, the states reported a total of 5.1 million ELLs in that

TABLE 2.2. Speakers of LOTEs and Emergent Bilinguals (EBs), 5 to 17 Years Old

	TOTAL 5–17 yrs*	Speakers of LOTEs*	Total speakers of LOTEs (%)	EBs	Total who are EBs (%)**	Speakers of LOTEs who are identified as EBs (%)
1979	44.7	3.8	8.5	1.3	2.8	34.2
1989	42.3	5.2	12.3	1.8	4.3	34.6
1995	47.5	6.7	14.1	2.4	5.2	35.8
2000	52.5	9.5	18.1	2.9	5.5	30.5
2004	52.9	9.9	18.8	2.8	5.3	27.9
2008	53.0	10.9	20.5	2.7	5.1	24.7

* Numbers are given in the millions.

**This number represents the number of English language learners in the entire population.

Sources: U.S. Census Bureau (1979), U.S. Census Bureau (1989), U.S. Census Bureau (1995), U.S. Census Bureau (2005); National Center for Education Statistics, 2006; U.S. Census Bureau (2008).

age group for the same year. This discrepancy has to do with some of the factors that we identified above, namely that the Census Bureau relies on self-reports and asks only whether or not students speak English and not whether they can read and write English. In addition, the census under-counts the undocumented population, which the states are more likely to count, since they collect their data through the schools themselves. It is also important to note that, although the percentage of youths who speak LOTEs at home is increasing (8.5% in 1979 compared with 20.5% in 2008), the percentage of LOTE speakers who are also emergent bilinguals seems to be decreasing (34.2% in 1979 compared with 24.7% in 2008). That is, there is a rise in the number of *bilingual* students who are both speakers of other languages and also fluent speakers of English.

In fact, the increase in the number of bilingual students who are profi-cient in both English and another home language in the U.S. school popula-tion has been immense. For example, from 1979 to 2004, there was only an 18% increase in the total number of school-age children. However, in the same period, according to census data, the number of school children who spoke a LOTE at home increased by 161% from 3.8 million to 9.9 million. As Table 2.3 shows, from 1979 to 2008, while the number of LOTE children who spoke English less than very well increased by 107%, the number who were proficient in English and thus fluent bilinguals increased by 220%. Certainly the growth of bilingual English proficient students is greater than that of emergent bilinguals, making bilingualism a central educational topic for teachers of *all* U.S. students, not just those who are learning English.

Although the growing bilingual student population is an important resource in a globalized world, we focus in this book *only* on emergent bilinguals because they are the students who need the most support from the educational system. We warn, however, that as García recently noted (2006a), English language learners are "only the tail of the elephant"—2.7 million of the 10.9 million bilingual and multilingual U.S. children. By fo-cusing only on the elephant's tail, or those students who are not proficient

TABLE 2.3. Speakers of LOTEs, Both Emergent Bilinguals and Fluent Bilinguals, 5 to 17 Years Old

LOTE Speakers*	1979	2008	Growth (%)
Emergent Bilinguals	1.3	2.7	107
Fluent Bilinguals	2.5	8.1	220
TOTAL SPEAKERS of LOTEs	3.8	10.9	187

*Numbers are given in the millions.

Source: U.S. Census Bureau (1979); U.S. Census Bureau (2008).

in English, we lose sight of the incredible potential of the millions of bilingual and multilingual children in this country who can become national resources in building a peaceful coexistence within a global society and helping the United States remain economically viable in an increasingly multilingual world.

HOW ARE THEY DESIGNATED?

The question of how many emergent bilinguals there are has to do with the ways in which they are designated/redesignated as a specific category of student. Unlike other categories of identification such as ethnicity, race, and gender, the limited English proficient/English language learner classification is fluid, that is, children move in and out of being classified according to their progress toward becoming bilingual and the kind of policy that the state or district mandates.

Since the 1970s, based on federal civil rights legislation and federal case law, states have had to identify English language learners and ensure that their schools serve them (Linquanti, 2001). Most states use the federal definition of an LEP student as "one who has sufficient difficulty in the use of English to prevent that individual from learning successfully in classrooms in which the language of instruction is English" (Kindler, 2002, p. 9). But, as we noted above, the criteria used to identify emergent bilinguals vary by state and sometimes even by districts within a state (Zehler et al., 2003).

Usually, when students first register for a new school, they are given a *home language survey*, which contains questions about the language used at home with caregivers, siblings, and peers. About 80% of all state educational authorities make use of home language surveys (Kindler, 2002). Students are then referred for language proficiency assessment, although the assessment instruments vary greatly, with some school districts using language proficiency tests, others achievement tests, and others locally designed tests (see Chapter 8). Most assessments measure the students' English listening comprehension and speaking skills for kindergarten through second grade, and reading and writing skills for third grade and up.

Most tests are commercially produced and are either norm referenced, which means each exam is measured against scores of other students, or criterion and standards based, meaning each exam is compared to a specific body of knowledge (see Center for Equity and Excellence in Education Test Database, 2005; Vialpando & Linse, 2005). The most commonly used language proficiency tests are the Language Assessment Scales (LAS), the IDEA Language Proficiency Tests (IPT), and the Woodcock-Muñoz Language Survey (Woodcock-Muñoz) (Kindler, 2002). Among the most commonly used achievement tests are the Stanford Achievement Test (SAT 9) and the Iowa

Tests of Basic Skills (ITBS) (Kindler, 2002). Some states and school districts have designed their own tests.[4] Recently, a consortium of states known as World-Class Instructional Design and Assessment (WIDA) have developed an English language proficiency test for English language learners, along with standards, known as ACCESS for ELLs.[5]

For the most part, school districts designate English language learners through a combination of information on the home language survey, previous school achievement, informal teacher assessments, and formal assessment. Sometimes, if the school district is able to provide support or instructional services in the students' home language, they are also assessed in their home language.

HOW ARE THEY RECLASSIFIED?

Equally important to the question of how students are classified as emergent bilinguals in U.S. public schools is the question of how these students get reclassified as English proficient. Even though *language proficiency* should be the focus for designation as English language learner, *academic achievement in English* is key to their reclassification as English proficient students (Linquanti, 2001).[6] This means that the assessment used for the reclassification process should be much more complex, since multiple dimensions of communicative competence have to be considered (Bachman, 1990; Canale & Swain, 1980). In other words, to be reclassified, students must be able to not only comprehend and communicate effectively, but also do cognitively demanding work in the content areas at the appropriate grade level in English (Bachman, 2002; Linquanti, 2001).

And yet the most common measure used by educators to reclassify a student as English proficient is an oral proficiency test in English. They also use assessments of classroom performance, literacy tests in English, achievement tests in English, and teacher judgment (Zehler et al., 2003). The tests most commonly used for reclassification are the same as those used for identification—LAS, IPT, and Woodcock-Muñoz—along with the SAT 9, the CTB Terra Nova, and various state achievement tests (Kindler, 2002). As we will see in Chapter 8, these tests have little validity and reliability for use with emergent bilinguals (Figueroa & Hernández, 2000). And because not all tests focus on the same skill domains, children reclassified in one state would not be reclassified in another.

Reclassification rates are lowest in kindergarten through second grade as well as in Grade 9, when many emergent bilinguals first enter the school system. This is because developing academic literacy in an additional language takes time (see Chapter 4). Third- and fifth-grade emergent bilinguals get reclassified at the highest rates (Kindler, 2002). We suspect that this is because of a combination of two factors. On the one hand, many of these children have been in school since kindergarten, having had 4 to 6 years of exposure to academic English. On the other hand, unlike assessment at the middle school or high school level, the kind of English language academic competency required in elementary school and measured by elementary-level assessments is easier to achieve.

WHERE DO THEY LIVE AND GO TO SCHOOL?

Emergent bilinguals are heavily concentrated in six states. Table 2.4 gives the states with the largest number of public school emergent bilinguals in 2005–6 and their numbers.[7]

Emergent bilingual students make up a large proportion of the total K–12 population in several other states, even if their actual numbers are not as large as in these six states. For instance, emergent bilingual students make up 25% of the total school enrollment of California, with New Mexico running a close second with 24%. After California and New Mexico, the greatest *proportion* of emergent bilingual school students is in Nevada (18%), Texas (16%), Alaska (15%), and Arizona (15%) (NCELA, 2006).[8]

However, the greatest *growth* in the number of students who are developing English proficiency in the past decade has been clearly outside all these states, in a new set of southeastern and midwestern states, including South Carolina and Indiana, as is shown in Table 2.5.

According to Kindler (2002), in the school year 1999–2000 alone, the greatest growth in ELL students in public schools was in South Carolina

TABLE 2.4. Number of Public School Emergent Bilinguals, 2005–06

State	Number
California	1,571,463
Texas	640,749
New York	234,578
Florida	233,165
Illinois	204,803
Arizona	152,962

Source: OELA (2008).

TABLE 2.5. Percentage Growth by State of Emergent
Bilinguals, 1994–95 to 2004–05

State	Growth (%)
South Carolina	714
Kentucky	417
Indiana	408
North Carolina	372
Tennessee	370

Source: NCELA (2006).

(82%), followed by Minnesota (67%). And, in the 2001–02 school year, the greatest growth was in Georgia, followed by Montana and then Mississippi (Kindler, 2002). Beyond these, the states of Kansas, New Hampshire, and Oregon have also had significant increases in their emergent bilingual school population (Kindler, 2002; Crawford, 2002).

Despite the spread of emergent bilinguals across the United States, they seem to be concentrated in fewer than half the school districts in the country. In fact, nearly 70% of all emergent bilingual students are enrolled in 10% of elementary schools (De Cohen, Deterding, & Chu Clewell, 2005). Further, school districts that have more than 5,000 emergent bilinguals enroll 54% of all English language learners in Grades K to 12 (Zehler et al., 2003). This points to the high degree of racial and ethnic segregation in the United States and the importance of the concept of *ethnic enclave* (Portes & Rumbaut, 1996), not only for immigrant ethnic subsistence and economic well-being, but also for educating the children of recent immigrants who are ethnic minorities. This concentration is also reflected in the fact that approximately 91% of all emergent bilinguals live in metropolitan areas (Fix & Passel, 2003), and nearly 70% of emergent bilinguals in elementary grades enroll, on average, in just 10% of the public schools in a metropolitan area (De Cohen et al., 2005).

As a result, the majority of emergent bilinguals—53%—go to schools where more than 30% of their peers are also emergent bilinguals (Fix & Passel, 2003). In contrast, 57% of students who are proficient bilinguals attend schools where less than 1% of all students are emergent bilinguals (Van Hook & Fix, 2000). Thus, emergent bilinguals often attend schools with others who, like them, speak little English. Furthermore, the level of linguistic segregation in the United States seems to be rising (Fix & Passel, 2003).

WHAT LANGUAGES DO THEY SPEAK?

While emergent bilinguals in the United States are speakers of more than 460 languages[9] (Kindler, 2002), Spanish remains by far the most frequently spoken language. Estimates of the percentage of emergent bilinguals who speak Spanish at home range from 75%—according to census data—to 80% (see Kindler, 2002; Office of English Language Acquisition, 2008; Zehler et al., 2003).[10] After Spanish, the most common language is Vietnamese, which is spoken at home by 2.4% of emergent bilinguals. Vietnamese speakers are followed by those who speak Hmong (1.8%), Korean (1.2%), Arabic (1.2%), Haitian Creole (1.1%), and Cantonese (1.0%) (Zehler et al., 2003). These six most represented language groups among emergent bilinguals are followed by speakers of Tagalog, Russian, Navajo, and Khmer (Cambodian) (see Hopstock & Stephenson, 2003b; Zehler et al., 2003). Speakers of Armenian, Chuukese, French, Hindi, Japanese, Lao, Mandarin, Marshallese, Polish, Portuguese, Punjabi, Serbo-Croatian, and Urdu each constitute more than 10,000 emergent bilinguals, although their percentage of the whole is very small (Kindler, 2002). Table 2.6 provides the distribution of the categories of languages other than English spoken by students in the United States, including those who are emergent bilinguals, according to calculations from the U.S. Census Bureau[11] (2007). It shows the number of LOTE speakers and the number of emergent bilinguals who speak each language or language category. The table also shows the percentage

TABLE 2.6. Numbers and Percentages of Languages Spoken by Emergent Bilinguals (EBs), 5 to 17 Years Old

Language Group	Number of LOTE Speakers	Number of EBs	All EBs (%)	EBs Within Language Group (%)
Spanish	7,781,437	2,007,637	75	26
Indo-European*	1,512,901	276,110	10	18
Asian Pacific**	1,153,290	314,267	11	27
Other	43,872	82,070	4	19
TOTAL	10,871,500	2,680,084		

Source: American Community Survey, 2006-2008, 3-year estimates.

* Indo-European is not synonymous with European languages. In this survey, the category Indo-European includes all languages of this linguistic family except English and Spanish. French, German, Hindi, and Persian are all classified as Indo-European. Hungarian, on the other hand, is lumped into the "Other Language" category.

** Asian Pacific languages include languages indigenous to Asia and Pacific Island areas that are not also Indo-European languages. Chinese, Japanese, Telugu, and Hawaiian are all in this category.

of emergent bilinguals speaking a given language compared with other languages. In addition, the last column of the table shows the percentage within each language group who are emergent bilinguals.

Despite the fact that the greatest proportion of emergent bilinguals are Spanish speaking (75%), it is important to point out that, proportionately, Latinos do *not* report being less proficient in English than those who speak Asian languages. In fact the proportion of speakers of Asian/Pacific languages who are emergent bilinguals is greater than that of the Spanish-speaking group.

WHAT ARE THEIR DEMOGRAPHIC CHARACTERISTICS?

Ethnicity/Race and Socioeconomic Status

According to Hopstock and Stephenson (2003b), in 2001–2 Latinos accounted for 77% of the emergent bilingual population. After Latinos, most emergent bilinguals were Asians and Pacific Islanders (13%). They were followed by non-Latino Whites (6%), non-Latino Blacks (3%), and finally, American Indian and Alaskan Natives (2%).[12]

Meanwhile, the most reliable figures related to the socioeconomic status of emergent bilinguals also come from the study by Zehler et al. (2003). Using the figures for the number of free or reduced-price lunch among emergent bilinguals, the authors suggest that more than 75% of English language learners are poor. The authors also note that the real poverty rate could be significantly higher, since not all poor families provide the needed documentation to receive subsidized school lunches.

As we noted above, De Cohen et al. (2005) report that nearly 70% of emergent bilinguals are enrolled in only 10% of the schools within a given metropolitan area. These schools are predominantly located in urban poor areas. Their study shows that 72% of children in what they call "high-LEP schools" (schools with a high proportion of limited English proficient students) qualify for free or reduced-price school lunches compared with about 40% in "low-LEP schools."[13] We also know that, of the 11 million immigrant children and children of immigrants in the 2000 census, about half were in low-income families (Capps et al. 2005). Forty percent of the principals at the high-LEP schools in the study by De Cohen et al. (2005) cite poverty as a serious issue and identify student health problems as "serious" or "moderate." August, Hakuta, and Pompa (1994) report that the majority of emergent bilinguals live in high-poverty school districts and indicate the need to ameliorate funding inequities among districts. According to a congressionally mandated evaluation of Title I, the federal compensatory education program targeted at poor students, a large percentage of emergent bilinguals attend schools where between 75 to 100% of the students live in poverty (Moss & Puma, 1995).

The educational level of family members is equally difficult to ascertain. Zehler et al. (2003) estimate that 54% of the parents of emergent bilinguals have not completed 8 years of schooling. Of the 16- to 24-year-olds, 42% of emergent bilinguals had dropped out of school, compared with 10.5% of those who spoke English (August & Hakuta, 1998, p. 9). Furthermore, as we noted above, emergent bilinguals frequently attend poor urban schools, which are often crowded and segregated and where teachers lack adequate credentials.

In describing schools that have high concentrations of English language learners, De Cohen et al. (2005) summarize:

> High-LEP schools are more likely to be located in urban areas and therefore have many characteristics associated with urban schools: larger enrollments; larger class sizes; greater racial and ethnic diversity; higher incidences of student poverty, student health problems, tardiness, absenteeism, and lack of preparation; greater difficulty filling teaching vacancies; greater reliance on unqualified teachers; and lower levels of parent involvement. (p. 19)

Age Distribution and Access to Pre-K Programs

In the United States, the growing bilingual student population is younger than the average K–12 student and thus clustered more in elementary schools. In 2000–01, for instance, 44% of all emergent bilingual students were in pre-K through Grade 3, and only 19% were enrolled at the high school level (Kindler, 2002).[14] In 2001–02, 70% of the emergent bilingual students were in Grades pre-K to 5, pointing to the potential of having bilingual citizens if we truly cultivated this aspect of these young students' education (Hopstock & Stephenson, 2003b). Moving higher up in the grades, we find that the number of emergent bilinguals decreases; in the same period, over a quarter (26%) were in Grades 4 through 8, and only 14% were in secondary school (Grades 9 through 12) (Hopstock & Stephenson, 2003b).

Finally, although the population numbers for high school emergent bilingual have been significantly lower than those in elementary school, between 2000 and 2001 there was a rapid increase of 73% in the high school population, much higher than the 44% increase at the elementary level (Kindler, 2002). It is, then, also important to be mindful of the growing number of adolescent English language learners in our high schools.

At the same time that the total number of emergent bilinguals is increasing and more of these students are moving up in the educational pipeline, we see evidence that relatively few of these students are getting the kind of head start they need prior to entering school in kindergarten. In 2000–01, only

1.5% of all emergent bilinguals were in prekindergarten (Kindler, 2002). In 2005, 43% of Latino children 3 to 5 years old attended some form of center-based childcare or preschool compared with 59% of White children and 66% of Black children (Education Law Center, 2007; National Task Force on Early Childhood Education for Hispanics, 2007). These numbers suggest that there is a dearth of public preschool programs available for these students and, thus, a disturbing gap exists in the early childhood education of most emergent bilinguals. If these children are not enrolled in educational programs in their prekindergarten years, and there is no funding available for the types of bilingual preschool programs that are most effective at helping the youngest ones to achieve an equitable education, then it is no wonder that we often see these same students falling behind as they grow older (García & González, 2006; Kindler, 2002).

Nativity

Despite popular perceptions, emergent bilinguals are by no means all foreign born. Although there is some disagreement about the exact percentage of English language learners who were born in the United States, estimates range from just under 50% to nearly 66% and even higher for younger students. Several studies confirm this fact: According to Zehler et al. (2003), 47% of emergent bilinguals were born in the United States. These include children of immigrant or refugee parents, but also children who are Native Americans and Alaskan Natives, as well as U.S. Latinos. Capps et al. (2005) also report a higher proportion of native-born English language learners. Fix and Passel (2003) put the figure of U.S.-born English language learners at nearly two thirds of all emergent bilinguals. Finally, NCELA (2008) reports that 74% of emergent bilinguals in 2005–06 were born in the United States and started U.S. schools in kindergarten and first grade.

Another way to examine the U.S.-born versus foreign-born distinction is to look at the percentage of first-generation immigrant students in K–12 public schools who are emergent bilinguals, which is 36% (Fix & Passel, 2003). But this number declines substantially with the second-generation U.S.-born children of immigrants, only 16% of whom are classified as English language learners (Fix & Passel, 2003).

Meanwhile, foreign-born students vary in terms of the number of years they have been in the United States, and this, in turn, affects the percentage of them who are classified as emergent bilinguals. In fact, it turns out that nearly a third of emergent bilinguals, or 31%, have been in the United States for less than a year. Another 41% have been in the United States for 1 to 4 years, and 28% have been in the United States for 5 years or more (Zehler et al., 2003). Thus, almost three fourths of all foreign-born English language learners have been in the United States for less than 5 years. However, it is also important to note the presence of those students called *long-term ELLs* in the population—that is, the 28% of students who have lived in the United States longer than 5 years and who have still not mastered academic English (Menken & Kleyn, 2009). They represent more than one in four of all emergent bilinguals.

It is also difficult to determine the number of foreign-born emergent bilinguals who are immigrants, refugees, or children of temporary sojourners[15] or migrant workers.[16] Overall, the foreign-born population in the United States is made up of naturalized citizens (31%), documented immigrants (31%), undocumented immigrants (26%), refugees (7%), and documented nonimmigrants (5%) (Fix & Passel, 2003). But we know little of how these figures relate to children enrolled in schools. We also know that approximately 1.6 to 1.8 million children under the age of 18 are undocumented immigrants, and an additional 3 million are native-born U.S. citizens who have undocumented parents (Jensen, 2001; Passel, Capps, & Fix, 2004; Suárez-Orozco, Suárez-Orozco, & Todovara, 2008). But again, we do not know how many of these students are emergent bilinguals.

Whichever estimate we accept, it is important to understand that the education of emergent bilinguals is not just about immigrant or refugee education alone. Their education is, in fact, an educational issue that concerns a large proportion of native-born U.S. citizens, who represent anywhere from half to nearly two thirds of all emergent bilinguals.

DO THEY LIVE IN HOMES WHERE ENGLISH IS SPOKEN?

An important issue that overlaps with immigrant status and how many generations their families have lived in the United States is the issue of whether or not emergent bilinguals live in homes where English is spoken. We know that approximately 80% of them live in families where the parents are themselves learners of English (Fix & Passel, 2003). The census data accounts for households in which everyone over 14 speaks English "less than very well." It refers to these households as "linguistically isolated."[17] In 2000, six out of seven emergent bilinguals in Grades K through 5 and two out of three in Grades 6 through 12 lived in households where no one over the age of 14 spoke English very well.

WHAT ARE THEIR LANGUAGE SKILLS IN ENGLISH AND THEIR HOME LANGUAGES?

Approximately 85% of emergent bilinguals are able to communicate orally in English; however, they have difficulty using English for academic functions in classrooms (Zehler et al., 2003). This is important to keep in mind as we debate whether census figures are reliable in identifying this population. The Census Bureau only asks families about spoken English, but it is the ability to complete academic work in English, and especially academic English literacy, that is the issue for educational attainment. Therefore, relying on Census Bureau figures may be misleading and may underestimate the population of students who are emergent bilinguals.

Estimates of the percentage of emergent bilinguals who have academic proficiency in their home language also vary, but school coordinators think that approximately 39% of these students nationwide have lower levels of literacy in their home language compared with what might be expected of students going to school in a country where the language is dominant (Zehler et al., 2003). This fact should be of vital importance to those who coordinate and plan for the education of these students because it turns out that the benefits of what is known as "linguistic transfer" of literacy skills from one language to another will not be completely enjoyed by emergent bilinguals who are not literate in their home language.

Linked to the issue of emergent bilinguals' proficiency in their home language is the fact that many have experienced interrupted schooling because of poverty, migratory patterns, or war in their country of origin (see Klein & Martohardjono, 2009). Most of these students with interrupted schooling histories are in secondary school. In fact, approximately 11% of emergent bilinguals in middle schools and high schools have missed more than 2 years of schooling since the age of 6 (Zehler et al., 2003).

WHO ARE THE LATINOS?

Spanish is the language spoken by the vast majority (approximately three fourths) of those classified as English language learners. In the case of Spanish-speaking emergent bilinguals, 50% have been born in the United States. Among the foreign born, 60% of Spanish-speaking emergent bilinguals were born in Mexico, followed in number by children from South America (14%), Central America (10%), Puerto Rico (8%) and Cuba (2%) (Zehler et al., 2003).[18] Among first-generation Mexican K–12 students, almost half, or 47%, are emergent bilinguals (Fix & Passel, 2003). Spanish is the dominant language of English learners in all but eight states, where other languages dominate: Montana (Blackfoot), Maine (French), Minnesota (Hmong), Hawaii (Ilocano), South Dakota (Lakota), North Dakota (Native American languages), Vermont (Serbo-Croatian), and Alaska (Yupik) (see Kindler, 2002).

Latino immigrant children account for more than half (58%) of all immigrant youth in the United States, with more of these students in the upper grades than in the lower. Although we do not have good data on undocumented immigrants, we know that many Latino immigrant children are undocumented or are children of undocumented immigrants (Capps et al., 2005). One of the most alarming facts about Latino emergent bilinguals is that more than 59% end up dropping out of high school; in comparison, only 15% of Latino students who are proficient bilinguals drop out of high school (Fry, 2003). When thinking about the education of emergent bilinguals, Latinos must be the focus of attention, for they constitute the overwhelming proportion, approximately 75%, of this important population.

EDUCATING EMERGENT BILINGUALS: KNOWING WHO THEY ARE

Despite the differences among emergent bilinguals that we have identified in this chapter, a few generalizations can be gleaned from our prior discussion:

- most are Spanish-speaking Latinos (75-80%)
- most are poor (75%)
- most live in households in which no one over the age of 14 is a speaker of English (80%)
- most live in urban areas and attend underresourced schools (91%)
- half live with parents who have not completed 8 years of schooling
- half were born in the United States
- although approximately half are in elementary schools, the greatest increase is in high school–aged students
- there is a dearth of early childhood programs for them, and few are enrolled in school prior to kindergarten.

It is with these general characteristics in mind that we turn to reviewing the educational policies that surround the education of emergent bilingual students.

STUDY QUESTIONS

1. Identify some of the contradictions in counting, classifying, and reclassifying emergent bilinguals. What are some of the inconsistencies in the data and how do numbers from the census differ from those of state reports?
2. Describe the population of emergent bilinguals in the United States. What do all of these students have in common?

3. Find out who the emergent bilinguals are in your school district. How many are there? What are their characteristics and what languages do they speak? How have they been counted? What method is used to identify, classify, and reclassify them?
4. Why is bilingualism a vital topic in the education of all children in the United States?

CHAPTER 3

Programs and Policies for Educating Emergent Bilinguals

This chapter, which considers programs and policies for educating emergent bilinguals:[1]

- Describes types of educational programs for emergent bilinguals
- Reviews educational policies for these students in historical context, including:

> Antecedents
> Title VII: The Bilingual Education Act
> Legal precedents
> The 1990s
> No Child Left Behind
> The present

Since the 1960s, language minority students have been the focus of many U.S. educational policy decisions—at the national, state, and local levels and in all three branches of government. As a result of top-down educational policies and negotiations with teachers and communities, different types of educational programs for these students exist in the United States. In what follows, we first review the educational programs that are available for emergent bilinguals. We then turn to a brief historical section in which we discuss the evolution of policies to educate these students. It will become evident that federal bilingual education policy has changed over the past 4 decades from taking into account the students' home languages and being flexible about educational approaches to being far more rigid in emphasizing English-only for English language learners. As we also illustrate, the high-stakes standardized testing movement spurred by NCLB (2001) has had much to do with this new rigidity. These developments mean that there is even greater dissonance between the policy and the research today than there has been in the past.

EDUCATIONAL PROGRAMS FOR EMERGENT BILINGUALS

Within the U.S. public educational system, there are different educational programs used in schools for working with emergent bilinguals. These programs range from those that expect students to learn English by simply exposing them to it and treating them like all other students, to those specifically designed to help English learners gain proficiency while at the same time supporting their academic development in all areas through the use of their home language when possible. The educational policies we discuss in this chapter are critical to the form of instruction that emergent bilinguals receive because they either support or provide incentives for schools or districts to make choices about which program to adopt.

As we will see, the tendency over the past decade has been for policy makers, and the public more generally through initiative processes, to provide more English-only programs and move away from programs that use children's home languages, despite abundant research evidence to the contrary. Before we discuss this shift and its connection to the research literature, we briefly describe these different programs/approaches below.

In the first approach, known as *submersion* or *sink or swim* programs, schools and educators provide emergent bilinguals with exactly the same educational services provided to monolingual English speakers. That is, they neither provide alternative educational services nor use the students' home languages to teach them. These submersion programs were prevalent before 1970 and still are used in many parts of the country, especially in light of recent English-only initiatives in certain states.

A second category of educational program, called *pullout ESL* programs, provides some support for students in special sessions outside the regular classroom. There are also *push-in ESL* programs, in which an ESL teacher works collaboratively with the content-area teacher to support emergent bilingual students in the class. Still another category of programs, called *structured English immersion*, also known as *sheltered English* or *content-based ESL*, provide emergent bilinguals with a great deal of pedagogical support and scaffolding in a program tailored specifically for these students. Usually only English is used for instruction in these programs.

Moving toward the other end of the pedagogical spectrum, there are also programs that take a more bilingual approach, in that they do use the children's home languages for a variety of reasons—sometimes to support their transition to English and other times to develop their bilingualism and biliteracy. The first such program is known as *transitional bilingual education*, also known as *early exit bilingual education*. This transitional program uses students' home languages to some degree, but the focus is on students' acquiring English as quickly as possible and in exiting them into "mainstream" English-only classrooms. Another program, known as *developmental bilingual education* (also known as *late exit bilingual education*), supports both students' acquisition of English and the development of their home language. *Two-way bilingual education* (also called *two-way dual language, two-way immersion, dual immersion,* or *dual language*)[2] pushes the developmental model even further by supporting fluency in both English and the home language within classrooms that enroll two types of emergent bilinguals—LOTE speakers and English speakers. In these language-integrated settings students learn both languages together, and all students emerge bilingual from these programs.

While all the programs described above develop from institutional structures that are either monolingual or bilingual as policy makers and teachers enact different language ideologies and policies, a different educational program for emergent bilinguals is gaining in popularity. Unlike the programs above where language practices in classrooms are rigidly controlled in top-down fashion by the school and classroom teacher, in these programs that we call *dynamic bi/plurilingual programs* emergent bilinguals themselves use hybrid language practices that are necessary as English is developing. That is, students are given agency to negotiate their linguistic repertoires, although the teaching, at least in a teacher-led discussion, is in English. This dynamic bi/plurilingual type of program has become prevalent in some newcomer programs, especially at the high school level (García, Flores, & Chu, in press).

To help differentiate these programs in terms of their pedagogy, philosophy, and focus, we display all programs below in Table 3.1, which is adapted and expanded from Crawford (2004, p. 42).

As this table illustrates, the student's home language can be used in a wide variety of ways within educational programs. For instance, the home language can either be used *fully*, as in the case of bilingual education programs in which it is a medium of instruction, or *partially*, as when teachers teach only in English but use the student's home language to ensure comprehension, to scaffold instruction in English, or to encourage bilingual practices as students work on collaborative projects. For example, the Sheltered Instruction, Observation Protocol (SIOP) model, a widely used program of sheltered English instruction for English language learners, supports the use of the student's home language to clarify concepts and assignments in situations in which the teacher knows the home language well enough to do this. The developers of this approach state:

> We believe that clarification of key concepts in students' L1 [first language] by a bilingual instructional aide, peer, or through the use of materials written in the students' L1 provides an important support for the academic learning of those students who are not yet fully proficient in English. (Echevarria, Vogt, & Short, 2004, p. 107)

Likewise, the model of international small high schools in New York City encourages their multilingual students[3] to work collaboratively on projects using their home languages to make sense of the material, but then having English become the academic and social lingua franca. As students develop

Table 3.1. Types of Educational Programs for Emergent Bilinguals

PROGRAM	LANGUAGE USED IN INSTRUCTION	COMPONENTS	DURATION	GOALS
Submersion (Sink or Swim)	100% English	Mainstream education; no special help with English; no qualified teachers	Throughout K–12 schooling	Linguistic assimilation (shift to English only)
ESL Pull Out (Submersion plus ESL)	90–100% in English; may include some home language support or not	Mainstream education; students pulled out for 30–45 minutes of ESL daily. Teachers certified in ESL	As needed	Linguistic assimilation; remedial English
ESL Push-in	90–100% in English; may include some home language support or not	Mainstream education; ESL teacher works alongside the subject teacher as needed. Teachers certified in ESL	As needed	Linguistic assimilation; remedial education within mainstream classroom
Structured Immersion (Sheltered English, Content-based ESL)	90–100% English; may include some home language support or not	Subject matter instruction at students' level of English; students grouped for instruction. Teachers certified in ESL, should have some training in immersion	1–3 years	Linguistic assimilation; exit to mainstream education
Transitional Bilingual Education (Early-Exit Bilingual Education)	90–50% home language initially; gradually decreasing to 10% or less	Initial literacy usually in home language; some subject instruction in home language; ESL and subject matter instruction at students' level of English; sheltered English subject instruction. Teachers certified in bilingual education	1–3 years; students exit as they become proficient in English	Linguistic assimilation; English acquisition without falling behind academically

Type	Language Allocation	Instructional Features	Duration	Goals
Developmental Bilingual Education (Late-Exit Bilingual Education)	90% home language initially; gradually decreasing to 50% or less by grade 4 / or / 50/50 from beginning	Initial literacy in home language; some subject instruction in home language; ESL initially and subject matter instruction at students' level of English; teachers certified in bilingual education	5–6 years	Bilingualism and biliteracy; academic achievement in English
Two-Way Bilingual Education (Two-Way Dual Language, Two-Way Immersion, Dual Immersion, Dual Language)	90/10 model: 90% language other than English, 10% English; 50/50 model: parity of both languages	English speakers and speakers of a LOTE taught literacy and subjects in both languages; peer tutoring. Teachers certified in bilingual education	5–6 years, usually at the elementary level	Bilingualism and biliteracy, academic achievement in English
Dynamic Bi/Plurilingual Education	English and students' home languages in dynamic relationship; students are the locus of control for language used; peer-teaching.	Teacher-led activities in English, coupled with collaborative project-based student learning using home and hybrid language practices	4–6 years, usually at the high school level and especially for newcomers	Bilingualism, academic achievement in English

English language proficiency, however, students' many home languages do not merely support English language acquisition, but also facilitate content-rich, interdisciplinary, and collaborative work.

Whether to use the child's home language as a medium of instruction or simply a scaffolding mechanism often has to do with the number of students of the same language group in the same school and classroom, as well as the ability to find teachers who speak that language. Clearly, in classrooms where emergent bilinguals are from different language backgrounds, traditionally structured bilingual education is not feasible, although some form of bilingualism in education always is, as demonstrated by the work of the international high schools in New York (Sylvan & Romero, 2002) and other schools (García et al., in press). But, as we noted in Chapter 2, fully 75% to 79% of all emergent bilinguals in the United States speak Spanish as their home language. Therefore, the recent shift toward increased efforts to teach Spanish-speaking emergent bilinguals exclusively in English, thereby omitting the use of Spanish to scaffold their learning, has to do with lack of knowledge in the public sphere about the nature of bilingualism and its benefits, as well as cultural politics that have little to do with what is educationally sound for the students.

Further, Table 3.1 shows that the length of different programs for emergent bilinguals varies considerably. These variations need to be considered in light of the research evidence that we introduce in Chapter 4, which suggests that to become academically proficient takes considerably longer than to become conversant in a second language. But first, we demonstrate how American language-in-education policy changes have placed limits on these program options.

A BRIEF HISTORY OF EDUCATIONAL POLICIES FOR EMERGENT BILINGUALS

The Antecedents

In 1954, the U.S. Supreme Court ruled in *Brown v. Board of Education* that segregated schools were unconstitutional, ushering in a new era in the struggle for civil rights in the United States. Congress passed The Civil Rights Act in 1964, prohibiting discrimination on the basis of race, color, or national origin. According to Title VI of this act: "No person in the United States shall, on the ground of race, color, or national origin, be excluded from participation in, be denied the benefits of, or be subjected to discrimination under any program or activity receiving Federal financial assistance" (Civil Rights Act, sec. 601, 1964). Thus, Title VI of the 1964 Civil Rights Act has played an important role in protecting the educational rights of language minority students in the United States (see Crawford, 2004; E. Garcia, 2005; and, especially, NCELA, 2006).

Title VII: The Bilingual Education Act

In 1968, the U.S. Congress reauthorized the landmark Elementary and Secondary Education Act, the largest and most influential federal education policy to date. Title VII of that act, known as the Bilingual Education Act, established a federal goal of assisting limited-English speaking students in the quick acquisition of English. Only poor students were eligible to participate at first. Title VII of the Elementary and Secondary Education Act did *not* require bilingual education. Rather, Congress put aside money for school districts enrolling large numbers of language minority students that chose to start up bilingual education programs or create instructional material. The Bilingual Education Act (1968) stated:

> In recognition of the special educational needs of the large numbers of children of limited English-speaking ability in the United States, Congress hereby declares it to be the policy of the United States to provide financial assistance to local educational agencies to develop and carry out new and imaginative elementary and secondary school programs designed to meet these special educational needs. (sec. 702)

When the Bilingual Education Act was first reauthorized in 1974, eligibility for educational services was expanded to include students of any socioeconomic status who had limited English-speaking ability (LESA). The subsequent 1978 reauthorization of the Bilingual Education Act expanded eligibility for services even further, from students with limited English-speaking abilities to students with more general limited English proficiency. The central focus during this time of expanding access was to ensure that students who needed bilingual education services were receiving them; the pedagogy was left to the educators.

By the 1980s, the tone and focus of the Bilingual Education Act had begun to shift support to English-only programs. In 1984, for the first time, reauthorization of the act also provided funding for programs that used only English in educating English language learners, although only 4% of the funding was reserved for these kinds of programs. The 1988 reauthorization of the act further expanded the funding for programs in which only English was used to 25% of programs funded. Additionally, it imposed a 3-year limit on participation in transitional bilingual education programs, meaning that schools had 3 years to move English language learners to fluency in English.

In 1994, Congress reauthorized the provisions of the Elementary and Secondary Education Act, including bilingual education, this time under the new Improving America's Schools Act. Although this reauthorization gave increased attention to two-way bilingual education programs, the cap for English-only programs that was previously legislated was lifted.

These legislative efforts, beginning with the Elementary and Secondary Education Act in 1968, were the first to focus on the need to provide language minority students with adequate education. Shortly after the 1968 legislation, a legal battle was waged for the rights of these students. It is on this legal front that the battles for an equitable education for emergent bilinguals have been fought most mightily, as we illustrate below.

Legal Precedents

In the early 1970s, a group of Chinese American parents brought a judicial case against the San Francisco School Board on the grounds that their children were not receiving an equitable education. The case was brought under the Equal Protection Clause of the Fourteenth Amendment of the Constitution and Title VI of the Civil Rights Act. The case, known as *Lau v. Nichols*, was eventually appealed up to the U.S. Supreme Court and was decided on the basis of Title VI. Justice William O. Douglas wrote the majority opinion of the Court, stating,

> There is no equality of treatment merely by providing students with the same facilities, textbooks, teachers and curriculum; for students who do not understand English are effectively foreclosed from any meaningful education. . . . Basic skills are at the very core of what these public schools teach. Imposition of a requirement that, before a child can effectively participate in the educational program, he must already have acquired those basic skills is to make a mockery of public education. (Lau v. Nichols, 1974)

The Court offered no specific method of instruction as a remedy. It merely instructed school districts to take "affirmative steps" to address the educational inequities for these students and called upon the federal Office of Civil Rights, as part of the executive branch, to guide school districts. The Office of Civil Rights set up a task force that eventually promulgated guidelines for schools and districts. These guidelines eventually became known as the Lau Remedies (1975). In addition to instructing school districts on how to identify and serve emergent bilinguals, the guidelines specifically required bilingual education at the elementary level and permitted the introduction of English as a second language (ESL) programs at the secondary level. Emphasizing that ESL was a necessary component of bilingual education, the guidelines continued, "since an ESL program does not consider the affective nor cognitive development of the students . . . an ESL program [by itself] is not appropriate" (as cited in Crawford, 2004, p. 113). In 1979, the Lau Remedies were rewritten for release as regulations. However, they were never published as official regulations and, in 1981, were withdrawn by Terrel Bell, the incoming secretary of education under Ronald Reagan, who called them "harsh, inflexible, burdensome, unworkable, and incredibly costly" (as cited in Crawford, 2004, p. 120).

Yet even as the executive branch of the federal government was signaling retrenchment from meaningful bilingual education, limited English speakers continued to have the courts on their side. In another important federal court case, *Castañeda v. Pickard* (1981), the U.S. Court of Appeals for the Fifth Circuit upheld the *Lau* precedent that schools must take "appropriate action" to educate language minority students. Such action must be based on sound educational theory, produce results, and provide adequate resources, including qualified teachers and appropriate materials, equipment, and facilities. The case, however, did not mandate a specific program such as bilingual education or ESL.

English-Only Education at the Polls: The 1990s

In the 1990s, the use of the child's home language to support learning came under political siege. The most effective attack against bilingual education was spearheaded by a Silicon Valley software millionaire by the name of Ron Unz. Proposition 227 (California Proposition 227, 1998, sec. 300-311), also known as the English for the Children Initiative, was presented to California voters in June 1998. The proposition prohibits the use of home language instruction in teaching emergent bilinguals and mandates the use of sheltered English immersion programs, where English only is used for a period not to exceed a year, after which students are put into mainstream classrooms. Parents may request waivers from the 1-year immersion program if the child is over 10 years of age, has special needs, or is fluent in English. Sixty-one percent of Californians voted in favor of this proposition, and as a result, it became state law. The Latino vote was two to one against the initiative.

This proposition passed despite the fact that only a minority of English learners were in bilingual programs in California in the first place. Twenty-five percent of California students are not proficient in English. Yet prior to the passage of Proposition 227, only 30% of these emergent bilinguals were in bilingual programs, with the rest in either ESL programs or regular classrooms (Crawford, 2003). Of the 30% of California English learners in bilingual programs, less than 20% were being taught by a credentialed bilingual teacher (Cummins, 2003). A year after the passage of Proposition 227, California students in bilingual programs declined from 29.1% to 11.7% (Crawford, 2007). Four years after Proposition 227 was passed, only 590,289 English learners (just 42% of the total in 1998) had become proficient in English, and annual redesignation rates, that is, the rates of

English acquisition, remained unchanged. According to the California Department of Education (2006a, 2006b), as of 2006, only 7.6% of English learners in California were in transitional bilingual education classrooms because their parents signed waivers requesting these programs. In 1998, 30% of emergent bilinguals had been in such transitional programs. In 1998, 29% of teachers were providing transitional bilingual education to English learners in California. By 2006, just 4.4% of California teachers were providing such programs (California Department of Education 2006a, 2006b; Rumberger & Gándara, 2000). And more than a half million children who participated in these programs have now been "mainstreamed," meaning that they receive no special help, even though they continue to be classified as English learners (Crawford, 2003). Curiously enough, two-way bilingual education programs are now growing in California.

A year after California's Proposition 227 was passed, Unz took his English-only efforts to Arizona. In 2000, 63% of Arizona voters approved Proposition 203, which banned bilingual education in that state. Arizona's statute is even more restrictive than California's. It limits school services for emergent bilinguals to a 1-year English-only structured immersion program that includes ESL and content-based instruction exclusively in English. Waivers are almost impossible to obtain.

In 2002, a similar proposition in Massachusetts (Question 2, G.L. c. 71A) to replace transitional bilingual education with structured English immersion programs for emergent bilinguals passed with 68% of the votes. However, in that same year, Amendment 31 to Colorado's state constitution, which would have made bilingual education illegal, was defeated with 56% of voters opposing it. In an interesting twist, the campaign to defeat the amendment focused on the threat to parental choice and local control of schools, as well as the possibility that non-English-speaking children would be in the same classrooms as other children. A TV commercial warned that the Unz-backed English-only amendment would "force children who can barely speak English into regular classrooms, creating chaos and disrupting learning" (Crawford, 2004, p. 330).

No Child Left Behind

The final stage to date of this policy movement away from bilingual education and toward an English-only approach is the most recent reauthorization of the Elementary and Secondary Education Act, in 2001, when that act became the more ambitious No Child Left Behind Act (NCLB) and was signed into law by President George W. Bush in January 2002. NCLB (2001) mandates that, by the 2013–14 school year, all students must achieve the level of "proficient" in state assessment systems. To accomplish this lofty goal, NCLB requires schools and districts to ensure that all their students meet specific state-developed annual targets of Adequate Yearly Progress (AYP) for reading, math, and science. In addition, it is not enough for schools or districts to meet their goals in terms of their aggregate data; they must also show that all subgroups of students—meaning students of different races, ethnicities, income groups, gender, and so on—are meeting AYP goals.[4] One of the subgroups that NCLB requires schools and districts to keep track of is limited English proficient students. As a result, local school officials must pay attention to their emergent bilinguals' yearly progress in terms of academic and English proficiency (Capps et al., 2005).

NCLB (2001) requires assessments for emergent bilinguals under Title I (funding for poor students)[5] and Title III (funding for limited English proficient students) of the act. Under Title I, which, as we noted, is the federal compensatory education program for poor students, if English language learners or other subgroups do not meet their test score targets, their schools can be designated "schools in need of improvement" (SINIs) and can be subject to interventions. Parents whose children attend SINIs are permitted to send their children to a non-SINI school in the same school district, provided that the school has room and the services each student requires. Students in schools designated as SINIs are offered supplemental services such as after-school tutoring programs. If the schools continue to fail to meet the performance targets, they must eventually be restructured or closed (NCLB, 2001).

Meanwhile, the purpose of Title III of NCLB, now titled Language Instruction for Limited English Proficient and Immigrant Students (the old Title VII under the Elementary and Secondary Education Act) is "to help ensure that children who are limited English proficient, including immigrant children and youth, attain English proficiency" (NCLB, 2001, sec. 3102). Schools must evaluate the English proficiency of all students enrolling for the first time in school, establish criteria to determine eligibility for programs and services for emergent bilinguals, and implement appropriate educational services. States must hold Title III subgrantees accountable for meeting three annual measurable achievement objectives (AMAOs) for their emergent bilinguals:

1. make annual progress;
2. attain English proficiency; and,
3. meet AYP requirements set by their states and measured by state standardized tests.

If the local educational agency (i.e., the school district) fails to meet the AMAOs for emergent bilinguals for 2 consecutive years, it must develop an improvement plan. But if it fails to meet the AMAOs for 4 consecutive years, the school district will have to develop a corrective plan. At this point, the state may intervene and may withdraw Title III funds. This places unprecedented demands on the states for improvements in both the academic proficiency and the English proficiency of emergent bilinguals.

One way in which states have tried to cope with the unreasonable demands of large-scale assessments of English language learners under NCLB (2001) is by defining how the subgroup must be counted, thereby avoiding having a subgroup. For example, Kossan (2004) has shown that, in 2004, an Arizona decision that schools must have at least 30 emergent bilinguals in the same grade in order to have a limited English proficient subgroup made it possible for 680 schools to avoid keeping separate data on emergent bilinguals and risk a failing subgroup designation. Texas has set its minimum group size at 50 students, representing 10% of all students (Castro, 2005). As Wright (2006) has pointed out, this is a mechanism by which schools without large emergent bilingual populations can avoid having data on their limited English proficient subgroup scrutinized.

As to the use of "reclassification" data—data on how many emergent bilinguals become fluent bilinguals and English proficient and are transitioned into mainstream classes—to gauge the success of states in educating English language learners, many believe these data to be meaningless. Usually states calculate reclassification by putting the number of reclassified students in the numerator and the rest of all English language learners in the denominator (Linquanti, 2001). However, this is futile, as it only creates a moving target. The remaining emergent bilinguals include the students who have just arrived and therefore cannot possibly be ready for reclassification. So, depending upon where particular schools' emergent bilinguals are in their trajectory towards exit—the number of years of schooling in the United States, their preparation in English prior to arriving in the United States, their literacy in their home language—their reclassification rates may appear to be higher or lower.

Under a 2004 NCLB regulation, states are permitted to exempt recently arrived immigrant students—those who have attended schools in the United States for less than a year—from taking their state's reading/language arts assessment. Although all students, including the most recently arrived, must be tested in mathematics and science, this new regulation regarding the reading tests permits states to omit the scores of students who have been in U.S. schools for less than a year when they make their AYP determinations.

Unlike other subgroups, emergent bilinguals eventually become bilingual, and thus, they move out of the category of "limited English proficient." Therefore, the progress toward proficiency of English language learners is difficult to demonstrate, since only those who fail to progress remain in the category. Realizing this, the 2004 NCLB regulation permits states to include former limited English proficient students within the limited English proficient category for up to 2 years after they have been reclassified for the purposes of making AYP determinations. However, these former emergent bilinguals cannot be included in the limited English proficient subgroup for state or local educational agency report cards.

NCLB defines *limited English proficient* as those whose "difficulties in speaking, reading, writing, or understanding the English language may be sufficient to deny the individual the ability to meet the State's proficient level of achievement on State *assessments*" [emphasis added] (2001, sec. 9101(37)). This signals a significant shift in political culture and ideology, from an earlier era that provided language minority students and their families greater access to educational resources and more equal educational opportunities to become truly bilingual, to an era that is focused solely on closing the achievement gap through testing and English immersion.

The Silencing of Bilingualism and Bilingual Education

NCLB (2001) is simply the most recent iteration of a broader change in policy orientation toward the education of language minority students in the United States. In fact, as many have remarked, the word *bilingual*—what Crawford has called "the B-Word"—is disappearing; public discourse about bilingualism in education has been increasingly silenced (Crawford, 2004; García, 2006b; Hornberger, 2006; Wiley & Wright, 2004). García (2009a) portrays this silencing of the word *bilingual* within the context of federal educational policy by illustrating some of the key name/title changes that have occurred in legislation and offices in Washington, DC, since the passage of No Child Left Behind. For example, the Office of Bilingual Education and Minority Languages Affairs (OBEMLA) has now been renamed the Office of English Language Enhancement and Academic Achievement for LEP Students (OELA). In addition, the replacement of Title VII of the Elementary and Secondary Education Act (the Bilingual Education Act) by Title III (Language Instruction for Limited English Proficient and Immigrant Students) is indicative of the shift away from the support of instruction in students' home languages through bilingual education. Zehler and colleagues (2003) have established that although between 1992 and 2002 the number of emergent bilinguals in Grades K–12 grew by 72% nationwide, their enrollment in bilingual programs declined from 37% to 17%. Crawford (2007) estimates that approximately half of emergent bilinguals in California and Arizona who would have been in bilingual classrooms in 2001–2 were reassigned to all-English programs.

EDUCATING EMERGENT BILINGUALS: UNDERSTANDING THE SHIFTS IN PROGRAMS AND POLICIES

In this chapter, we have laid out the range of educational programs for emergent bilinguals and shown how U.S. language-in-education policies have shifted the program options away from a focus on the home language and toward English-only instruction. In the following five chapters, we uncover the fallacies of these shifts in policy and pedagogy. We explore what has been learned through research in sociolinguistics and psycholinguistics, education and curriculum, sociology, economics, psychometrics, and assessments about educating emergent bilinguals to achieve to high standards. We focus on the following questions: *What does the research tell us about how best to educate and assess emergent bilingual students? Are we using accepted theories and evidence in the education of these students?* We provide evidence that, as we noted in our introduction, the gap between the policy and practices and the research is indeed wide. In addition, we provide descriptions of alternative practices that do benefit emergent bilinguals.

STUDY QUESTIONS

1. What are the different types of educational programs for emergent bilinguals? Discuss how they differ in practices and goal.
2. How are emergent bilinguals being educated in your district? Give specific examples.
3. Discuss how it is possible to use students' home languages in all classrooms regardless of whether there are a few or many who speak a language other than English, whether the group is diverse, or whether the teacher speaks their home language.
4. Discuss the development of educational policies targeting emergent bilinguals in our recent past. Make sure you address the changes in the Bilingual Education Act, as well as *Lau v. Nichols* and *Castañeda v. Pickard*.
5. What have been the changes in educational policies with regard to emergent bilinguals since No Child Left Behind?

CHAPTER 4

Language and Bilingualism: Theoretical Constructs and Empirical Evidence

In this chapter we:

- Review the following theories related to language and bilingualism:
  Cognitive benefits
  Linguistic interdependence and common underlying proficiency
  Development of academic language and literacy
  Dynamic bilingualism and translanguaging

- Consider the empirical evidence on bilingualism and academic achievement in English

So far, we have seen that a growing number of language education programs and policies have failed to recognize language minority students' evolving bilingualism and the role of their home language in supporting their learning. In this chapter, we consider the theoretical constructs and empirical findings that support the use of a student's home language in the classroom. Within this context of the home language, we also examine the theories and research on bilingual and second-language acquisition that speak to the developmental process of acquiring English not just for verbal communication but also for academic work.

THEORETICAL LANGUAGE CONSTRUCTS

Over the past 4 decades, researchers have developed frameworks for understanding the relationship between bilingualism and academic achievement. We describe here some of the theoretical frameworks that are useful in considering the equitable education of emergent bilinguals.

Cognitive Benefits

Since the seminal article by Peal and Lambert (1962) that found that bilingualism is an important factor in cognitive development, the literature on this topic has been extensive. In their Montreal study, Peal and Lambert found bilingual 10-year-olds to be "more facile at concept formation, and [to] have greater mental flexibility" than monolingual students (1962, p. 22). Since then, many empirical studies have detailed various aspects of cognitive advantages for bilingual children (for a review of these, see Baker, 2006; Blanc & Hamers, 1985, p. 49, García, 2009a, chap. 5; Hakuta, 1986).

Bialystok (2004, 2007), for instance, has pointed out that children's knowledge of two language systems results in a more analytic orientation to language, a facility that is known as greater *metalinguistic awareness*. Bilingual children also have two ways to describe the world and thus possess more flexible perceptions and interpretations, that is, more *divergent or creative thinking*. Finally, bilingual children have more practice in gauging communicative situations, giving them more *communicative sensitivity* (Ben-Zeev, 1977).

The development of academic proficiency in two languages has been associated with enhancements in cognitive function. August and Hakuta (1997) conclude: "Bilingualism, far from impeding the child's overall cognitive linguistic development, leads to positive growth in these areas. Programs whose goals are to promote bilingualism should do so without fear of negative consequences" (p. 19). All programs that successfully teach English to emergent bilinguals are thus enabling learners to capitalize on the cognitive advantages of bilingualism. Since bilingualism develops cognitive capacities, educational programs for emergent bilinguals can be effective if they apply the home language and English judiciously to the learning process.

Linguistic Interdependence and Common Underlying Proficiency

Jim Cummins has been a pioneer in developing theoretical frameworks that help us understand the relationship between a student's home language and the development of an additional language. It might seem counterintuitive to imagine that using the home language at school can support higher levels of English proficiency. However, the benefits of such practices are explained by the concept of *linguistic interdependence*, which means that both languages bolster each other in the student's acquisition of language and knowledge (Cummins 1979, 1981). Cummins explains linguistic interdependence by saying: "To the extent that instruction in Lx [one language] is effective in promoting proficiency in Lx [that language], transfer of this proficiency to Ly [the additional language] will occur provided there is adequate exposure to Ly" (2000, p. 38). Cummins is not positing here that the child's home language needs to be fully developed before the additional language is introduced, but he argues that "the first language must not be abandoned before it is fully developed, whether the second language is introduced simultaneously or successively, early or late, in that process" (p. 25).

Linguistic interdependence is stronger in the case of languages that share linguistic features (such as, for example, Spanish and English) where students can derive interdependence from similar linguistic factors, as well as familiarity with language and literacy practices and ways of using language. Yet even in cases where the two languages are not linguistically congruent such as Chinese and English, Chinese-speaking students learning English will benefit academically if they have developed literacy in Chinese because they will understand, for example, that reading is really about making meaning from print and that writing requires the ability to communicate to an unknown and distant audience. In addition, they will have had practice in decoding, a sense of directionality of print, and the mechanics of writing in their own language—useful metalinguistic understandings that help orient learners to texts in another language.

A related theoretical construct called *common underlying proficiency* (Cummins, 1979, 1981), posits that knowledge and abilities acquired in one language are potentially available for the development of another. Researchers have consistently found that there is a cross-linguistic relationship between the student's home and additional language, and proficiency in the home language is related to academic achievement in an additional language (Riches & Genesee, 2006). This is particularly the case for literacy. Lanauze and Snow (1989), for example, found that emergent bilinguals, even those students who were not yet orally proficient in their second language, exhibited similar complexity and semantic content in their writing in both their home and additional languages.

Academic Language and Literacy

Skutnabb-Kangas and Toukomaa (1976), working with Finnish immigrants in Sweden, proposed that there is a difference between the way in which language is used in academic tasks as opposed to conversation and intimacy. The *surface fluency* so evident in conversational language or in writing to someone we know intimately is most often supported by cues that have little to do with language itself—gestures, repeating, providing examples. Cummins (1981) has called this use of language, which is supported by meaningful interpersonal and situational cues outside language itself, *contextualized language*. Contextualized language, supported by paralinguistic cues, is what one uses for *basic interpersonal communication* (BICS) (Cummins, 1981). Contextual support, Cummins (2000) explains, can be *external*, having to do with aspects of the language input itself. But contextual support can also be *internal*, having to do with the shared experiences, interests and motivations that people engaged in "languaging"[1] may have.

To complete school tasks, and especially assessment tasks, a different set of language abilities is needed. Students in school must be able to "language" with little or no extralinguistic support, which is very different from "languaging" during everyday informal communication. That is, more *abstract language*, or in Cummins's terms, *decontextualized language*,[2] is what is needed in order to participate in most classroom discourse, in order to read texts that are sometimes devoid of pictures and other semiotic cues or texts requiring background knowledge that students do not always have. Students also need this abstract language to write the academic essays that require an unknown audience with whom communication is important, and in taking multiple-choice tests that force students to choose only one answer. Cummins (1979, 1981, 2000) refers to the mastery of these abstract language abilities as Cognitive Academic Language Proficiency (CALP) and proposes that it takes *5 to 7 years* to develop these skills in an additional language. Meanwhile, students can usually acquire the language of everyday communication in a second language in just 1 to 3 years. As shown in Table 3.1 in Chapter 3, many programs provided to emergent bilinguals do not afford sufficient time to gain these language skills.

The finding that it takes 5 to 7 years to develop academic proficiency in an additional language is supported by other empirical research. Hakuta et al. (2000) have found that it takes 5 years or longer to fully develop academic skills in English. They add: "In districts that are considered the most successful in teaching English to EL students, oral proficiency takes 3 to 5 years to develop and academic English proficiency can take 4 to 7 years" (p. 13). Likewise, Thomas and Collier (1997) found that it takes students between 4 and 10 years to achieve "on grade" levels of performance in reading in English. Gándara (1999) reports that by Grade 3, listening skills in English may be at 80% of native proficiency, but reading and writing lag behind this number. High school students need a vocabulary of approximately 50,000 words, and the average student learns 3,000 new words each year (Graves, 2006; Nagy & Anderson, 1984). Thus, in 4 years of high school, emergent bilinguals might have acquired 12,000 to 15,000 words, falling short of what they would need to engage with the complex coursework of high school (Short & Fitzsimmons, 2007).

Brian Street, a key figure in new literacy studies (NLS), challenges scholars and educators to examine the uses of academic language as a series of *social practices*. Rather than thinking of literacy as a monolithic construct made up of a discreet set of skills, he recommends that we consider, first, that literacies are multiple and, second, that they are embedded in a web of social relations that maintain asymmetries of power (Street, 1985, 1996, 2005). In other words, learning academic language is not a neutral activity, easily divided into two modes of communication—spoken and written. Rather, as recent scholarship has shown, learning academic literacy entails much more: full academic literacy requires skills that are multimodal—spoken and written modes intricately bound up with other visual, audio, and spatial semiotic systems (Jewitt & Kress, 2003; Kleifgen, in press; Kress, 2003; New London Group, 2000). These literacy scholars note that the acquisition of these complex technical skills is contingent upon wider societal factors beyond the school.

Likewise, Nancy Hornberger's (2003) model of the continua of biliteracy framework identifies the major social, linguistic, political, and psychological issues that surround the development of biliteracy, as they relate to each other. The interrelated nature of Hornberger's (2003) continua supports the potential for positive transfer across literacies. Hornberger (2005) says that "bi/multilinguals' learning is maximized when they [students] are allowed and enabled to draw from across all their existing language skills (in two+ languages), rather than being constrained and inhibited from doing so by monolingual instructional assumptions and practices" (p. 607). The nested nature of Hornberger's (2003) continua also shows how transfer can be promoted or hindered by different contextual factors (Hornberger & Skilton-Sylvester, 2003).

Building on the frameworks developed by Street and Hornberger, García, Bartlett, and Kleifgen (2007) propose the concept of *pluriliteracy practices*, which are grounded in an understanding that equity for emergent bilinguals must take into account the power and value relations that exist around the various language practices in the school setting and in society. The notion of pluriliteracies recognizes the more dynamic and hybrid uses of literacies in and out of schools in a context of new technologies and increased movements of people, services, and goods in a globalized world. Schools that value the use of pluriliteracy practices—including diverse languages and scripts—are providing an equitable education for emergent bilinguals; they are enabling students to develop a powerful repertoire of multiple literacies, academic English being one of them.

Dynamic Bilingualism and Translanguaging

Wallace Lambert (1974), working in the context of Canadian immersion bilingual education for Anglophone majorities,[3] proposed that bilingualism could be either *subtractive* or *additive*. According to Lambert, language minority students usually experience subtractive bilingualism as a result of schooling in another language. Their home language is subtracted as the school language is learned. This is the case of all ESL/English-only programs, as well as of transitional bilingual education. On the other hand, Lambert claims that language majority students usually experience additive bilingualism as the school language is added to their home language. These models of bilingualism are represented in Figure 4.1.

Responding to the intensified movements of peoples across national borders and attendant language contact and change in the 21st century, García (2009a) has proposed that bilingualism is not *linear* but *dynamic*. This conceptualization of bilingualism goes beyond the notion of two autonomous languages and of additive or subtractive bilingualism, and instead suggests that the language practices of *all* bilinguals are complex and interrelated; they do not emerge in a linear way. Bilingualism does not result in either the balanced wheels of two bicycles (as the additive bilingual model purports) or in a unicycle (as the subtractive bilingual model suggests). Instead, bilingualism is like an all-terrain vehicle with individuals using it to adapt to both the ridges and craters of communication in uneven terrains (see Figure 4.2). Like a banyan tree, bilingualism is complex as it adapts to the soil in which it grows (see García, 2009a).

Dynamic bilingualism refers to the development of different language practices to varying degrees in order to interact with increasingly multilingual communities. In some ways dynamic bilingualism is related to the concept of plurilingualism as defined by the Council of Europe (2000): (1) the ability to use several languages to varying degrees and for distinct purposes and (2) an educational value that is the basis of linguistic tolerance. The difference is that within a dynamic bilingual perspective, languages are not seen as autonomous systems that people "have," but rather as practices that people "use." Thus, educating for dynamic bilingualism for *all* students builds on the complex and multiple language practices of students and teachers. Unlike additive and subtractive models of bilingualism, a dynamic bilingualism model proposes that complex bilingual language practices are both the center of how languaging occurs and the goal for communication in an increasingly multilingual world.

In the case of language minority communities who have experienced language loss and who attend bilingual schools, these speakers undergo a process of *recursive dynamic bilingualism*. They do not start as simple monolinguals (as is assumed in the subtractive and additive models). Instead, they recover bits and pieces of their existing ancestral language practices as they develop a bilingualism that continuously reaches back in order

Figure 4.1. Subtractive versus Additive Bilingualism

Subtractive Bilingualism	Additive Bilingualism
L1 + L2 - L1→ L2	L1 + L2 = L1 + L2

Figure 4.2. Types of Bilingualism

Subtractive Bilingualism	Additive Bilingualism	Dynamic Bilingualism

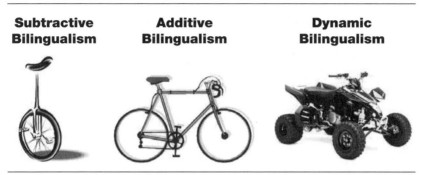

to move forward. But their bilingualism is not in any way balanced, as in the two wheels of a bicycle, because their language practices need to adapt to the bilingually complex terrain in which they interact. This is the case, for example, in many Native American communities in the United States, where language practices have been deeply influenced by contact with English and resulting language loss.

A representation of the two models of dynamic bilingualism is in Figure 4.3. Language practices intermingle as both students and teachers make meaning in multilingual classrooms. In most bilingual encounters in the 21st century, bilingualism in multilingual classrooms is portrayed in the graphic on the right in Figure 4.3. Often, however, the dynamism refers not only to the synchronic interrelatedness of language practices taking place in a present interaction, but also to diachronic intermingling of practices as speakers blend together remnants of past practices with some features of those of the present. This languaging is often exhibited by Indigenous peoples and ethnolinguistic groups who have lived in the United States for more than three generations.[4] This recursive dynamic bilingualism is portrayed in the graphic on the left in Figure 4.3.

Educators meaningfully educate when they draw upon the full linguistic repertoire of all students, including language practices that are multiple and hybrid, as we will see below. Any language-in-education approach—be it monolingual or bilingual—that does not acknowledge and build upon the hybrid language practices in bilingual communities is more concerned with controlling language behavior than in educating (Cummins, 2007; García, 2009a; García et al., in press). Effectively educating emergent bilinguals, even in programs that teach through the medium of English, must include and support the dynamic bilingual practices by which bilinguals construct knowledge and understandings.

Figure 4.3. Kinds of Dynamic bilingualism

Recursive Dynamic Bilingualism   Dynamic Bilingualism

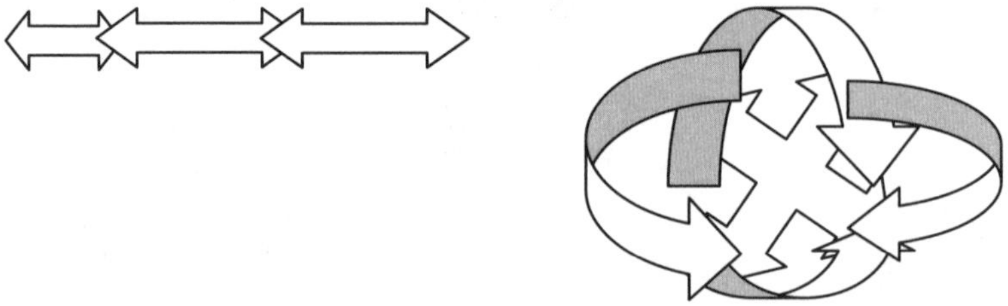

This conceptualization of dynamic bilingualism is in keeping with that of others in the 21st century. It builds on, as well as challenges, early second-language acquisition work. In the 20th century, researchers in the field of second-language acquisition (SLA) were concerned with the degree to which a language learner's "interlanguage" (Selinker, 1972) conformed to the target language. They often cataloged what is called *fossilization* behavior, that is, "errors" associated with their interlanguage. Selinker and Han (2001) name some of these fossilizations: low proficiency, non-targetlike performance, backsliding or the reemergence of "deviant" forms, and errors that are impervious to negative evidence. The emphasis on fossilization and "ultimate attainment" in second-language acquisition studies have affected the ways in which some language educators view their learners—as somehow incomplete. In this view, learning an additional language is linear, as if a static and complete set of grammar rules were available for acquisition.

However, recent scholarship has increasingly questioned the idea of a "native speaker" and of "native-like proficiency" (Canagarajah, 1999; Cook, 2008; García, 2009a; Valdés, 2005). Kramsch (1997) has argued that the concept of native speaker, which had been considered a privilege of birth, is closely linked to social class and education, since the ways of speaking of many poor and working-class native-born citizens are considered suspect and excluded.

In addition, scholars in the field of bilingualism have long argued that bilinguals are not two monolinguals in one (Grosjean, 1985, 1989). Speaking of these bilinguals as first-language/second-language, or L1/L2, users, Guadalupe Valdés adds:

> L1/L2 users have acquired two knowledge systems that they use in order to carry out their particular communicative needs, needs that may be quite unlike those of monolingual native speakers who use a single language in all communicative interactions. (2005, p. 415)

By proposing the concept of *multicompetence*, Cook (2002) argues that second-language users are different from monolingual speakers because their lives and minds are also different; that is, they hold knowledge of two languages in the same mind. Likewise, Herdina and Jessner (2002) propose that speakers of more than one language have dynamically interdependent language systems whose interactions create new structures that are not found in monolingual systems. This view of bilingualism has implications for teaching English to emergent bilinguals. As Larsen-Freeman and Cameron (2008) explain:

> Learning is not the taking in of linguistic forms by learners, but the constant adaptation of their linguistic resources in the service of meaning-making in response to the affordances that emerge in the communicative situation, which is, in turn, affected by learners' adaptability. (p. 135)

Emergent bilinguals are developing a complex multicompetence. Educators who are aware of this complexity support home language practices and facilitate the adaptations of these practices as their students make meaning in new social and academic situations.

García (2009a), extending Williams (cited in Baker, 2001, 2003, 2006), calls the process by which students and teachers engage in complex discursive practices in order to "make sense" of, and communicate in, multilingual classrooms *translanguaging*.[5] Translanguaging includes code-switching—the shift between two languages in context—but differs from it in significant ways, for it includes other bilingual practices that go beyond a simple switch of code, such as when bilingual students read in one language and then take notes, write, or discuss in another. In addition, the term helps to make the point that while it is true that, when seen from the outside, bilingual children tend to do their languaging through linguistic features that are socially categorized as belonging to one or another language, from the point of view of the bilingual speaker, his or her discourse can just as reasonably be viewed as resulting from a single, coherent communicative system (Otheguy, 2009). This system is used by bilinguals to make sense of bilingual communities, bilingual families, and classrooms with multilingual students. Translanguaging thus focuses on the complex languaging practices of bilinguals in actual communicative settings, and not on the use of language codes whose distinctness is monitored by the standardizing agencies of nation-states such as language academies, grammar books, and, of course, schools.

Direct methods and communicative approaches have traditionally excluded the students' home language practices from ESL and bilingual classrooms. In ESL classrooms, many teachers continue to believe that it is best to use English exclusively. In bilingual classrooms, the separation of languages has been the most accepted practice, with a clearly demarcated

English-only and LOTE-only curricular schedule. Jacobson and Faltis explain the reasons for this practice: "By strictly separating the languages, the teacher avoids, it is argued, cross contamination, thus making it easier for the child to acquire a new linguistic system as he/she internalizes a given lesson" (1990, p. 4).

Recently, however, scholars around the world have challenged these approaches by demonstrating that translanguaging in the classroom, if properly understood and suitably applied, can in fact enhance the complex cognitive, linguistic, and literacy abilities that students need (Cummins, 2007; Fu, 2009; Gajo, 2007; Heller & Martin-Jones, 2001; Lewis, 2008; Martin-Jones & Saxena, 1996; Serra, 2007; Li Wei, 2009). Speaking of bilingual education, Duverger (2005) has pointed out that both macro-alternation (in the sense of allocating languages to periods of the day, teacher, or subject matter) and micro-alternation (or the use of translanguaging by both teachers and students) have been used in bilingual schools. "Macro-alternation is programmed, institutionalized, demanding; micro-alternation adds suppleness, flexibility, and efficiency. The combination of the two is subtle" (Duverger, 2005, p. 93).

Teachers of emergent bilingual students—mainstream, ESL, and bilingual—who understand the potential of translanguaging as a sense-making mechanism have the tools to provide a rigorous education for these students. Of course, it is important for all teachers, but especially for bilingual teachers, to have a clear language-in-education policy, which for Duverger (2005) includes an explicit policy of macro-alternation. But having defined the allocation of language in the classroom, teachers must then provide space for translanguaging as an important sense-making mechanism within these instructional spaces. Developing standard academic English effectively does not rely solely on transfer from standard academic uses of the home language, but on the interdependence of complex translanguaging practices that support academic language development (García, 2009a).

EMPIRICAL EVIDENCE ON ACHIEVEMENT IN ACADEMIC ENGLISH

Around the world there is near consensus among researchers that greater support for students' home language, and academic development in that language, is "positively related to higher long-term academic attainment by LEP pupils" (Ferguson, 2006, p. 48). Because in the United States the notion of bilingual education itself is so politically loaded, research about the question of whether bilingual education or monolingual, English-only education works best for emergent bilinguals is often contradictory. Nevertheless, and on balance, there is much research support for the positive effects of bilingual education over monolingual education for these students. Let us review some key historical findings from empirical studies.

In the late 1970s two nationwide studies on bilingual education were conducted—one by the General Accounting Office (GAO) (1976), which is the investigative arm of Congress, and the other by the American Institutes for Research (AIR) (see Danoff, 1978). The GAO (1976) panel concluded that transitional bilingual education produced positive effects on students' English-language competence, and also pointed to more limited data that supported the use of the home language for learning in subjects other than English. The AIR study (Danoff, 1978), on the other hand, concluded that participation in Title VII Spanish-English transitional bilingual education programs did not produce gains in English language arts or mathematics. But a review and analysis of 12 studies performed by Rudolph C. Troike concluded that "students in the bilingual programs exceeded the achievement levels of control groups or district norms, and in several instances they exceeded national norms in English, reading, and math" (1978, p. 5).

In 1981, Baker and de Kanter concluded that there was no consistent evidence for the effectiveness of transitional bilingual education and therefore "exclusive reliance on this instructional method is not justified" (p. 1). But in 1985, Willig conducted a meta-analysis of the studies that had been reviewed by Baker and de Kanter in 1981, in which she measured the program effect in each study, even if not statistically significant. Willig (1985) concluded that there were positive effects for transitional bilingual programs for all academic areas. In 1987, The GAO surveyed 10 experts and found that they looked favorably on the use of bilingual education to teach language minority children and were quite critical of approaches that used English-only (Crawford, 2004).

In fact, several large-scale evaluations (Ramírez, 1992; Thomas & Collier, 1997) demonstrate that using the home language in instruction benefits language minority students. For instance, the Ramírez (1992) study was a longitudinal study of 554 kindergarten-to-sixth-grade Latino students in five states (New York, New Jersey, Florida, Texas, and California) who were in English-only structured immersion programs, transitional early exit programs, and late-exit developmental bilingual programs. (In this study, two-way dual-language education programs were not evaluated.) The results of the Ramírez (1992) study favored late-exit developmental bilingual programs, that is, programs that use students' home languages for 5 to 6 years. Although there were no differences between programs among students in the third grade, by sixth grade students in late-exit developmental programs were performing better in mathematics, English language arts, and English reading than students in the other programs.

Collier (1995) stresses that four factors are important for the equitable and successful education of emergent bilinguals: (1) a socioculturally supportive environment; (2) the development of the students' home languages to a high cognitive level; (3) uninterrupted cognitive development, which best occurs through education in the home language; and (4) teaching the additional language with cognitively complex tasks. Thomas and Collier provide evidence that development of home-language skills provides a sound foundation for subsequent academic success in and through English as an additional language. They state:

> The first predictor of long-term school success is cognitively complex on-grade level academic instruction through students' first language for as long as possible (at least through grade 5 or 6) and cognitively complex on-grade level academic instruction through the second language (English) for part of the day. (1997, p. 15)

Thomas and Collier concluded that two-way bilingual education (dual language) is the best program for children at the elementary level because students develop academic and second language proficiency, as well as cognitive understanding, through their first language. As in the Ramírez (1992) study, these advantages are not evident until students reach the sixth grade.

In 2002, Thomas and Collier released a study of the effectiveness of different kinds of educational programs for language minority student achievement. They compared the achievement on nationally standardized tests[6] of students in different kinds of programs, who entered school in kindergarten or first grade with little or no proficiency in English, and followed them to the highest grade level reached. They concluded that bilingually schooled students outperformed comparable monolingually schooled students in all subjects. Furthermore, the strongest predictor of English language achievement was the amount of formal schooling the students received in the home language. Developmental bilingual education programs and two-way bilingual education programs were the only kinds of programs that enabled emergent bilinguals to reach the 50th percentile in both languages in all subjects. These bilingual education programs also produced the fewest dropouts. Two types of two-way and developmental bilingual education programs were included in the study: (1) the 50:50 model, meaning that 50% of the instruction is in the child's home language and 50% in the additional language; (2) the 90:10 model, meaning that *initially* 90% of the instruction is in the child's first language and 10% in the other language as it gradually moves to a 50:50 arrangement. Thomas and Collier (2002) found that the 90:10 type of instruction was more efficient than the 50:50 instructional model in helping students reach grade-level achievement in their second language. To completely close the achievement gap, it is important for students to stay on grade level in their primary language and for bilingual programs to continue through the end of middle school years (V. Collier, personal communication, October 30, 2009).

Lindholm-Leary (2001) conducted a comprehensive evaluation of programs serving emergent bilinguals in California. These included (1) English-only programs, (2) transitional bilingual education, and (3) two types of two-way bilingual education (what she called simply dual-language education, or DLE—90:10 and 50:50). Like Thomas and Collier (2002), Lindhom-Leary (2001) concluded that students who were in instructional programs in which initially English was used for only 10 to 20% of the time (whether transitional or 90:10 dual language) did as well on English proficiency tests as those in English-only programs or 50:50 dual-language programs. By Grade 6, however, Latino students in dual-language education (two-way bilingual education) outperformed transitional bilingual education students. In mathematics all students in dual-language education outperformed by 10 points those educated only in English.

Oller and Eilers (2002) conducted a large-scale study of two-way bilingual education programs and English immersion in Miami. They compared 952 bilingual and monolingual students from kindergarten to fifth grade in two-way bilingual education and English immersion classrooms. By the fifth grade, there was no gap in English language test performance between students, while those in bilingual programs also gained academic literacy in Spanish.

A recent meta-analysis of the literature on the teaching of emergent bilinguals shows that those in bilingual education programs outperform those in English-only programs on tests of academic achievement (Krashen, Rolstad, & McSwan, 2007). This was also the conclusion of the two recent reviews of the research literature (Rolstad, Mahoney, & Glass, 2005; Slavin & Cheung, 2005). Slavin and Cheung (2005) reviewed 16 studies comparing structured English immersion with transitional bilingual education. They found that most of the studies favored transitional bilingual education and that none of the studies they reviewed significantly favored structured English immersion programs. Rolstad et al. (2005) meta-analysis found evidence that the use of a child's home language was more beneficial for emergent bilinguals than was structured English immersion. Likewise, the National Literacy Panel on Language Minority Children and Youth, appointed by the administration of President George W. Bush, concluded that bilingual education approaches, in which the student's home language is used, are more effective in teaching students to read than are English-only approaches (see August & Shanahan, 2006).

In their synthesis of the research evidence in the education of emergent bilinguals, Genesee, Lindholm-Leary, Saunders, and Christian (2006) confirm that students who are in educational programs that provide extended instruction in their home language through late-exit bilingual education programs (developmental and two-way bilingual education/dual language) outperform students who only receive short-term instruction through their home language (early-exit transitional bilingual education). They also found that bilingual proficiency and biliteracy were positively related to academic achievement in both languages. Finally, these researchers found that emergent bilinguals who participated in primary school programs providing home language support had acquired the same or superior levels of reading and writing skills as students in English-only programs by the end of elementary school, while developing their bilingualism and biliteracy.

Goldenberg (2008) points out that five independent meta-analyses of experimental studies (August & Shanahan, 2006; Greene, 1997; Rolstad et al., 2005; Slavin & Cheung, 2005; Willig, 1985) concluded that learning to read in the child's home language promotes reading achievement in an additional language. Goldenberg (2008) adds that no other area in educational research with which he is familiar can claim five meta-analyses based on experimental studies that converge on the same finding. Thus, the evidence that learning to read in the student's home language promotes reading achievement in English is strong.

Despite the evidence that two-way bilingual education programs (dual-language bilingual education) are quite successful in developing the academic language of emergent bilinguals, we cannot conclude that they are the only way to educate language minority children bilingually. In reality, and despite the promise of two-way bilingual education, not all localities can implement these programs because many language majority communities are not eager to have their children schooled with language minority children. What is evident from the research is that the use of the student's home language is crucial for their long-term cognitive growth and academic achievement in English. And thus, all teachers, those who are required to deliver instruction in English only and those who do so bilingually, can take a more effective pedagogical path by constructing bilingual instructional spaces. Describing how all teachers can include the students' home language practices in instruction, Cummins suggests that "When students' L1 is invoked as a cognitive and linguistic resource through bilingual instructional strategies, it can function as a stepping stone to scaffold more accomplished performance in the L2" (2007, p. 14). Cummins believes that adding "bilingual instructional strategies open up the pedagogical space in ways that legitimate the intelligence, imagination, and linguistic talents of ELL students" (2009, p. 11). Translanguaging practices in the classroom hold much promise in educating emergent bilinguals to fully contribute to the communicative dynamism of a globalized world.

EDUCATING EMERGENT BILINGUALS: BUILDING ON DYNAMIC BILINGUALISM

While additive schooling *practices* continue to exist, as we have seen, additive conceptions of bilingualism fail in capturing the complexity of bilingual acquisition and development in the 21st century. We retain the term *subtractive bilingualism* to characterize the kind of bilingualism promoted by some educational programs. However, because a linear conception of *additive bilingualism* does not describe adequately the ever-changing multilingualism of the 21st century, we choose instead to use the term *dynamic bilingualism*. We make evident that some language minority students who speak languages that are not prevalent in the school community cannot be schooled bilingually given the ways in which many bilingual education programs have been constructed. It is, of course, easier to build bilingual education programs for large language groups—especially Spanish speakers, the largest and most rapidly growing ethnolinguistic minority in the United States. And yet every teacher, even those teaching in spaces that are formally denominated as ESL or English-only, can draw on students' linguistic practices in helping them make sense of academic tasks. Translanguaging, as we will see in Chapter 5, is an important pedagogical practice to educate emergent bilingual students.

By way of summary, Table 4.1 shows the types of educational programs described in Chapter 3, alongside linguistic goals, and the kind of

TABLE 4.1. Types of Educational Programs and Bilingualism

Program	Goal	Bilingualism
Submersion	Monolingualism	Subtractive
ESL Pullout	Monolingualism	Subtractive
ESL Push in	Monolingualism	Subtractive
Structured Immersion	Monolingualism	Subtractive
Transitional Bilingual Ed.	Monolingualism	Subtractive
Developmental Bilingual Ed.	Bilingualism	Recursive Dynamic
Two-Way Bilingual Ed.	Bilingualism	Dynamic
Dynamic Bi/Plurilingual Ed.	Bilingualism	Dynamic

bilingualism that they promote according to the understandings that we have proposed in this chapter.

STUDY QUESTIONS

1. What, according to a number of studies, are the cognitive benefits of bilingualism?
2. Discuss Cummins's theories of "linguistic interdependence" and "common underlying proficiency." Indicate the distinction, according to Cummins, between basic interpersonal communication skills and cognitive academic language proficiency.
3. Discuss the difference in conceptions between language and literacy, on the one hand, and languaging and literacy practices, on the other.
4. Identify models of bilingualism. Discuss why dynamic bilingualism fits closely with the concept of multicompetence and the complexity of bilingualism.
5. What is translanguaging? How can translanguaging practices be used in classroom instruction in ESL and bilingual education?
6. In bilingual education programs, what is the difference between macrolanguage alternation and translanguaging? What is the importance of each?
7. Discuss the research evidence that exists for drawing on home language practices in the schooling of emergent bilinguals.

CHAPTER 5

Language and Bilingualism: Practices

In this chapter, we will:

- Identify two inequitable practices with regard to language use in education:

    Insufficient support and development of home languages, and "Bracketing" of English.

- Consider four alternative practices:

    Bilingualism in education for all
    Translanguaging pedagogy
    Critical multilingual awareness, and
    English academic literacy through complex language use.

In the previous chapter, we considered theoretical constructs and empirical evidence supporting the use of bilingualism in the education of emergent bilinguals. Here, in Chapter 5, we first review the inequitable language-education practices often handed down by schools, and then we describe alternative language-education practices to show that educators can negotiate educational policy in ways that benefit emergent bilinguals (Menken & García, 2010).

INEQUITABLE LANGUAGE/LITERACY PRACTICES

We now turn to our central question: *Given what we know theoretically and research-wise about the role of emergent bilinguals' home language practices and the development of academic English, are these students being educated according to accepted theories and research evidence about language and bilingualism?* The answer to this question is a resounding *no*. As suggested in Chapter 3, the use of languages other than English in the education of emergent bilinguals has increasingly come under serious question. The inequities of insufficient support and inadequate development of home language practices contradicts theory and research findings we discussed in Chapter 4, which have provided us knowledge about

- The cognitive benefits of bilingualism
- Linguistic interdependence and the common underlying proficiency
- The characteristics and development of academic language and literacy

We have seen a kind of *bracketing* of English—a strict separation of English from instruction in other languages. This form of opposition impedes the dynamic nature of bilingualism and the complex nature of bilingual acquisition, as well as emergent bilinguals' translanguaging. In what follows, we examine more closely two inequitable school practices—insufficient support and inadequate development of home languages in instruction, and the bracketing of English.

Insufficient Support and Inadequate Development of Home Languages

As reported in Chapter 3, bilingual education programs are in decline all over the United States, despite the growth of the bilingual student population. Some states (Arizona, California, and Massachusetts) have even outlawed bilingual education programs. Most emergent bilingual students are in English-only programs, including ESL pullout, ESL push-in, and structured English immersion (59% of them in 2001–02, according to Zehler et al., 2003). Zehler et al. (2003) found that only 20% of emergent bilinguals were being educated with significant use of the native language, such as in bilingual education programs. An additional 20% of their sample was receiving instruction that made some use of the native language, although that support might have been very limited.

Hopstock and Stephenson (2003a), found that the most common instruction received by emergent bilinguals was exclusively in English, and only 24% were receiving extensive services in ESL. Only 16% of the emergent bilinguals were provided with services that significantly used their native languages, and of these, most were Spanish speakers. Schools that had a majority of Spanish speaking students also had more two-way bilingual immersion programs (10% versus 0.7% for other schools). In California, where most emergent bilinguals live, 20 to 25% of these students were in submersion classrooms in 1997—that is, they were educated exclusively through the medium of English—and between 1995 and 1997 only about 30% of California's emergent bilinguals were enrolled in any kind of bilingual education (Crawford, 1997; Gándara, 1999). All this occurred prior to the passage of Proposition 227.

Many more emergent bilinguals are now in classrooms where nothing is done differently to help them. Zehler et al. (2003) report that in 2001–02, 12% of emergent bilinguals were receiving no special services at all, and only

36% were receiving some services, meaning they were getting at least ESL pullout support. According to the survey (Zehler et al., 2003), only 52% of those identified as English language learners were receiving an educational program substantially different from that of their monolingual counterparts.

It is noteworthy that although the numbers of emergent bilinguals are increasing and there is near consensus in the research community about the crucial role of the home language in their education, there has been a significant decrease in the use of the students' language in their instruction over the past decade. Between 1992 and 2002, the percentage of these students who received ELL services exclusively in English increased substantially from 34% to 48% (Zehler et al., 2003). At the same time, the percentage of emergent bilinguals whose education made significant use of the native language, such as in bilingual education programs, decreased by more than half—from 37% to just 17% (Zehler et al., 2003). While transitional and developmental bilingual education programs significantly decreased, two-way bilingual education programs were the only services to increase. Although this might be positive news for this type of program and for the future possibility of a less monolingual society, it is less optimistic in terms of the number of emergent bilinguals who can participate in these programs, since at least half the students in each two-way bilingual class are students whose home language is English. Thus, these two-way bilingual programs, on average, serve fewer language minority students.

Given the backlash against bilingual education and the push for English-only instruction in the United States, this decrease in the use of students' home languages in their education might not surprise us. It is significant to find that between 1992 and 2002, the percentage of students who qualify for ELL services but received only mainstream (regular classroom) instruction also increased from 4% to 12% (Zehler et al., 2003). Thus, emergent bilinguals are increasingly being educated in mainstream classrooms with little specialized educational support either in English or in their home languages. Another interesting fact is that although emergent bilinguals at the secondary level arguably have a more difficult task than students at the elementary level given the complexity of the subject matter they must master to graduate, elementary students are far more likely to have instruction in which the native language is used in any significant way. Zehler et al. summarize the declining conditions in which emergent bilinguals are being educated: "Compared to prior years, LEP students are now more likely to receive instructional services provided in English, and less likely to receive extensive ELL services" (2003, p. 35).

New York City exemplifies the decline of the use of students' home language practices in education. Although the Aspira Consent Decree of 1974 mandated transitional bilingual education programs for Latino students (Reyes, 2006), bilingual education programs are today in decline. In the school year 2002–03, 53% of emergent bilinguals in New York City were in ESL programs; by school year 2007–08, 69% were instructed in ESL programs. Likewise, while 37% of emergent bilinguals were in transitional bilingual education in 2002, only 21% participated in bilingual instruction in 2007–08 (NYCDOE, 2008). Although much is said about New York's development of "dual-language programs" (bilingual education programs that are either two way [for more than one ethnolinguistic group] or developmental [for one ethnolinguistic group but where the two languages are used in instruction throughout the program], in reality the growth has been minimal. In 2002, 2% of emergent bilinguals were in such programs, while only 3.6% were in such programs in 2007–08 (NYCDOE, 2008). Thus, in 2008 almost three fourths of the 148,401 emergent bilinguals in New York City were in English-only programs. New York is not different from other cities in the United States where inadequate use is made of emergent bilinguals' home languages at school.

The pullout ESL approach continues to be the program of choice in the United States (Crawford, 1997). In this approach, students are taken from their regular classrooms (usually daily for one to two periods of instruction) and given one-on-one or small-group instruction in English. The content taught during these sessions is often unrelated to the content-area instruction they receive while in their mainstream classrooms. In a study conducted by Thomas and Collier (1997), pullout ESL classrooms made up 52% of their sample. Although it has been found that ESL taught via content-area instruction (social studies, math, science, and so on) is associated with higher long-term educational attainment than ESL pullout (Thomas & Collier, 1997), there are more pullout ESL programs that focus only on the language than there are programs that teach English via ESL with a focus on content-area instruction.

Finally, despite the substantial research evidence that it takes between 5 to 7 years to develop academic proficiency in English, many states insist that emergent bilinguals may stay in special programs for only 1 year (California, Arizona, and Massachusetts) or for a maximum of 3 years (New York State and Washington, for example). Zehler et al. (2003) report that, according to their national survey, emergent bilinguals, on average, maintain their ELL status for 3.55 years and receive some type of service for 3.51 years. Thus, according to the research, emergent bilinguals are receiving educational support for about half the time that they will most likely need it.

As we have said, even when the students' home languages are used in bilingual programs, most programs in the United States are "early exit" programs, meaning that native languages are used for only 2 to 3 years before the children are completely mainstreamed into English classrooms. These early exit bilingual education programs often have the secondary consequence of tracking emergent bilinguals into remedial programs (Ovando &

Collier, 1998). The effect of such policies is that academic *bilingualism* does not *emerge*; instead, academic failure is on the horizon for these students.

Even in bilingual education programs there is little importance given to the language other than English and pressure to exit children from programs as early as possible. As we have seen, NCLB (2001) requires schools to meet AYP targets, which include rapid academic English development for emergent bilinguals. As a result, many schools have stopped taking the development of academic literacy in the home language seriously because teachers feel that they do not have the time. Instead, most bilingual education programs are using, at best, the home language sparingly in an effort to facilitate the acquisition of academic English.

Because bilingual education programs exist primarily at the elementary school level, there is insufficient development of students' home literacies in middle and secondary schools. Consequently, most children who attend bilingual elementary programs then go to middle schools and high schools where instruction is exclusively in English. Middle and high school bilingual programs most often serve recent immigrants, except in the case of students coming from elementary school classrooms who have been unable to pass the English proficiency assessments. These students (often referred to by school systems as "long-term English language learners") have not developed appropriate academic English. In addition, they have often experienced much home language loss, and some have even become monolingual English speakers. Although these students are emergent bilinguals, they do not share the characteristics of those for whom instruction is usually planned. That is, they are often fluent speakers of English who are weak in academic literacy in English. Usually they have not had a consistent or quality educational experience, as they have shifted between ESL and bilingual education programs (Menken & Kleyn, 2009; Menken, Kleyn, & Chae, 2010).

Bracketing of English

Most education programs for emergent bilinguals are based on the fact that English only should be used—that English is best taught monolingually (Phillipson, 1992). Harmer (1998) summarizes this common advice to ESL teachers, saying that "the need to have [students] practicing English (rather than their own language) remains paramount" (p. 129). The popularity of Communicative Language Teaching (CLT) with its focus on developing communicative competence in English is partly responsible for these views (see Littlewood, 1981). The reasoning behind this practice has to do with the belief that emergent bilinguals should think in the additional language without interference of the home language (Cummins, 2007).

The recent emphasis on getting emergent bilinguals to perform as English proficient on assessments, which by definition they cannot be, means that ESL teachers are increasingly proscribing the use of students' home languages from their classrooms. They do so with the false belief that if home languages are used, teachers fail to adapt instruction in the additional language (Cloud, Genesee, & Hamayan, 2000).

As García (2009a) points out, bilingual education programs have also fallen prey to a monoglossic ideology that treats each of the students' languages as separate and whole and views the languages as bounded autonomous systems. Thus, they strictly separate the languages in what Cummins (2007) calls "the two solitudes." It was Wallace Lambert (1984) who perhaps best expressed this ideology of language separation in his discussion about French immersion programs in Canada:

> No bilingual skills are required of the teacher, who plays the role of a monolingual in the target language . . . and who never switches languages, reviews materials in the other language, or otherwise uses the child's native language in teacher-pupil interactions. In immersion programs, therefore, bilingualism is developed through two separate monolingual instructional routes. (p. 13)

This practice of strict language separation and sheltering of languages has prevailed in bilingual education. Heller speaks of parallel monolingualism to refer to practices in which "every variety must conform to certain prescriptive norms" (1999, p. 271). García (2009a) describes the four strategies used to separate languages:

- Time-determined, with one language exclusively used half of the day, on alternate days or even alternate weeks
- Teacher-determined, with one teacher speaking one language exclusively
- Place-determined, with one room or even building used for one language exclusively
- Subject-determined, with one language being exclusively used to teach one subject.

We agree that educational programs for emergent bilinguals must have a clear language policy, and understand that bilingual programs need to have an arrangement for the use of the two or more languages; nevertheless, the *rigid adherence* to one language or another contradicts research findings and what we know about dynamic bilingualism and translanguaging.

ALTERNATIVE LANGUAGE/LITERACY PRACTICES

Whether teaching in English only or teaching bilingually, effective educators make room for bilingualism in classrooms. How do they manage this, given policies that many times run counter to these practices? By negotiating education policies for the benefit of their students, thus becoming policy makers themselves (Menken & García, 2010). In what follows, we describe educational practices that work for emergent bilinguals given the nature of bilingualism and education that we have laid out above.

We describe four language-focused educational practices that build on theoretical constructs and research evidence regarding academic language development we have been considering:

- Bilingualism in education for all
- Translanguaging pedagogy
- Critical multilingual awareness programs
- English academic literacy through complex language use

Bilingualism in Education for All

As García has said, "Bilingual education *is the only way* to educate children in the twenty-first century" (2009a, p. 5). That is, *all* children, regardless of language background, need to develop bi/plurilingual abilities to meet the communicative challenges of the 21st century.

A meaningful and rigorous education for emergent bilinguals will always use the home language as much as possible. Some educators may be constrained by program structures that release students from bilingual education programs too early or structures that require English-only instruction. Other educators might be inhibited because the emergent bilinguals in their classrooms speak many languages. But *all* educators—bilingual, ESL, and mainstream—can draw upon the bilingualism of their students for a meaningful education. Instead of bilingual education consistently being structured from the top down, educators can build on bilingualism from the bottom up, that is, from the students' own language use. Educators can bring bilingualism into play as an important resource not only for emergent bilinguals, but also for the growing bilingual student population in the United States and for those who are speakers of English only and potentially emergent bilinguals themselves.

There are many schools in the United States where *all* students are in bilingual programs. That is the case of, for example, some of the high schools for Latino newcomers (see Bartlett & García, in press) or some two-way bilingual elementary schools (see Freeman, 1998). This is also the case of many bilingual private schools that serve different ethnolinguistic groups, such as Hebrew day schools. Bilingual education in schools like these enables teachers to use the two languages extensively while developing students' academic abilities in both English and the additional language.

Nevertheless, there are many other classrooms in the United States where educators are finding ways of using the students' home languages regardless of the program structure. As Cummins says, "Bilingual instructional strategies can be incorporated into English-medium classrooms, thereby opening up the pedagogical space in ways that legitimate the intelligence, imagination, and linguistic talents of ELL students" (2009, p. xi). Communicative Language Teaching with its emphasis on the use of English only, especially in oral communication, does not suffice when emergent bilinguals have to meet high academic targets and use academic English in complex ways. García et al. (in press) have described how bilingualism in education is practiced in two small high schools where instruction is formally in English—one for newcomer immigrants with students with very different languages, the other a school with a broad range of language proficiencies but where emergent bilinguals are mostly Spanish speaking. In both schools, students are given agency to control their language use in order to learn and make sense of the new language. In one school, for example, Spanish-speaking emergent bilinguals are paired with other bilingual Spanish-speaking students for projects, and the work is conducted bilingually. Some emergent bilingual students complete their projects in Spanish and then share the oral presentation in English. Others choose to complete their projects in English and then present them in Spanish, with translation provided by the bilingual student.

In the other school, where everyone is an emergent bilingual of different language backgrounds, students decide what languages they want to use both when researching topics and when reading and writing about them. Students develop their own strategies for learning and making sense of the academic lesson and its language, often using Google Translate and the Web as a resource. During the course of the projects, students teach each other phrases not only in English but also in additional languages. Whenever possible, the teacher interacts with small groups and individual students in the languages they are using. When students are using a language the teacher does not understand, one of the more advanced emergent bilinguals provides translation (García, Flores & Chu, in press).

In an ESL elementary school classroom, Christina Celic "stretches" her self-contained ESL class by getting students to read and write in languages other than English. Most of her emergent bilinguals are Spanish speaking, but there are also Mandarin speakers and children from Nepal, India, and Bangladesh. Students are paired strategically so that fluent bilingual students work with emergent bilingual students. Celic uses a workshop model of teaching literacy (Calkins, 1994). During mini-lessons in reading and writing,[1] students "turn-and-talk," which means they practice what the teacher has been modeling with their partner using all the language and other semiotic resources at their disposal—Spanish, English, language prompts, and drawings. During the reading workshop, Celic meets regularly with emergent bilinguals in guided reading groups. As a fluent Spanish speaker, Celic uses Spanish to help students preview the text and discuss what they think it will be about. Then, as students read the text in English, Celic encourages her emergent bilinguals to use what they know in both English and Spanish to make sense of what they are reading. For independent reading, Celic makes sure that leveled reading material is available for each of her emergent bilinguals in their own language. These books have often been written by students' parents, past students, or even other students in the same classroom. During the writing workshop, students have the option to write in any language. Emergent bilinguals are encouraged to write extensively in their home languages, and they add on English writing as they develop their English language skills. This includes labeling drawings with vocabulary they have developed in English, using basic sentence frames, and using writing they have created collaboratively with a more English proficient partner. As emergent bilinguals develop their English proficiency, they often write fully bilingual texts, similar to the bilingual children's books that Celic uses as read-alouds (C. Celic, personal communication, October 31, 2009). Celic also helps emergent bilinguals develop their understanding of new vocabulary in English by making explicit connections between languages and building on Spanish-English cognates. Sometimes she asks her students if they know what the word means in their language, and whenever possible has them add the translation to the class word wall.

In the middle schools studied by Danling Fu (2003, 2009) the students use Chinese writing as a stepping-stone to English writing. Teachers allow beginning ESL students to write in Chinese, using the few words they know in English. Gradually, more English writing emerges. Fu says:

> Learning to write in English for ELLs who are literate in their native language is actually a process of becoming bilingual writers, rather than merely replacing one language or writing ability with another or mastering two separate language systems. . . . If writing reflects who and what the writers are, then ELLs' native language (voice and expressions) will either visibly appear or be blended with English. (2009, p. 120)

The work of Cummins and his colleagues (2005) in Canadian classrooms also clearly demonstrates how teachers can use bilingual instructional strategies in supposedly English-only classrooms. Cummins (2006) calls for the use of "identity texts," as students use both languages to write about their own immigration and education experience. Cummins quotes Madiha, one of the girls involved in the project of producing bilingual identity texts:

> I think it helps my learning to be able to write in both languages because if I'm writing English and Ms. Leoni says you can write Urdu too it helps me think

of what the word means because I always think in Urdu. That helps me write better in English. (2009, p. x)

In some classrooms—mainstream, ESL, and bilingual—teachers encourage students to write double-entry journals. In this assignment, students react to the academic texts they are reading from their own personal perspective, contributing both their experiences and their cultural and linguistic understandings to make sense of the text. Sometimes, these reactions/reflections are written in the students' own languages. At other times, they are written in the class language with the hybrid use that a personal reflection enables. These double-entry journals are then shared with fellow classmates as a way to build multicultural and multilingual understandings of the same text and to generate different understandings from multiple perspectives (see García & Traugh, 2002).

Especially in high schools and middle schools, the students' many languages are often taught in programs referred to as "heritage language"[2] (Valdés, 2000, 2001). Besides developing literacy in the home language of bilingual students, these classrooms often act as "safe spaces" (Pratt, 1991) in which support and advice is offered to language minority students. One particular high school we know offers classes in Spanish, Chinese, Urdu, and Arabic. In another high school, the Urdu class is significant for Pakistani students even though the teacher doesn't speak Urdu and instead offers culture and history (Ghaffar-Kucher, 2008). In some high schools a number of these heritage language classes are taught by an ESL or bilingual teacher, extending the responsibility of teachers hired for the development of English to language development in general. In yet another school that does not offer any form of bilingual or heritage language instruction, there are "native language projects" in which bilingual students interview adults in languages other than English about the adults' immigration and education experiences. These interviews are transcribed in those languages, and then students write linguistic summaries in English (García et al., in press).

Lucas and Katz (1994) document other practices of bilingualism in education used with emergent bilinguals which do not require teachers to be bilingual:

- Teachers devise a writing assignment in which students use their home language;
- Students read or tell stories to each other using their home language and then translate them into English to tell other students;
- Students from same language backgrounds are paired together so that students who are more fluent in English could help those less fluent;
- Students are encouraged to use bilingual dictionaries;

- Students are encouraged to get help at home in their home languages;
- Books are provided in students' home languages;
- Awards are given for excellence in languages not commonly studied (cited in Cummins, 2007)

All the practices described above are ways in which bilingualism in education is used in all types of educational programs for emergent bilinguals. These practices are consonant with theoretical and empirical evidence for how the home language supports students' development of academic English.

Translanguaging Pedagogies

Translanguaging pedagogies include all practices that work against the bracketing of English, building instead English proficiency using the home language as a scaffold. A translanguaging pedagogy was first developed by Cen Williams in Wales and involved having the input and output of the lesson deliberately in different languages. For example, the hearing or reading of lessons is in one language, and the development of the work (the oral discussion, the writing of passages, the development of projects and experiments) is in another (Baker, 2001).

In many classrooms for emergent bilinguals—both in ESL and bilingual education programs—educators extend Williams's translanguaging pedagogy in complex ways. For example, many educators encourage emergent bilinguals to look up resources on the Web in their home languages, as students go back and forth from Web pages that are in one language or the other. In these classrooms, emergent bilinguals make frequent use of dictionaries and glossaries. Likewise, as we saw before, students frequently conduct discussions in languages other than English when reading in English. Frequently they write first in the home language, then translate the writing piece into English.

In primary classrooms where a workshop model of balanced literacy is followed, students are taught to ask questions of the reading they do independently or in collaborative groups by using stick-on notes. It is common to see such notes written in the home language of the students or in hybrid forms of English and the home language. Educators who understand the power of translanguaging encourage emergent bilinguals to use their home languages to think, reflect, and extend their inner speech.

In some states, subject matter assessment for emergent bilinguals is given in languages other than English. But many times, especially if the student is in English-only instruction, students prefer to take the exams in English. Nevertheless, they are given the two versions of the exam—one in English and another in their home language. Going from text in one language to the same text in the other language is a practice that educators encourage the students to develop; it is a translanguaging practice that helps them make sense of the exam.

Manyak (2001, 2002, 2004), working in a primary ESL classroom of Spanish speakers in California, documents the frequent use of Spanish in order to have students make sense of the material. In fact, even in English-only classrooms where teachers attempt to keep the language other than English at bay, students are often observed talking to each other in Spanish. Manyak (2004) documents how what he calls "acts of translation" play an important role in making meaning accessible for emergent bilinguals and fostering their English literacy development.

Because of the large number of Latino emergent bilinguals and the large number of Spanish speakers in the United States, there are English-only classrooms in which the teacher, with some knowledge of Spanish, can use a preview-view-review pedagogy that is common in some bilingual class-rooms. Although English is the official language of the lesson, the teacher gives the gist of the lesson in Spanish, making the message comprehensible to the emergent bilinguals. Many times a written synopsis is given to stu-dents in Spanish before the teacher starts to teach. Other times, the writ-ten materials that teachers distribute are annotated in Spanish or contain translations.

Another effective translanguaging activity is to have students identify cognates in their languages. Cognates are important ways in which emer-gent bilinguals make sense of a new language, and teachers can encourage that activity even when they themselves do not know the language (Cum-mins, 2007).

Effective translanguaging pedagogies have also been documented in the United Kingdom, especially in the context of what are known there as complementary schools organized by ethnolinguistic communities (Creese & Blackledge, 2010; Creese et al., 2008; Kenner, 2004; Kenner, Mahera, Gregory, & Al-Azami, 2007). For example, Robertson (2006) shows how community language teachers of Pakistani students routinely use the chil-dren's knowledge of English and Pahari to teach and learn Urdu. In another program, Bengali bilingual students use transliteration by writing Bangla words using the English alphabet (Al-Azami, Kenner, Ruby, & Gregory, in press).

Critical Multilingual Awareness Programs

Emergent bilingual and bilingual students bring to the foreground language practices that differ significantly from the ways in which standard aca-demic English is used in school. Additionally, these different language prac-tices are often manifestations of social, political, and economic struggles.

Critical multilingual awareness programs build students' understandings of the social, political, and economic struggles surrounding the use of many languages (see Fairclough, 1992, 1999; García, 2008; Kleifgen, 2009). Shohamy (2006) reminds us that it is important for all students to reflect on ways in which languages are used to exclude and discriminate. Critical multilingual awareness programs must generate greater linguistic tolerance among all students and communities.

An exemplary program in critical multilingual awareness for young children was developed in Alsace, France, by Hélot and Young (Hélot, 2006; Hélot & Young, 2006). In that program, mothers who speak different languages come into their children's classroom so that all can familiarize themselves with the child's language, script, and essential stories. The children greet each other, repeat phrases, and sing songs in the other language. In addition, the mothers often bring artifacts or food that are associated with their linguistic and cultural identity. The presence of these immigrant mothers in the school as experts who hold important knowledge—and not just as helpers of the children—can be instrumental not only for the children in the class, but also for the mothers and the community who feel more empowered in the school. We discuss parental involvement in greater detail in Chapter 7.

Yet another way in which educators are enacting these multilingual awareness programs is by having read-alouds in different languages, sometimes of a story with which students are familiar. These read-alouds are sometimes conducted by mothers but also by the students themselves. Cummins (2007) describes a library class in which students with different language backgrounds read aloud the same story in different languages, bringing consciousness to the rest of the class of the differences and similarities across language groups.

In other multilingual awareness programs, students with different language histories write their own linguistic biographies and interview family members about language practices at home and in the community, as well as their migration stories. Another practice is to have students write biographies of famous bilingual persons, thus making students aware of the cognitive and social benefits that can be accrued as bilinguals.

Another important multilingual awareness activity is to have students of different language backgrounds read the same news in different languages. Through translating the news into English, the students can then analyze the different messages transmitted in different languages and reflect on the reasons for those differences.

García et al. (2009) describe one multilingual awareness activity where students studied some ways of mapping sentences and diagramming syntax as well as some verb tenses in English. Students then worked collaboratively in groups to produce a teaching project in which they taught their classmates about the features of some other language. While a few groups chose to teach about features of English, most groups chose a language other than English.

In classrooms with older students, teachers engage them in becoming critical ethnographers of language communities—looking at the ways in which different languages are represented in public space or what Shohamy (2001) calls *linguistic landscapes*. Multilingual awareness activities include students taking photographs of signs in the community and then conducting analyses of whether the same or different messages are enacted in various languages. Students also analyze bilingual signs and their hybrid language practices. Other students can analyze the hierarchy of power with regard to languages by studying the order in which languages appear in print and whether this order changes in different communities. Yet other students can study the nature of signage in their communities and determine whether some languages are professionally printed while others are relegated to hand-made production.

Ethnographies of language communities that are part of these multilingual awareness practices can also include oral language. Teachers can ask students to study the language use in an upper-scale store and one in a bodega in a Latino neighborhood. Students are then asked to focus on questions such as the following: Which languages are selected for use in different places in the neighborhood such as in business, government offices, places of worship, and parks? Who is served first in businesses and offices—English speakers or speakers of the other language? Which languages are used in these situations?

Educators can also engage students in studying the languages represented in the press and magazines found in their neighborhood stands. Students can also study how languages are used in the media—in television, on the radio, and on the Internet—and the different uses to which different languages are put. Furthermore, students can study how different language groups are represented in film, television, and other media outlets.

To ensure that students also reflect on translanguaging in society, banks of examples in media, print, as well as oral discourse can be generated. These problem sets are then subjected to further analysis and become the focus of explicit language and literacy instruction.

The best multilingual awareness programs are those in which students study their own school—how are the different languages used in their school? Who uses what language with whom and for what purpose? What languages are spoken by administrators, teachers, paraprofessionals, office and cafeteria staff, and janitorial staff? What is the meaning of this language use?

The students can also be engaged in close observation and description of how language and literacy is used by the teacher and the students within the classroom—in lessons, assignments, and testing. Students can then examine how particular discourses are used by the teacher and students to include or exclude individuals.

In describing language and literacy practices within the classroom, students can draw from the data they have gathered outside the classroom and in the community. This comparison can serve well to help student anchor language use in particular domains and for specific purposes.

As part of a multilingual awareness program, educators also present students with an explicit curriculum of multilingualism in the United States and in the world. Educators engage students in researching the following questions: What languages are spoken in different regions of the United States and what are the historical, social, and economic reasons for those differences? What countries speak what languages, what is the role of those languages, and who are their language minorities? Students engage in making links between socioeconomic characteristics and the official status of their languages. And they search the Internet as they become aware of different scripts used to write different languages and the relationship, in some cases, between script and cultural history.

English Academic Literacy Through Complex Language Use

Educators who understand theories about bilingualism in education, as well as the empirical evidence, understand that English academic literacy must be developed through a challenging curriculum combined with explicit, overt instruction. Teachers present complex ideas that develop the students' metacognitive skills: that is, plans of attack that enable learners to successfully approach academic tasks and that monitor their thinking (Walqui, 2006). Effective teachers do not oversimplify the English language or offer remedial instruction. Instead, they scaffold instruction in English by offering intensive support, while providing challenging instruction. This is consonant with Cummins's model of pedagogy that suggests that "language and content will be acquired most successfully when students are challenged cognitively but provided with the contextual and linguistic supports or scaffolds required for successful task completion" (2000, p. 71). The best scaffold for English academic language is, of course, the use of the students' language practices.

García (2009a, p. 331) identifies six other scaffolding strategies:

- Routines in which language is used consistently and predictably;
- Contextualization not only through home language support, but also by body language, gestures, manipulatives, realia, technology, word walls, and graphic organizers;
- Modeling thorough think-alouds and verbalization of actions and processes of lessons, including asking questions;

- Bridging and schema building by weaving new information into pre-existing structures of meaning;
- Thematic planning by which vocabulary and concepts are repeated naturally;
- Multiple entry points, allowing some children to use the language of instruction fully without adaptation, while others might use their home languages, and others might use gestures or drawings.

Besides using complex language in teaching subject and offering appropriate scaffolding, emergent bilinguals also need some explicit overt instruction. Genesee and his colleagues summarize their findings from a major meta-analysis by saying: "The best recommendation to emerge from our review favors instruction that combines interactive and direct approaches" (2006, p. 140). There are syntactic structures and vocabulary that must be taught explicitly. For example, all disciplines have different linguistic registers, and students must be made aware of such differences (Gibbons, 2002, 2009). Vocabulary is most important in teaching emergent bilinguals. And educators who understand theories of bilingualism and the empirical evidence teach vocabulary directly and systematically, focusing on both meaning and form (Lapkin & Swain, 1996). This means identifying words from texts; posting them on word walls; and then having students use them in discussion, reading stories, and writing (Carlo et al., 2004). Every lesson for an emergent bilingual must have both a content objective and a language objective. Thus, it is important to both identify and blend process approaches with direct explicit instruction so that both goals can be accomplished.

EDUCATING EMERGENT BILINGUALS:
INCORPORATING MULTILINGUAL PEDAGOGIES

This chapter has focused on effective practices to teach emergent bilinguals. After exploring the theories and empirical evidence in the previous chapter, we have now considered inequitable practices that occur in schools and have provided evidence of alternative practices that are also present in many schools. However, language is not the sole aspect of the education of emergent bilinguals. In the chapter that follows, we consider issues dealing with inequitable curriculum opportunities and pedagogical practices that affect the equitable education of emergent bilinguals.

STUDY QUESTIONS

1. What is the situation today of the use of languages other than English in U.S. education? How is it done in your school district?

2. What does bracketing English mean? What are some of the ways in which this is done?
3. How could bilingualism be for all? Describe some ways in which you might be able to do this in your classroom.
4. How could mainstream teachers use the home languages of their students for more effective academic instruction? Describe one way in which this might be done regardless of program structure.
5. What are translanguaging pedagogies and how might they be used in classrooms?
6. Describe a critical multilingual awareness activity that you might be able to conduct.
7. What are some ways in which teachers could develop English academic literacy with emergent bilinguals?

CHAPTER 6

Curriculum and Pedagogy

In this chapter, we will:

- Review theoretical constructs that support curricular opportunities and pedagogical practices for emergent bilinguals:

  Orientation of social justice and linguistic human rights
  Curriculum that is challenging and creative
  Pedagogy that is transformative/intercultural and collaborative

- Identify inequalities in curricular opportunities and pedagogical practices:

  Inequitable curricular opportunities; lack of early childhood programs, remedial education and tracking, special education placements, exclusion from gifted and AP classes,
  Inequitable resources, including funding inadequate instructional materials, school facilities, and funding
  Inequitable access to quality educators

- Consider some alternative practices:

  A challenging inclusive curriculum that starts early
  Preparation of caring, creative, and qualified teachers

> When we narrow the program so that there is only a limited array of areas in which assessment occurs and performance is honored, youngsters whose aptitudes and interests lie elsewhere are going to be marginalized in our schools. The more we diversify those opportunities, the more equity we are going to have because we're going to provide wider opportunities for youngsters to find what it is they are good at.
> —Elliot Eisner, "What Does It Mean to Say a School Is Doing Well?"

In this chapter, we focus on curricular opportunities and pedagogical practices affecting the education of emergent bilinguals. Gándara and Contreras say: "The problem of English learners' underachievement . . . is more likely related to the quality of education that these students receive, regardless of the language of instruction" (2009, p. 145). We consider here the quality of the education that emergent bilingual students are receiving, beyond the issue of language of instruction; in doing so, we continue to give attention to the central question in this book: *What does research tell us about how best to educate and assess emergent bilingual students? Are we using accepted theories and evidence in the education of these students?* Just as we observed a gap in Chapters 4 and 5 between language education theory and practice, we note in this chapter a gap between accepted theoretical foundations for curriculum and pedagogy and the classroom realities for many emergent bilinguals. We conclude the chapter by laying out alternative practices that can do much to accelerate the academic achievement of these children.

THEORETICAL CURRICULAR AND PEDAGOGICAL CONSTRUCTS

In this section we draw on three theoretical constructs that are useful in considering equity in curriculum and pedagogy for emergent bilinguals—an orientation of social justice and linguistic human rights, a curriculum that is challenging and creative, and a pedagogy that is transformative/intercultural and collaborative.

Social Justice and Linguistic Human Rights

Social justice in education is derived from the work by the American philosopher John Rawls in *A Theory of Justice* (1971). Applied to education, the concept of social justice refers to the appropriate distribution of benefits and burdens among groups, based on the principles of human rights and equality. As such, social justice theories demand that we analyze discriminatory structures and practices within institutions such as schools; these theories also require that part of educating youth includes engaging them in taking action to remedy social wrongs (Adams, Bell, & Griffin, 2007; Adams, Blumenfeld, Castañeda, & Hackman, 2000; Anyon, 1997, 2005; Ayers, Hunt, & Quinn, 1998; Cochran-Smith, 2004). This analysis of structures and practices is especially important in the teaching of emergent bilinguals. As we saw in Chapter 2, most emergent bilinguals are poor, and many are students of color. Many emergent bilinguals, although not all, are immigrants who are feeling dislocation and separation from both their countries of origin and sometimes families they have left behind. And as we have also seen, more than half (approximately 1.8 million) of the 3 million foreign-born immigrant children in the United States are undocumented (Jensen, 2001; Suárez-Orozco et al., 2008), thus intensifying feelings of dislocation and not belonging. Others are Native Americans, having experienced subjugation and oppression in their own lands. All these students have the right to an education that includes a rich and rigorous curriculum.

The idea of teaching for social justice has roots in the United States' social history of democracy and oppression. In defense of the basic human rights and freedoms guaranteed under the Bill of Rights of the U.S. Constitution, educating for social justice requires that teachers and students act in the construction of a socially just world. This was the case, for example, in the Freedom School movement of the 1960s when Black students in the segregated South participated in programs that engaged them not only in a rigorous academic curriculum, but also in a citizenship curriculum, enabling them to understand their rights and their role in bringing about change. Movements like this one to teach for social justice have been inspired by the work of the Brazilian scholar Paolo Freire. In his *Pedagogy of the Oppressed* (1970) Freire urges educators to engage students in a dialogical praxis so that they can act upon the world in order to transform it.

The humans' right to education is at the core of these social justice efforts. In this regard, UNESCO has been most influential. In the UNESCO Convention Against Discrimination in Education (adopted December 14, 1960; put into force May 22, 1962), Article 1 reads:

> For the purposes of this Convention, the term "discrimination" includes any distinction, exclusion, limitation or preference which, being based on race, colour, sex, language, religion, political or other opinion, national or social origin, economic condition or birth, has the purpose or effect of nullifying or impairing equality or treatment in education. (UNESCO, 1960)

The focus on social justice and human rights, coupled with the rise of critical theory on the role that language has played in asymmetrical power relations, has led to the call for linguistic human rights (Skutnabb-Kangas, 2000, 2006; Skutnabb-Kangas & Phillipson, 1994). Skutnabb-Kangas and Phillipson (1994) identify two categories of linguistic human rights, which are important to consider in educating emergent bilinguals:

- Individual rights, including the right to identify with one's own language and to use it both in and out of school, and the right to learn the official language of the state;
- Community rights, including the right of minority groups to establish and maintain schools and other educational institutions and to control their curricula.

Taking these categories into account, we can argue that in the United States linguistic human rights are not fully observed. For example, although many languages other than English are spoken, the use of these languages in everyday situations is sometimes considered suspect. When it comes to using these languages in the schools, many are excluded, especially in the elementary school years; in high schools, foreign language classes may be offered, but usually only Spanish, French, German, and lately Chinese (Center for Applied Linguistics, 2009) are the languages taught. As for minority groups' linguistic rights, although these groups have the right to establish their own complementary schools (often known as "heritage language" or bilingual community schools), where their languages and cultures are taught after school and weekends, they do not receive state funding for these schools (see García, Zakharia, & Otcu, in press; Peyton, Ranard, & McGinnis, 2001). One of the questions for educators, then, is how to extend these language rights to all students in the curriculum. Social justice and linguistic human rights are the philosophical values that motivate a challenging and creative curriculum for emergent bilinguals, a subject to which we now turn.

Curriculum That Is Challenging and Creative

Research on teaching and learning indicates that all students need to be given opportunities to participate in challenging academic work that promotes deep disciplinary knowledge and encourages higher-order thinking skills (Newman et al., 1996). Goldenberg summarizes it thus:

> As a general rule, all students tend to benefit from clear goals and learning objectives; meaningful, challenging, and motivating contexts; a curriculum rich with content; well-designed, clearly structured, and appropriately paced instruction; active engagement and participation; opportunities to practice, apply, and transfer new learning; feedback on correct and incorrect responses; periodic review and practice; frequent assessments to gauge progress, with re-teaching as needed; and opportunities to interact with other students in motivating and appropriately structured contexts. (2008, p. 17)

And yet, as Gibbons points out, "the development of curriculum distinguished by intellectual quality and the development of higher-order thinking has in reality rarely been a major focus of program planning for EL learners" (2009, p. 2).

Many have called attention to the importance of maintaining high expectations for emergent bilinguals and of providing them with challenging academic work (Carrasquillo & Rodriguez, 2002; Walqui, 2006). As with all students, emergent bilinguals require practice in complex thinking and deserve teachers who engage them in combining ideas to synthesize, generalize, explain, hypothesize, or arrive at some conclusion or interpretation (Walqui, García, & Hamburger, 2004). Gibbons (2009, pp. 21–30) advances seven intellectual practices for emergent bilinguals:

1. Students engage with the key ideas and concepts of the discipline in ways that reflect how "experts" in the field think and reason.
2. Students transform what they have learned into a different form for use in a new context or for a different audience.
3. Students make links between concrete knowledge and abstract theoretical knowledge.
4. Students engage in substantive conversation.
5. Students make connections between the spoken and written language of the subject and other discipline-related ways of making meaning.
6. Students take a critical stance toward knowledge and information.
7. Students use metalanguage in the context of learning about other things.

Along with offering challenge and rigor, it is important to provide students, especially emergent bilinguals, with a creative curriculum that provides space for them to experiment and innovate. There is not a more creative and innovative human activity than learning how to make meaning through another language. Research has shown that there is a relationship between bilingualism and creativity, meaning cognitive and linguistic production that is both original and valuable. That is, bilinguals can often think of something new by extending conceptual boundaries, something cognitive psychologists call "creative conceptual expansion."

Therefore, responsive schools will not only provide emergent bilinguals with a challenging and rich curriculum, but also with a creative one. By having teams of multicultural and multilingual students, who work collaboratively as equals using all their linguistic and cultural resources to address educational challenges presented to them, schools can foster the creative conceptual expansion of all students. To do so, schools must have teachers who can deliver a transformative/intercultural pedagogy, the subject of our next section.

Pedagogy That Is Transformative/Intercultural and Collaborative

Cummins calls for a "transformative/intercultural pedagogy" (2000, p. 45) to be used with language minority students where the students' language and cognitive abilities are included in the learning process and where students' identities are affirmed. Cummins defines transformative/intercultural pedagogy as "interactions between educators and students that attempt to foster collaborative relations of power in the classroom" (p. 253). In addition, he notes that such an approach "recognizes that the process of identity negotiation is fundamental to educational success for all students, and furthermore that this process is directly determined by the micro-interactions between individual educators and students" (p. 253). Important in Cummins's conceptualization is the intercultural aspect. That is, this transformative/intercultural pedagogy not only authorizes language minority students to engage in collaborative critical inquiry, but by affirming their cultural practices this pedagogy also recognizes their knowledge and identities. Thus, the process is transformative and intercultural, including majority and minority children and affecting the school culture and society in general.

Focusing on teaching by building on the ethnolinguistic identities of language minority students, other scholars have also advocated a "culturally relevant pedagogy" for minority students (Gay, 2002; Ladson-Billings, 1994, 1995; Valdés, 1996; Villegas & Lucas, 2002). Besides aligning classroom experiences with the students' home cultures and languages, culturally relevant pedagogies attempt to counteract inequitable power relations in society and empower minority students to develop their literacy and agency to work against oppression (Freire, 1970; Giroux, 1988).

Research on teaching and learning has also validated the importance of pedagogy that builds on collaborative social practices in which students try out ideas and actions and thus, socially construct their learning (Vygotsky, 1978). Lave and Wenger describe learning within a given social group as a process of participation that moves gradually from being 'legitimately peripheral' to being fully engaged in what they call a *community of practice*: "a set of relations among persons, activity and world, over time and in relation with other tangential and overlapping communities of practice" (1991, p. 98). This social view of learning and pedagogy takes the position that emergent bilinguals do not get to "possess" or "have" academic English; rather, they learn by "doing" and "using" English repeatedly over the course of a lifetime in communities of practice. As Van Lier explains:

> The ecologist will say that knowledge of language for a human is like knowledge of the jungle for an animal. The animal does not have the jungle; it knows how to use the jungle and how to live in it. Perhaps we can say by analogy that we do not have or possess language, but that we learn to use it and to live in it. (2000, p. 253)

A collaborative pedagogy relies, then, on a great deal of practice of talk or what Tharp, Estrada, Dalto, and Yamauchi (2000) call *instructional conversation* or what Padrón and Waxman (1999) call *teaching through conversation*. We know, for example, that quality literacy instruction for emergent bilinguals must include "efforts to increase the scope and sophistication of these students' oral language proficiency" (August & Shanahan, 2006, p. 448). That is, a focus on reading and writing alone is insufficient to develop emergent bilinguals' abilities to use and live in English.

To build this community of practice, groups of students need to be engaged in *cooperative learning* (Kagan, 1986; Kagan & McGroarty, 1993). The National Literacy Panel review found that having students work cooperatively on group tasks increases the literacy comprehension of emergent bilinguals (August & Shanahan, 2006).

For this transformative/intercultural and collaborative pedagogy to be delivered, highly prepared teachers and school leaders are needed. For example, value-added assessment studies in Tennessee have shown that students who have high-quality teachers over a period of 3 years achieve, on average, 50 percentile points more on standardized tests than those who have low-quality teachers (Sanders & Rivers, 1996). Furthermore, teachers with less teaching experience produce smaller gains in their students compared with more experienced teachers (Murname & Phillips, 1981). Studies have shown that teacher preparation and certification are the strongest correlates of student achievement in reading and mathematics (Darling-Hammond, 1999), and many others have affirmed that teacher quality matters (Rice, 2003; Wenglinsky, 2000).

Despite research that shows the importance of having curricular programs that emphasize social justice and that are academically challenging and creative, and pedagogy that is transformative and intercultural, emergent bilinguals are often excluded from meaningful educational programs and rigorous instruction. Their teachers are also often poorly prepared. We discuss these inequitable curricular and pedagogical practices before turning to what is being done about it.

INEQUITABLE CURRICULAR
AND PEDAGOGICAL PRACTICES

We describe here curricular, pedagogical, and educator-quality issues that result in inequities in the education of emergent bilinguals. And because quality instruction does not happen without adequate resources, we also consider funding needed to provide quality education for emergent bilinguals.

Inequitable Curricular Opportunities

It all starts early. When emergent bilinguals enter kindergarten they are already disadvantaged. According to the Early Childhood Longitudinal Study (ECLS), about half of kindergarteners who speak English at home but no more than 17% of kindergartners who speak a language other than English at home perform above the 50th percentile in California (Gándara, Rumberger, Maxwell-Jolly, & Callahan, 2003). This disparity has to do with the fact that emergent bilingual kindergarteners cannot understand

English well enough to be assessed in that language. From the very beginning, then, these children are often placed in remedial education.

It has been shown that early childhood education programs can help narrow gaps in preparation for elementary school especially among poor children (Haskins & Rouse 2005; Takanishi, 2004, in Capps et al., 2005). Additionally, researchers have demonstrated the benefits of early childhood education programs that contribute positively to children's health, emotional adjustment, and cognitive functioning (Karoly & Bigelow, 2005; García & González, 2006). For example, in a study of the effects of a preschool program on poor children in Ypsilanti, Michigan, a control group received no preschool services. At the age of 40 those who had attended preschool had not only increased earnings, but also decreased reliance on public assistance and had lower rates of criminal activity and substance abuse (Nores, Belfield, Barnett, & Schweinhart, 2005). A study in North Carolina obtained similar results—the group that had attended preschool had higher IQs, increased levels of high school graduation and college attendance, as well as decreased rates of grade retention and rates of special education classification than a control group that did not attend preschool (Barnett & Masse, 2007).

The benefit of preschool education for Latino emergent bilinguals has also been demonstrated. Gormley (2008), for example, showed that Hispanic emergent bilinguals in a prekindergarten program did better in all aspects of the Woodcock-Johnson Test and the Woodcock-Muñoz Battery—assessing letter-word identification, spelling, and answers to applied problem items.

And yet, emergent bilinguals are less likely to be enrolled in any early childhood program than their monolingual counterparts. Furthermore, we know that the best form of early childhood education for emergent bilinguals would be one that builds on the linguistic and cultural strengths they bring from home, and such programs are extremely rare (García & González, 2006).

Remedial education and tracking. Kindergarteners and others who score low on tests are likely to be placed in remedial education (Gottlieb, Alter, Gottlieb, & Wishner, 1994). Because emergent bilinguals are seen as only English language learners from whom little is expected, their schooling often consists of remedial programs where the emphasis is on drill and remediation (De Cohen et al., 2005). As a result, the learning of emergent bilinguals is frequently about compensating for their limited English language skills (Harklau, 1994; Olsen, 1997). They are often given multiple periods of classes in English as a second language instead of meaningful content, a product of the emphasis on developing English. To accomplish this English-acquisition goal at the expense of other learning, these students are often taken from their regular classes for "pullout ESL," creating further inequities (Anstrom, 1997; Fleischman & Hopstock, 1993). Furthermore, although it is widely accepted that a balanced approach to literacy that incorporates more time to discuss, create, read, and write, alongside some phonics instruction, is central to literacy development (Birch, 2002; Honig, 1996), most English language learners are taught to read exclusively through heavily phonics-based approaches.

For academic courses other than English, the English language learners are also regularly tracked into courses that do not provide them with challenging content (Callahan, 2003, 2005; Oakes, 1990). In some cases, they are given shortened day schedules whenever courses are not considered relevant to them (Olsen, 1997), or the extra time blocks are filled with physical education or art classes rather than core subject content courses (García, 1999). In fact, many times their learning of content-area academics is delayed until English has been acquired (Miniucci & Olsen, 1992). Alternatively, when newcomers are taught subject matter exclusively through English, instruction often takes on a slower pace and less content is covered (Minicucci & Olsen, 1992). In California, only 41% of teachers reported being able to cover the same material with emergent bilinguals as with all students (Gándara et al., 2003). Only when the home language is used to teach academic subjects in recognition of these students' emergent bilingualism can challenging academic content be taught (Bartlett & García, in press; García & Bartlett, 2007).

In a study of secondary schools in California, less than one fourth of the schools surveyed offered the full range of content courses for emergent bilinguals (Minicucci & Olsen, 1992). This in turn results in an inferior education, for by the time the emergent bilinguals develop their full proficiency in English, they have not taken the appropriate high-level courses compared with their grade-level English speaking counterparts, and thus, they score lower on college admission tests (Durán, 1983; Mehan et al., 1992; Pennock-Roman, 1994). In a major test case on the viability of curriculum tracking as an educational practice, *Hobson v. Hansen* (1967), the Washington, DC, Superior Court noted that sixth-grade students who are taught a Grade 3 curriculum are likely to end the year with a third-grade education (Gándara et al., 2003).

Special education. English language learners are also overrepresented in some categories of special education, particularly in specific learning disabilities and language and speech impairment classes, and most especially at the secondary level (Artiles, Rueda, Salazar, & Higareda, 2002). Emergent bilinguals who are in bilingual programs are less likely to be in special education than those students who are in English-only programs (Artiles et al., 2002). Gándara et al. (2003) have shown that English language learners who have low proficiency in both English and their home language are even more vulnerable. They are 1.5 times more likely at the elementary level, and twice more likely at the secondary level, to be diagnosed as speech impaired and learning disabled.

The overrepresentation of emergent bilinguals in the learning disability category (57% in this category vs. 53% in this category among the rest of the student population) and in the speech/language category (24% in this category vs. 19% among the rest of the population) suggests that many educators may have difficulty distinguishing students with disabilities from those who are still learning English (Yates & Ortiz, 1998). Many emergent bilinguals in special education have been classified erroneously as having a speech/language disability (Zehler et al., 2003). This error comes as a result of the shortage of special educators who are trained to understand issues of bilingualism and second-language development (Ortiz, 2001).

According to Zehler et al. (2003), approximately 9% of the total ELL population in public schools was in special education classes in 2001–02.[1] Of these, 61% were male, indicating an overrepresentation of male emergent bilinguals with disabilities, since only 51% of all emergent bilinguals were male (Zehler et al., 2003). Most emergent bilinguals in special education programs were at the elementary level (50.5%), followed by middle school (22.8%), and then high school (18.6%) (Hopstock & Stephenson, 2003a).[2]

Spanish-language English learners represented 80% of the total special education emergent bilingual population, indicating that they are slightly overrepresented in special education programs compared with English learners overall (Zehler et al., 2003). This overrepresentation may have to do with the increased availability of special education Spanish-English bilingual teachers and bilingual school psychologists, as well as the abundance of assessment instruments in Spanish, compared with other languages. It could also relate to cultural biases against Latino students.

Exclusion from gifted programs and Advanced Placement. The other side of the coin for emergent bilinguals when it comes to access to the most challenging educational programs is their underrepresentation in "gifted and talented" programs. Only 1.4% of English language learners nationwide are in gifted and talented programs, in contrast to 6.4% of the English proficient population (Hopstock & Stephenson, 2003a). Although 3.2% of all high school students are enrolled in Advanced Placement mathematics and science, only 0.8% of English language learners are enrolled in Advanced Placement science and 1.0% in Advanced Placement math (Hopstock & Stephenson, 2003a). Although other data on participation by emergent bilinguals in college preparatory courses is not available, their placement in remedial literacy and mathematics courses and lower-level core academic courses is well documented (Gándara et al., 2003; Parrish et al., 2002). Yet the data suggest that because of emergent bilinguals' performance on invalid standardized tests, they are too often judged unfit for mainstream college preparatory classes (Koelsch, n.d.).

Inequitable Resources

Instructional materials and technology. Oakes and Saunders (2002) have argued that there is a clear link between appropriate materials and curriculum and student academic outcome. Emergent bilinguals need developmentally appropriate materials to learn English, but they also need appropriate content materials in their home languages. However, more often than not, emergent bilinguals do not have appropriate resources. Only 25% of teachers surveyed in a study by The American Institutes for Research (AIR) reported that they used a different textbook for emergent bilinguals from that of their English proficient students; and only 46% reported using any supplementary materials for them (Parrish et al., 2002). More than one quarter of the teachers in California reported not having appropriate reading material in English, and almost two thirds of those with high percentages of emergent bilinguals in their classes had few instructional materials in Spanish or other languages (Gándara et al., 2003). In another study, teachers with high percentages of emergent bilinguals had higher rates of reporting that their textbooks and instructional materials were meager and that they and their students had less access to technology (Gándara et al., 2003).

Although Title III of NCLB (2001) requires states to have English language proficiency standards that are aligned with the state academic content standards, the alignment of instruction for emergent bilinguals with state standards is much poorer than for English proficient students (Gutiérrez et al., 2002; Hopstock & Stephenson, 2003a). There are also few instructional materials to support this alignment (Hopstock & Stephenson, 2003a).

Technology, and in particular access to the Internet for information seeking, holds much promise in teaching linguistically diverse students and emergent bilinguals (Cummins, Brown, & Sayers, 2007; Kleifgen, 1991; Kleifgen & Kinzer, 2009). Technology can, for example, assist emergent bilinguals in searching for content material in their home languages that would help to contextualize and supplement the lesson in English. However, these students often attend overcrowded schools with limited resources and funding. For example, California teachers report that their emergent bilingual students seldom have access to technology (Gándara et al., 2003).

Even in schools that provide computers, inner-city schools generally offer students only basic literacy and numeracy skills at the computer, and they are seldom given the opportunity to use the Internet at school. In contrast, affluent schools tend to provide opportunities to use the technology for critical thinking skills (Clark & Gorski, 2001). This situation is further exacerbated by the fact that emergent bilinguals often do not have access to computers and the Internet at home. The National Center for Education Statistics (NCES, 2003) provided data showing that, in 2001, 77% of White students used a computer at home, yet only 41% of students of color, including Latino students, had the same computer and Internet access at home. Liff, Steward, and Watts (2002) point to the real inequity for any student who has limited access to the technology: "The digital divide is not just about whether one has the technology or not but more about the ability of some people to become active participants in these new patterns of expanded network interactions" (p. 84). In short, emergent bilinguals who have little school or home access to computers and the Internet are robbed of opportunities to truly engage in meaningful self-directed learning and communication in a globalized world.

School facilities. Research has shown that classrooms for emergent bilinguals are often located on the periphery of, in the basement of, or outside the school building (Olsen, 1997). Emergent bilinguals also go to schools in buildings that are often not clean or safe. For example, in a Harris Poll conducted in 2002 of 1,017 California teachers, close to half the teachers in schools with high numbers of emergent bilinguals reported that their schools had unclean bathrooms and had seen evidence of mice, compared with 26% of teachers in schools with few if any English learners (Gándara et al., 2003).

In 2006 a report concluded that new school buildings were needed across the country and that minorities, in particular, were attending schools with decrepit facilities (BEST, 2006). Despite unprecedented spending and growth in school construction since then, resources for school construction have not been equally available in all school districts. For example, between 1995 and 2004, school districts with high minority student enrollment invested only $5,172 per student in school construction, while school districts with predominantly White student enrollment spent the most, $7,102 per student (BEST, 2006). In addition, high minority school districts used the money to fund basic repairs, such as new roofs and asbestos removal, whereas schools in wealthier districts funded science labs and performing arts studios. In sum, emergent bilinguals attend the most impoverished and underresourced schools, which is clearly related to their growing isolation and segregation within the public educational system (Orfield, 2001).

Inequitable funding. One of the most important equity issues surrounding the education of emergent bilinguals has to do with the ways in which programs are funded. Currently, the major funding source for public education programs for emergent bilinguals is the federal government, virtually all of which has come through what was Title VII of the Elementary and Secondary Education Act (ESEA). Title VII, known as the Bilingual Education Act, is now Title III of NCLB.[3] Until 2002, Title VII of ESEA had provided funding for projects and services for English language learner students at the state, district, and school levels on a competitive basis; that is, they were *discretionary grants* that states and districts applied for and used to fund schools and programs serving emergent bilinguals. In contrast, under Title III of NCLB, there are *performance-based formula grants that the federal government awards directly to the states*. These federal grants to the states are determined by two factors that are weighted differently in the formula:

1. the number of English language learners (80% of the formula) and
2. the population of recently immigrated children and youth[4] (relative to national counts of these populations) (20% of the formula).

Once the individual state departments of education receive their federal money, they award subgrants to local educational authorities, who apply for them based on the number of English learners and immigrant students in each district. States are allowed to set aside up to 5% of these funds for state-level activities, such as test development. In addition, Title III requires each state to use up to 15% of its formula grant to award subgrants to school districts with significant increases in school enrollment of immigrant children and youth, before distributing the remainder across school districts in proportion to the number of students who are categorized as English learners.

Despite this provision and the fact that total funding has increased with NCLB (Borkowski & Sneed, 2006), Title III reaches only approximately 80% of the 5 million English language learners nationwide (OELA, 2006). Furthermore, the funds are spread very thin as the program continues to be underfunded within NCLB. The Great City Schools Report found that the average Title III subsidy of $109 per student was insufficient to meet the educational needs of emergent bilinguals (Council of the Great City Schools, 2004).

As we noted in Chapter 2, there are numerous problems with efforts to count emergent bilinguals via the census or school reports, so the federal funding is not always accurately distributed across states and districts. As a result, some states have done better and others worse. For example, according to Jim Crawford (personal communication, March 17, 2007), in 2004–05, California served 516,000 more emergent bilinguals than the Census Bureau counted through its American Community Survey (ACS); Texas served 140,000 more; and Arizona served 53,000 more. By contrast, New York served 128,000 fewer emergent bilinguals than the ACS reported; New Jersey, 45,000 fewer; and Georgia, 28,000 fewer.

In addition, not every local educational authority applies to its state for Title III funding. For example, in 2006, fewer than 200 out of 780 districts in the state of New York applied (Pedro Ruiz, personal communication, February 2007). New York State gets $53 million to $54 million for Title III funding each year and 80% of this funding is targeted for "LEP allocations."[5] In 2008–09 New York State identified 272,046 LEP students. Each student was then allocated approximately $182 in additional funds per year (Pedro Ruiz, personal communication, 2009).

Per pupil funding figures also assume that schools target funds to those who need English language learner services and distribute funding somewhat evenly among them. In reality, the money allocated for each school is given directly to the principal in one lump sum, and the principal decides what to do with it. Little information exists on how these funds are allocated at the school level.

There are also problems with how funding is contingent on Annual Yearly Progress (AYP) for schools' and districts' Title I funding and Annual Measurable Achievement Objectives (AMAOs) for Title III.[6] According to the Legislative Analyst Office (2006), the first of the three required AMAOs, which mandated annual progress for English language learner students on the state's language proficiency test, may have created a set of perverse incentives for states. For instance, in 2004, California required that 51.5% of students move up at least one level on the scale, or score a 4 or 5 (Early Advanced or Advanced) and maintain that level. But analysts argued that these benchmarks could result in the delaying of reclassification of thousands of English language learners, and yet those schools that delay may be rewarded with more funding. The danger here is that schools may alter test scores in order to receive much needed funding.

Costing-out studies. Striving for transparency is a central part of seeking equitable funding, a process that some believe entails more public engagement and judicial oversight (American Institutes of Research [AIR], 2004; Rebell, 2007).[7] Since 1991, when the press for higher standards and more accountability became more intense, courts, state legislatures, and education advocacy organizations have requested "costing out" studies—to obtain more information on how to fund students, including English language learner students, equitably. Such research helps to inform the legal movement to seek adequate funding for groups deemed in need of additional resources, including emergent bilinguals (AIR, 2004; Rebell, 2007, 2009).

In examining this costing-out literature as it relates to emergent bilinguals, most studies have shown that it costs more to educate emergent bilinguals than it does to educate native English speakers (Baker, Green, & Markham, 2004; Parrish, 1994), although a few studies have argued otherwise (AIR, 2004). Still, estimates of these additional costs per emergent bilingual student vary greatly and range from 5% more to 200% more than the cost of educating mainstream students (Baker et al., 2004; J. Crawford, personal communication, March 17, 2007). In other words, there is great variation in this literature on the cost of a meaningful education for these students, but some consensus is beginning to emerge, as we will describe below.

Overall, it has been established that emergent bilinguals require additional personnel at rates of approximately 20 students with one full-time teacher and one or more instructional aide per teacher. This leads to an additional cost (above a regular program) of $2,403 to $3,822 per pupil at the elementary level and $2,851 to $4,937 per pupil at the secondary level, depending on the per pupil cost and teachers' salaries in a given state and district in optimally sized schools (Baker et al., 2004). These additional costs of educating emergent bilinguals can also vary by district size, concentration of students, and the type of instructional program offered.

Parrish (1994) has found that the most expensive educational programs for emergent bilinguals are English as a Second Language programs. In 1994, ESL programs cost $2,687 per pupil, more than two-way bilingual education (dual language) programs, which cost $2,675 per pupil. In the same year, the least expensive educational programs were transitional bilingual education programs, with early exit programs estimated to be the least expensive at $1,881 per pupil and late exit programs at $1,976 per pupil. Sheltered English programs follow, costing approximately $2,050 per pupil.[8]

Clearly, there is a need for additional funding to provide emergent bilinguals with the educational services they require, and deserve, so that they may achieve high standards in English. However, before anyone can establish precisely how much more is needed for their education, it is necessary to carefully examine the local context in which these emergent bilinguals are being educated and the goals for their education.

Inequitable access to quality educators. Teacher and principal quality are two of the most important factors in determining school effectiveness and, ultimately, student achievement (Blasé & Blasé, 2001; Clewell & Campbell, 2004). But few school leaders and not enough teachers are well versed in issues surrounding bilingualism. Additionally, there is high turnover among both administrators and teachers of language minority students. Thus, it is even more difficult to find quality teachers and school leaders for emergent bilingual students than it is for students in general.

Although principals and teachers at schools with large numbers of English learners are more likely to be Latino or Asian, both principals and teachers also tend to be less experienced and have fewer credentials than those at schools with few or no emergent bilingual students (De Cohen et al., 2005). Forty percent of Asian teachers and 45% of Latino teachers nationwide teach in schools with high levels of emergent bilinguals (De Cohen et al., 2005). These Latino and Asian teachers are more likely to be bilingual and knowledgeable of the children's cultures, thus enabling the support of the students' languages and identities. And yet these teachers tend to be less experienced in the classroom than their White counterparts. Teachers in schools with high numbers of English language learners have fewer credentials on average than teachers at schools with few or no emergent bilinguals (De Cohen et al., 2005). Although only slightly more than 50% of teachers in schools with high levels of emergent bilinguals have full certification, almost 80% of teachers in other schools do.

In California, the least experienced teachers are placed disproportionately in schools that have the greatest number of minority students (Esch & Shields, 2002; Esch et al., 2005; Gándara et al., 2003). In 2002, 25% of teachers of emergent bilinguals in California were not fully certified, as compared with 14% statewide (Rumberger, 2002). Schools with high concentrations of emergent bilinguals have more difficulties filling teaching vacancies; they are more likely to hire unqualified teachers and rely on substitutes (De Cohen et al., 2005). And although California's bilingual education certification—the BCLAD[9]—is the most comprehensive of all California certification, it is also the rarest. Only 5% of California teachers who instruct emergent bilinguals have a full credential with BCLAD authorization (Gándara et al., 2003). More than 40% of the teachers of emergent bilinguals report receiving only one in-service workshop that focused on the instruction of their students in the previous 5 years (Maxwell-Jolly, Gándara, & Mendez Benavidez, 2006).

The General Accounting Office (GAO) report of 2006 also reports that states have much difficulty in finding qualified personnel to teach emergent bilinguals. Only 11% of the teachers of emergent bilinguals are certified in bilingual education, whereas 18% are certified in ESL. And although being bilingual is an important asset for teachers of emergent bilinguals, only 15% are fluent in a language other than English (LOTE) (Crawford & Krashen, 2007).

Beyond teacher certification in specialized areas, most teachers in the United States have not had any preparation in how to teach emergent bilinguals. Nationwide, less than 20% of teacher education programs required at least one course focused on English learners and bilingualism, and less than a third exposed their students to any fieldwork experience with emergent bilinguals (GAO, 2009). Although 42% of teachers surveyed in a 2002 report of the National Center for Education Statistics indicated they had emergent bilinguals in their classrooms, only 13% of these teachers had received more than 8 hours of professional development related to emergent bilinguals.

The inadequate preparation of teachers on issues affecting language minority students negatively affects their ability to teach these children. It has been found that teachers who are certified in ESL or bilingual academic development, as well as those who have fluency in a LOTE, have more positive attitudes toward the bilingualism of the children and their classroom practice (Lee & Oxelson, 2006).

As the numbers of emergent bilinguals increase, the shortage of qualified teachers for these students has only been exacerbated. In 1986, there was one bilingual teacher for every 70 English learners students in California. By 1996, there was one for every 98 emergent bilingual students (Gándara et al., 2003).

According to Gándara et al. (2003), there is also a dearth of school professionals to assist emergent bilinguals. Bilingual speech pathologists are sorely needed, and guidance counselors with bilingual skills are also in short supply. In California, less than 8% of the school psychologists are bilingual and capable of conducting an assessment in an English language learner student's home language.

Although classrooms with large numbers of English language learners may have more teaching assistants, emergent bilinguals actually interact less with English-speaking adults. In fact, it turns out that parents and other adults spend *less time* in classrooms with emergent bilinguals (Gándara et al., 2003). In other words, although parental participation has been identified as a most important factor in furthering a child's education, as we will see in Chapter 7, the participation of parents in the education of their emergent bilingual children is underused, leading to the students' isolation from the school community.

From the foregoing discussion, it is evident that emergent bilinguals have to contend with much more than language inequities. With regard to Latinos, Gándara and Contreras say:

> Although Latinos have suffered many of the same inequities as blacks and other minority groups in schooling—inadequate and overcrowded facilities, underprepared teachers, inappropriate curriculum and textbooks, and segregated schools—the civil rights focus in education for Latinos has been primarily the issue of language. (2009, p. 121)

The fact that 80% of emergent bilinguals are Latinos means that more attention has been paid to the inequities of language use, than to the inadequacies of the educational opportunity they have been given. And yet, as we will see, to offer equitable curricular opportunities to emergent bilinguals would require a fundamental change in the ways in which we view the students' languages other than English, and in particular, Spanish.

ALTERNATIVE CURRICULAR AND
PEDAGOGICAL PRACTICES

A Challenging Inclusive Curriculum
That Starts Early

Emergent bilinguals are fully capable of developing academic English if given the same socioeducational opportunities as wealthy White children. "The same," however, does not always mean integrated educational programs in which emergent bilinguals would be overlooked, or worse, discriminated against. An equitable curriculum and pedagogy for emergent bilinguals must adapt to their needs. A challenging inclusive curriculum for emergent bilinguals must be ecologically adaptive, as students' bilingualism and biliteracy emerge.

In early childhood, emergent bilinguals must be given the opportunity to engage with caring adults who not only speak their home languages and understand their cultural practices, but also can guide their bilingual development by providing opportunities to practice listening to and speaking English. The beginnings of communication around print must occur in the child's home language, the language in which he or she can make meaning from print. Although it may be necessary to provide a separate instructional space away from English-speaking students to develop an emergent bilingual's literacy, care must also be taken to provide integrated spaces where emergent bilinguals can interact with other children who speak English. This can happen during the time for snack or lunch, play, nap, music, art, or dance, the range of activities in which very young children are involved. These integrated spaces must function not only as catalysts of English language acquisition for language minority children, but also of LOTE acquisition and familiarity with other linguistic and cultural norms for English-monolingual young children who will also be considered, in these integrated spaces, emergent bilinguals.

It is most important that culturally and linguistically relevant early childhood programs with bilingual instruction be created for very young emergent bilinguals (Garcia & Jensen, 2009). And it is crucial that this preschool education be state funded and provided free to all 3- and 4-year-olds. Such an investment in bilingual preschools for all emergent bilinguals would be richly compensated with the children's improved language development by the time they reach elementary school.

In Chapter 5 we discussed alternative practices that have to do with developing English academic literacy through complex language use. Much has been said about the ways in which a challenging academic curriculum can be delivered to emergent bilinguals while also developing their academic literacies and academic English (Celic, 2009; Chamot & O'Malley, 1994; Gibbons, 2002, 2009; Echevarría, Vogt, & Short, 2004; Freeman & Freeman, 2008). But in order to provide inclusive educational spaces and curricular opportunities for emergent bilinguals throughout schooling, while maintaining opportunities for emergent bilinguals to develop their bilingualism and biliteracy, the home language cannot be considered suspect. An inclusive and equitable society would provide the means by which emergent bilinguals are assessed for gifted and talented programs in the language they know best. In turn, these gifted and talented programs would then include these LOTEs and make the development of bilingualism and biliteracy a goal for all the children. As we have seen, bilingualism and biliteracy are important for improved cognitive functioning and creative performance. Thus, gifted and talented programs would not only include emergent bilinguals, but would be spaces where bilingualism and biliteracy would be a goal for all.

Likewise, if LOTEs were given their rightful place in the U.S. curriculum, as important tools for socio-cognitive and academic development, more advanced classes and Advanced Placement classes would be taught in those languages. Recent New York State policy that mandates translation of some math, science and social studies graduation exams into five LOTEs—Spanish, Chinese, Korean, Russian, and Haitian Creole—has resulted in a more challenging high school curriculum for emergent bilinguals because students who were previously relegated to ESL, music, art, and physical education classes are now included in content classes taught in these languages. Many high schools are also now teaching AP classes in LOTEs. In one high school we know, for example, AP Biology is taught in Spanish for Latino emergent bilinguals. Although the students read the advanced Biology text in English, they discuss and do experiments and scientific work in Spanish. Thus, a translanguaging pedagogy would be one way to offer more advanced courses in a LOTE. In fact, translanguaging would be precisely the tool that would allow all emergent bilinguals to participate in advanced classes, even those taught in English, as students are given responsibility to use their home languages to research and learn advanced content.

Finally, with deeper understandings of bilingualism, educators may be less inclined to immediately recommend special education placement for those students who have not yet developed academic English. Educators would know that the development of bilingualism and biliteracy takes practice over a lifetime, and that using academic English to perform the decontextualized tasks of schools comes with time and practice. With this knowledge, educators would ensure that students receive quality education throughout and that they follow an educational program that supports their linguistic and cultural differences.

Preparing Caring, Creative, and Qualified Educators

Perhaps no area is more crucial to the improvement of education of emergent bilinguals than the preparation of educators for emergent bilinguals—school leaders; teachers; and other school professionals such as school psychologists, guidance counselors, and therapists; and paraprofessionals. All school leaders today need to become experts in bilingualism and language learners (Reyes, 2006). Not only specialized bilingual and ESL teachers, but also "mainstream" teachers have to understand issues of bilingualism in education and how to include emergent bilinguals in a quality and challenging education (Lucas & Grinberg, 2008).

With the intensified migrations of peoples and convergences of languages and cultures in this 21st century, there cannot be language teachers on the one hand, and content teachers on the other (Téllez & Waxman, 2006). All language teachers must be content-area experts, while all content teachers must be language experts. To achieve this, teacher education programs would have to change significantly, making a commitment to include courses on bilingualism and academic language development in all curricula, thus ensuring that all their prospective teachers have clinical experiences with emergent bilinguals (Grant & Wong, 2003).

Teacher apprenticeship models have sprung up where prospective teachers team up with experienced teachers for a year of teaching, while pursuing university courses in partnership with the school district. One such model is that being pursued by the Internationals Network for Public Schools in New York City. Prospective teachers have a yearlong teaching apprenticeship in high-performing international high schools. After completing the program, apprentices receive New York State certification in TESOL and an innovative master's degree in TESOL from Long Island University. The program is designed around the tenet that, like students, teachers learn best when they apply the theories and content of teaching in an authentic learning context and develop teaching abilities by practicing alongside an experienced teacher.

Teachers who provide emergent bilinguals with a challenging and creative curriculum are those who are committed to the development of language minority communities, both socially and academically. A way to capitalize on this commitment would be to attract prospective teachers from the language communities themselves (Clewell & Villegas, 2001). Gándara and Contreras (2009) reminds us that there has never been a true effort to recruit these teachers and to prepare them to the highest standards. Gándara and Contreras give reasons why hiring qualified teachers from the students' own communities would be important:

> Such teachers not only better understand the challenges that students face and the resources that exist in those communities; they are also more likely to speak

the language of the students and be able to communicate with them and their parents. Moreover, teachers who come from the same community in which they work are more likely to stay in the job over time, developing valuable experience and expertise that has been shown to enhance the achievement of their students. (2009, p. 148)

The engagement of the community is crucial not only to ensure that there is a supply of committed and qualified caring and creative teachers, but also to provide an equitable education to students themselves. This will be the subject of Chapter 7.

EDUCATING EMERGENT BILINGUALS: EMBRACING CHALLENGE AND CARE

It is evident that providing an equitable education to emergent bilinguals is not only an issue of language. And yet unless the students' home languages are accepted in schools and not considered suspect, there will continue to be ways of excluding emergent bilinguals from the equal educational opportunities that they deserve. Given the ways in which schools are structured, only a language rights orientation based on principles of social justice will ensure that emergent bilinguals are given equitable curricular opportunities and be included in advanced courses and gifted and talented programs. But language rights have to be balanced with socioeducational rights, insisting that emergent bilinguals have equitable resources, equitable funding, and equitable access to quality teachers. Social justice for emergent bilinguals includes providing them with a challenging inclusive and linguistically and culturally relevant curriculum that empowers them to counteract the linguistic and social oppression in which they often live.

STUDY QUESTIONS

1. What is social justice? How is social justice related to language rights? What do you think about language rights?
2. What are the characteristics of a challenging and creative curriculum for emergent bilinguals? Describe inequities in curricula that emergent bilingual students face.
3. How would you define transformative/intercultural pedagogy? What is culturally relevant pedagogy? What are the similarities and differences in both approaches?
4. Why are emergent bilinguals often classified as special education students? Why are they often excluded from advanced courses and gifted and talented programs?

5. Discuss the inadequate instructional resources for emergent bilinguals. What would be necessary to alleviate this situation?
6. What is the situation regarding funding of quality educational programs for emergent bilinguals? What do costing-out studies say?
7. Why are many educators inadequately prepared to serve emergent bilinguals? What would be a way of attracting and preparing caring, creative, and qualified teachers of emergent bilinguals?
8. Discuss ways in which an inclusive and just curriculum for emergent bilinguals could be accomplished.

CHAPTER 7

Involving Parents and Communities

This chapter addresses the roles of parents and communities in the education of emergent bilinguals. The chapter focuses on:

- Theoretical constructs and empirical evidence for parent and community involvement:

    Research on parental and community involvement
    The funds of knowledge construct

- Inequitable practices:

    Stigmatization of language minority parents and communities
    Exclusion of the home language
    One-size-fits-all parent education programs

- Alternative approaches:

    Family engagement as a shared responsibility
    Broadening the view of parental engagement
    Community organizing

Both popular belief and research over the years have supported the notion of parental involvement in children's schooling, the premise being that several caring adults (school personnel and family members), working together, can accelerate students' learning. It is "the mantra of every educational reform program" (González, 2005, p. 42), including the current NCLB (2001) legislation, which requires schools to reach out to parents and involve them in their children's education. In this chapter, we start by examining what the research tells us regarding the benefits of parental involvement overall, and then we discuss specific benefits for families with emergent bilingual children. Next, we take a critical look at what actually happens to many of these families and children when they reach the schoolhouse door—the discrimination and marginalization they experience. Finally, we describe alternative approaches—more promising ways in which families, schools, and communities come together to support an equitable education for emergent bilinguals.

RESEARCH AND THEORIES ON PARENTAL
AND COMMUNITY INVOLVEMENT

Research Evidence

Research has shown that parents' involvement in their sons' and daughters' education leads to better attendance, higher achievement, improved attitudes about learning, and higher graduation rates. These benefits of parental involvement have been demonstrated for children in their early years of schooling (Weiss, Caspe, & Lopez, 2006; Caspe, Lopez, & Wolos, 2007) as well as for adolescents from middle school to high school (Eccles & Harold, 1993), although the parental role diminishes during these years, partially because of adolescents' desire for more autonomy (Kreider, Caspe, Kennedy, & Weiss, 2007). According to Kreider and her colleagues, three family involvement processes leading to students' school success include (1) parenting attitudes and practices in the home, (2) formal and informal home-school connections, and (3) parental responsibility for their children's academic growth.[1]

In addition, and of particular importance for this chapter, studies show that children from minority and low-income families gain the most from parent involvement (Epstein, 1990; Henderson, 1987; Henderson & Berla, 1994; Henderson & Mapp, 2002; Hidalgo, Siu, & Epstein, 2004; Jordan, Orozco, & Averett, 2001). A meta-analysis conducted by Jeynes (2005b) of 41 studies on urban elementary schools demonstrates a significant relationship between parental involvement and academic achievement; this relationship holds for Whites and minority groups as well as for both boys and girls. Jeynes (2004/2005) found positive effects for secondary school students, as well, in his meta-analysis of 52 such studies.

Psychology researchers have found what they describe as three overarching "determinants" of parental involvement. The first is parents' beliefs regarding the support roles they have in their children's education; the second is the extent to which they believe that they possess the knowledge and tools they need as educators of their children; the third relates to their perceptions regarding the schools' (or their children's) willingness to have them participate.[2]

Researchers who focus on social theory examine sociocultural and socioeconomic factors of parent involvement. These scholars point out that parents who possess certain kinds of social capital—social connections, relationships, and shared understandings that provide support and access to institutional resources (Bourdieu, 1985; Portes, 1998)—are successful in helping their children do well academically. Becoming involved in their children's schooling requires that parents understand how the school system functions, what curricular choices are available for their children, and whether they are aware of counseling and advice for accelerated learning and other college prep options. Studies show that many ethnolinguistic minority parents do not have access to these understandings (Gándara & Contreras, 2009), yet they do have uniformly high aspirations for their children (Delgado-Gaitán, 1990, 1992; Steinberg, 1996). Parents embrace the "opportunity narrative," a belief that with their sacrifices and hard work, their children can get ahead because school represents an opportunity for success (Bartlett, 2007).

Let us examine one such study on families' educative practices at home. Concha Delgado-Gaitán (1992) shows in her close ethnographic observation and interviews of six families that school *does* matter to Mexican American parents. Delgado-Gaitán examines family social interaction in the home, during which parents, within the broader context of their local community institutions, transmit their beliefs, values, and experiences to their children. She describes three categories of parental support for their children's education. The first she calls the physical environment, which addresses the economic and social resources in the home and surrounding community such as arranging study spaces and materials in close-knit quarters at home and consulting people they know in the church and workplace about their children's schooling. The second category includes emotional and motivational climates within the home such as encouraging their children to study so that they improve the weekly evaluations they bring home from school and ultimately grow up to be well educated. The third category includes the interpersonal interactions among family members around literacy in the home. Delgado-Gaitán found that these interactions, particularly families' approaches to homework activities, varied across the families and illustrated their incomplete knowledge about school literacy practices and expectations. She summarizes parents' dedication to their children's school success this way:

> Parents share a great deal with their children in the areas of aspirations, motivations, physical resources, and face-to-face interactions, which organize the total learning environment. (Delgado-Gaitán, 1992, p. 512)

Mexican American parents' aspirations for their children are a critical factor in these students' academic achievement. But more is needed on the part of the school. Delgado-Gaitán concludes that schools need to "open lines of communication with families and whole communities in a systematic way in order to facilitate the families' access to necessary academic and social resources" (p. 513).

The Funds of Knowledge Construct

Delgado-Gaitán's (1992) work resonates with other research on ethnolinguistic minority parents and families. A group of anthropologists from the University of Arizona have developed a program of research, spanning nearly 2 decades, on "funds of knowledge" for schooling (e.g., González, Moll, & Amanti, 2005; Greenberg, 1989, 1990; Moll, Amanti, Neff, & González, 1992; Moll & Greenberg, 1990). "Funds of knowledge" is a construct that refers to different strategies and ways of knowing needed for a household to function effectively. It is based on the notion that everyday practices, including linguistic practices, are sites of knowledge construction and that these resources can be brought into the classroom.

We all know that education begins in the home, and because children in U.S. schools come from diverse linguistic and cultural backgrounds, family educational practices can take on distinctive characteristics. In other words, emergent bilinguals' families possess endogenous knowledge and skills that are often overlooked by educators who too often ignore John Dewey's much earlier call to arrange teaching to take into account children's prior experiences (Dewey, 1938). Research has demonstrated variation in ways of knowing—that is, funds of knowledge—among families from different backgrounds. Philips's (1983) classic work on the Warm Springs Indian Reservation in Oregon showed that Indian children learn participation structures at home that are different from the participation structures in the school, resulting in White teachers' misinterpreting the children's turn-taking behaviors and other ways of speaking. Heath (1983) demonstrated how practices in the home sometimes clash with school practices in her research describing the home-school relationship of three communities in the Piedmont Carolinas: Maintown (representative of the middle class) and Trackton and Roadville, representing working-class Black and White mill communities, respectively. Literacy activities in the working-class communities differ from the literacy taught in schools, which represents middle-class "ways with words." Heath argues that literacy is practiced in all three communities in situations with rich mixtures of orality and literacy, but that teachers often fail to recognize and build upon the literacy practices of some communities, particularly those most marginalized in the larger society.

Other studies have shown how teachers can learn about communication patterns in the home, which can be adapted for improved learning opportunities in the classroom. For example, Rosebery, Warren, and Conant (1992) found that native speakers of Haitian Creole use certain discursive practices that are culturally congruent with the discourse of argumentation in science, thus demonstrating how the home language can be a resource rather than an impediment for learning, as is often assumed. In a similar vein, Au (1993) described efforts to meet the needs of native Hawaiian children, with particular attention to children's reading development, demonstrating that these students' reading improves when the participation structure of reading lessons maintains a close fit with the discourse of talk-story, part of the Hawaiian storytelling practice. These and similar studies show that, working with parents, school personnel can effectively draw on family and community linguistic and other knowledge to guide students toward educational attainment.

INEQUITABLE PRACTICES IN PARENTAL AND COMMUNITY INVOLVEMENT

Stigmatization of Language Minority Parents and Communities

Despite these findings, the parents of emergent bilinguals, who in many cases have limited formal schooling themselves and may not communicate proficiently in English, continue to be stigmatized and considered incapable educational partners (Ramirez, 2003) because of what are considered substandard language skills, lack of education, "inferior" family organizational structures and values, and "lack of interest" in their children's education. This deficit view is also applied to their children—even by researchers (e.g., Dunn, 1987). The home language is devalued, and family members' "accented" English may become a marker of difference and exclusion (Lippi-Green, 1997), especially if families are newcomers to the United States (Wiley & Lukes, 1996). Thus, not only do parents feel marginalized (Warriner, 2009), but also their children often experience a sense of failure during school and may feel unwelcome or even excluded from extracurricular activities (Gándara, O'Hara, & Gutiérrez, 2004).

Yet the research demonstrates that, in fact, it is the schools that are deficient—schools with the least funding and limited resources as well as teachers who have not been prepared to work with families for whom English is not their first language and to engage effectively with the parents (Gibson, Gándara, & Koyama, 2004). As Valenzuela (1999) has noted, schooling is too often a subtractive process, which ignores students' ways of knowing and speaking; opportunities for building on these resources are lost, and schooling eventually becomes complicit in producing failure (see also Varenne & McDermott, 1998). Schools are less apt to reach out to parents of color who speak a language other than English in spite of the positive effect such connections can have (Gándara & Contreras, 2009; Henderson & Berla, 1994). Teachers themselves admit that their weakest skills are in the area of making effective connections with parents of ethnolinguistic minorities (Gándara, Maxwell-Jolly, & Driscoll, 2005); Gándara and her colleagues tell us that teachers they interviewed reported

> their district's failure to devote resources to the training of teachers, aides, and other personnel to communicate with parents and/or to provide teachers the time to make useful contact with families. (2005, p. 7)

We argue that the schools have to revise their valuation of these parents' educative role and redouble their efforts at involving the parents in order to help pave the way for greater educational equity for emergent bilinguals.

Exclusion of the Most Significant Resource: The Home Language

Many educators still consider family practices to be barriers to student achievement. The practice that most often comes under attack is the home language. There is a kind of "exceptionalist" belief (DeGraff, 2005)—a deficit view of the home language as an inadequate vehicle for education. Linguist Michel DeGraff (2009) presents a critical examination of this deficit view of the home language using the example of school and community attitudes toward his native Haitian Creole; he shows the fallacy of this belief and its social cost for Haitian American children's education. DeGraff describes comments that readers once sent to the *Miami Herald* about the Haitian Creole language ("Creole is not even a language. It is slave lingo. . . . Why on earth are we spending public funds to teach kids in school the language of peasants?" [as cited in DeGraff, 2009, p. 124])—as not only demeaning but racist and classist. Contrary to these false beliefs, DeGraff demonstrates through detailed comparative analysis of Creole, English, and French language structures that Haitian American students' home language is a powerful linguistic resource.

A great deal of research shows the value of the home language as an educative tool. For example, we know that supporting Latino parents' use of the home language to speak and read to children from their early years can have a positive impact on their language and literacy development in school (López, Barrueco, & Miles, 2006). Sadly, immigrant parents are often exhorted to "speak English at home," in the mistaken belief that this will improve their children's English at school. This advice, while well intentioned, encourages inconsistent, often poor, "linguistic input" from parents who themselves are emergent bilinguals and, above all, devalues the home language (Gándara & Contraras, 2009; Ross & Newport, 1996). As we have argued in earlier chapters, the erasure of the home language through English-only school practices reinforces the deficit view that families and their children need to be linguistically "fixed" or "repaired" before they can succeed academically in the United States.

One-Size-Fits-All Parent Education Programs

There is, of course, the question regarding what parental involvement in the schools means. The "mainstream" view of parental involvement includes parental presence at school or parents' assistance with students' academic work. In general, it is the school that decides how parents can become involved with their children's education, which, according to Seeley (1993), is a "delegation" model.

One mainstream approach has been to develop "parent education" or "family literacy" programs. Parent education programs have been initiated to show parents how they can become involved in their children's education. The programs offer services such as providing information about the U.S. educational system; demonstrating ways to interact with teachers, school administrators, and other staff; and offering ways to help their children at home—for example, by reading to them, talking with them, and encouraging them in their studies (Chrispeels & Gonz, 2004; Chrispeels & Rivero, 2001).

Although parent education programs are valuable, some focus almost exclusively on what parents do not know. Many of these efforts have taken the "let us fix them" approach, assuming that these parents lack the requisite motivations and skills to support their children's education. We have already shown the fallacies in any deficit model that claims there is one best way for parents to be involved in their children's education, and other scholars concur with this criticism (Auerbach, 1995; Taylor, 1997).[3] In the concluding section that follows, we provide alternative routes to family engagement in children's education.

ALTERNATIVE APPROACHES TO PARENT
AND COMMUNITY ENGAGEMENT

Counteracting Stigmatization Through Parent
and Community Engagement

In recommending alternative approaches, we discuss efforts that are being made to lessen the chasm between parents of emergent bilinguals and school personnel. We begin by signaling more culturally sensitive programs to support parents as educators.

Since 1983, the Harvard Family Research Project (http://www.hfrp. org/) has sponsored a number of initiatives and provides tips, research reports, and policy briefs on family involvement (or what they currently call *family engagement*) in children's education. Their overarching approach is to demonstrate that family engagement is a shared responsibility among parents, the school, and the community.

The Family, School, and Community National Working Group (Weiss & Lopez, 2009) has developed an expanded definition of family engagement that entails three principles, which we cite here:

- First, family engagement is a shared responsibility in which schools and other community agencies and organizations are committed to reaching out to engage families in meaningful ways and in which families are committed to actively supporting their children's learning and development.
- Second, family engagement is continuous across a child's life and entails enduring commitment but changing parent roles as children mature into young adulthood.
- Third, effective family engagement cuts across and reinforces learning in the multiple settings where children learn—at home, in prekindergarten programs, in school, in after-school programs, in faith-based institutions, and in the community. (Weiss & Lopez, 2009, para. 6)

But even these more sensitive approaches to parent education programs acknowledge that schools must move beyond a unidirectional undertaking. Schools must also learn from families and come to understandings about how student learning occurs at home and in the community. A more useful way to benefit emergent bilinguals' success is to develop bidirectional school-community education programs.

As Rosenberg, Lopez, and Westmoreland (2009) argue, family engagement is a responsibility that must be shared by schools, parents, and communities. That is why the "funds of knowledge" program of research we introduced earlier, which is led by Luis Moll and his associates, is so important (e.g., Browning-Aiken, 2005; González, Moll, & Amanti, 2005; López, 2001; Mercado, 2005a, 2005b; Moll et al., 1992; Tenery, 2005). This research has focused on teachers' visits to the homes of Latino families to learn about a variety of skills that the families possess, such as carpentry, mechanics, music, knowledge about health and nutrition, household and ranch management, and extensive language and literacy skills and practices. López (2001) describes parents' efforts at teaching their children the value of hard work, a value that is transferable into academic life. Other researchers have documented children's first exposures to print, known as "local literacies": Bible reading, reading and writing family letters, record keeping, and following recipes (Delgado-Gaitan & Trueba, 1991; Mercado, 2005b).

Mercado (2005a) describes funds of knowledge in two New York Puerto Rican homes as developing in three areas: intellectual, social, and emotional resources. The families draw on both Spanish and English literacy to address their needs in health, nutrition, and legal matters and for spiritual development. As Mercado says, the funds of knowledge approach "is an approach that begins with the study of households rather than the study of pedagogy . . . and transforms relationships between and among families, students, and teachers" (2005a, p. 251). Browning-Aiken (2005) and Tenery (2005) both describe how social networks are formed with extended family, friends, and the wider community. In short, parents of emergent bilinguals have a great deal to teach teachers about knowledge and skills that originate in their households that can, and should, be translated into academic success in schools.

Broadening the View of Parental and Community Engagement

A broader definition of parental involvement that takes into account family and community practices is that provided by Pérez Carreón, Drake, and Calabrese Barton (2005), who developed the concept of *ecologies of parental engagement* to refer to the participation of parents in a child's schooling in a manner that goes beyond the physical space of the school and is rooted in the understanding of a family's cultural practices. The ecologies of parental engagement view takes into account the different styles of action taken by parents of diverse ethnolinguistic backgrounds. The authors offer the examples of Celia, a mother who engages with the teacher as a helper inside the classroom, and Pablo, an "undocumented" immigrant father, who engages with a network of neighbors and his son's teacher outside the classroom to question what is happening in school.

Let us examine two such studies of families' styles of action. Zentella's (1997, 2005) research in New York and Valdés's (1996) research in California provide evidence that parents of various Spanish-speaking backgrounds are involved in their children's education in a variety of ways, including rich linguistic exposure to storytelling and print in the native language at home. Zentella (1997) explores the lives and rich, varied language patterns of working-class Puerto Rican families with a focus on five girls, whom she follows from childhood until they become young adults. Her observations of family language practices lead her to emphasize the importance of teachers building on students' home language for learning—including vernacular varieties—to support students' self-worth and identity and to help children see connections with the standard variety, in this case, standard Spanish. For Zentella (2005), becoming bilingual—maintaining the home language and developing strong English language and literacy competencies—gives students a chance at economic advancement. She states that parental goals for their children also include becoming *bien educado* (well educated), a term that encompasses moral values and respect along with having book knowledge.

Valdés (1996) describes first-generation Mexican parents' beliefs about their role in their children's schooling. For these parents, the teachers were to be entrusted with the children's academic skills. Mothers and fathers, who did not feel that they had the academic preparation to help with these skills, focused instead on giving advice, instilling respect, and fostering moral values (see also Suárez-Orozco & Suárez-Orozco, 2001). Valdés makes a strong argument in this research that school officials' and teachers' response to these parental beliefs has been that the parents are disinterested in the children's education. As we have seen in the research reported throughout this chapter, this notion is far from the truth; parents want to learn how to help their children at home (Epstein, 1990), yet they have in some cases felt disregarded and left powerless in their attempts to be involved in the school (Pérez Carreón et al., 2005).

Community Organizing

Research shows that language minority parents are beginning to question the existing power relations in the home-school relationship. Some parents have begun to form grassroots organizations to address their schools about concerns they have regarding their children's education. According to a survey of 66 community-organizing groups by Mediratta, Fruchter, and Lewis (2002), 50 of these groups have been in existence since 1994. Although research on these groups' impact has been limited, we know about some of their efforts. Gold, Simon, and Brown (2002) interviewed 19 community-organizing groups and conducted a case study of 5 of these groups. The authors learned that members of the community make an impact on the quality of schools by, among other things, insisting on school-community connections and developing parents' leadership skills.

Delgado-Gaitán (2001) studied a Latino parent organization, Comité de Padres Latinos/Committee of Latino Parents (COPLA), where parents learned to make sense of the school system, build leadership, and become their children's advocates. Delgado-Gaitán explained: "Shaped by the lesson of their own pain, [the] parents placed their children's needs center stage, giving rise to and sustaining their activism in the community" (p. 8). Community organizations like these are beginning to require more equitable and responsive actions by the public education system.

EDUCATING EMERGENT BILINGUALS: RECREATING THE SCHOOL COMMUNITY

We can learn a great deal from research about appropriate school-family-community linkages. In addition, we have to recognize that parents are invested in their emergent bilingual children's learning and want them to excel. Further, we should recognize that the education of emergent bilingual students is a partnership with parents and the community. Schools can investigate the funds of knowledge that their students' families and communities hold and then build on them. The most important resource or fund that families possess is their home language, which should be celebrated as a source of knowledge. Teachers also need support: They must be provided the tools to communicate better with these families. And finally, assistance should be given to families to understand the workings of the school system, to build social networks, and to seek out school and community services that support their educational efforts. In short, the literature we report here suggests that there be a balance of power with school personnel, parents, and community working to achieve closer mutual engagement for the education of emergent bilinguals.

STUDY QUESTIONS

1. Describe what research tells us regarding the benefits of parental involvement for emergent bilingual children's success in school.
2. What are "funds of knowledge?" Give some examples of these from the research.
3. In what ways are families of emergent bilinguals sometimes stigmatized?
4. What are the problems and promises of parent education programs?
5. In what ways are parents showing leadership on behalf of their children's education?

CHAPTER 8

Assessments

In this chapter we will:

- Review theoretical constructs important for fair assessment of emergent bilinguals, specifically:

  The power of assessments
  The difference between academic language proficiency and content proficiency
  The validity and reliability of the tests for emergent bilinguals
  The fit of the assessment to the population
  The match of the language of the test to the language practices of the students

- Identify inadequacies in assessment practices by:

  Assessing prematurely and intensely
  Establishing arbitrary proficiencies
  Ignoring those that need it the most

- Consider some alternative practices, including:

  Accommodations
  Disentangling language and content
  Assessing in students' home languages: translations and transadaptations
  Assessing bilingually
  Assessing dynamically and bilingually
  Observing closely

One of the key equity issues surrounding the education of emergent bilinguals concerns the ways in which these students are assessed according to national mandates and state accountability systems. It has been widely demonstrated that as a result of inadequate high-stakes tests, emergent bilinguals experience more remedial instruction, greater probability of assignment to lower curriculum tracks, higher drop-out rates, poorer graduation rates, and disproportionate referrals to special education classes (Artiles, 1998; Artiles & Ortiz, 2002; Cummins, 1984).

Because the limited English proficiency (LEP) subgroup by definition cannot possibly meet the proficiency targets in these tests, *all* programs serving emergent bilinguals are being questioned, including those that are conducted exclusively in English. As Menken (2008) argues, mandating high-stakes tests in English for all has acted as language policy, accelerating students' immersion in English without the advantage of home language support. Valenzuela (2005) maintains that high-stakes testing in Texas has been the most detrimental policy for Latinos and emergent bilinguals and recommends that there be local control over assessment.

We agree with the assertion that all students have to be *included* in every assessment, and NCLB (2001) has indeed prohibited the exclusion of emergent bilinguals by requiring that 95% of all student cohorts be tested. But there are equity concerns regarding how assessments are currently being conducted and how the data they generate are being used. These equity issues have to do with misunderstandings of theoretical constructs for assessment that especially affect emergent bilinguals. These include (1) the power of assessments, (2) the difference between academic language proficiency and content proficiency, (3) the validity and reliability of the tests for emergent bilinguals, (4) the fit of the assessment to the population, and (5) the match of the language of the test to the language practices of the students. This chapter first considers these theoretical constructs and then describes some of the ill-considered practices that surround assessment of emergent bilinguals. As in other chapters, we note that there is a gap between accepted theories regarding assessment for these students and the testing that takes place. We end the chapter by proposing alternative assessment policies and practices based on theory and research evidence.

THEORETICAL CONSTRUCTS IN ASSESSMENT

The Power of Assessments

As Foucault (1979) has indicated, assessment can be a way to exercise power and control (see also Shohamy, 2001). Foucault explains:

> The examination combines the technique of an observing hierarchy and those of normalizing judgment. It is a normalizing gaze, a surveillance that makes it possible to quantify, classify and punish. It establishes over individuals a visibility through which one differentiates and judges them. (p. 18)

Since Alfred Binet developed his intelligence testing methods in the early 20th century, tests have been used to label and misclassify students. For example, the Stanford-Binet test developed by Lewis Terman was used to "prove" that "[Indians, Mexicans, and Blacks] should be segregated in special classes" (Terman, as cited in Oakes, 1985, p. 36). The history of assessment has been entangled from the very beginning with racism and linguicism (Wiley, 1996). Testing is used more often as a vehicle for allocating educational and employment benefits than as a means for informing teaching and developing learning. Thus, educators have to be extremely mindful of the power of tests and how they can be dangerous and discriminatory if used inappropriately.

Academic Language Proficiency and Content Proficiency

Every assessment is an assessment of language (AERA, APA, & NCME, 1985). Thus, assessment for emergent bilinguals, who are still learning the language in which the test is administered, is not valid unless language is disentangled from content. As we have noted, English proficiency for interpersonal communication is not the same as the more complex proficiency required for academic achievement in English. *Academic language proficiency* is usually assessed by evaluating the comprehension and use of specialized vocabulary and language patterns in the spoken and written modes, the linguistic complexity of these modes, and the appropriate use of the sound system (phonology), grammatical structure (syntax), and meaning (semantics) of the language (Gottlieb, 2006). *Content proficiency* refers to whether the student has actually acquired knowledge of the subject matter. When assessment uses academic English to test emergent bilinguals' content knowledge, both language and content proficiency are entangled and assessment lacks validity, an important concept to which we now turn.

Validity and Reliability for Emergent Bilinguals

In order for test results to be equitable, emergent bilinguals must be included in the design and piloting of the instrument so that the *norming* of the test is not biased; that is, the test must have both validity and reliability for bilingual students (Abedi, 2004; Abedi & Lord, 2001).

Reliability refers to the capacity of the test or of individual test items to measure a construct consistently over time. Abedi (2004), Abedi, Hofstetter, and Lord (2004), and Martiniello (2008) demonstrate that large-scale exams have differential reliability for students whose English language abilities do not match those of the test. Martiniello shows that emergent bilingual students and monolingual students with the same ability perform differently on particular math test items because of unfamiliar vocabulary and complex syntactic structures.

Chatterji defines *validity* as having to do with "the *meaningfulness* of an assessment's results given the particular constructs being tapped, purposes for which the assessment is used and the populations for whom the assessment is intended" (2003, p. 56). Given the fact that language and content are confounded in tests, as we have already discussed, there are concerns over the validity of standardized assessments for emergent bilinguals, since the test may not measure what it intends. Furthermore, tests may have little *content validity* for these students because the performance of emergent bilinguals does not reveal much about their learning (Lachat, 1999). Worse still is the *consequential validity* of these tests for emergent bilinguals, that is, the price students pay with regard to how they are taught (Cronbach, 1989; Messick, 1989). As we noted earlier, as a result of these tests, emergent bilinguals may be misplaced in special education and remedial classes.

Because tests are constructed for monolingual populations, they always contain a built-in content bias. Tests do not always include activities or concepts from the worlds of language minority students (Mercer, 1989). Nor do they take into account the cultural norms of the bilingual children being assessed. These tests for monolingual students reflect neither the cultural practices nor the language practices with which emergent bilingual students are familiar. This is the topic of the next section.

Fit of Tests to Population

Criterion-referenced assessments, in which students' performance is evaluated on a specific body of knowledge or skills, are a vast improvement over *norm-referenced assessments*, in which students' scores are measured against the performance of other students. But they are still not appropriate for testing emergent bilinguals. In criterion-referenced assessments, students are graded according to whether they have met a defined criteria or standard, which determines what students should know and be able to do in various subject areas. But emergent bilinguals by definition generally cannot meet the standard of language proficiency. Thus, they are often judged not to be competent.

Furthermore, because language and content are entangled, studies have found that there is a discrepancy between test assessments scores and student performance in the classroom. Katz, Low, Stack, and Tsang studied Spanish-speaking and Chinese-speaking emergent bilinguals in San Francisco and concluded: "Test data suggested that ELL students underperformed academically compared to EO (English-only) students, but ELL students turned out to be high achievers in the classroom context" (2004, p. 56).

It has been shown that *performance-based assessments*, tests that ask students to produce a product such as a portfolio or perform an action, are better for bilingual students because they provide a wider range of opportunities to show what they know and are able to do in both language and content areas (Estrin & Nelson-Barber, 1995; Navarrete & Gustke, 1996).

Genishi and Borrego Brainard say that performance-based assessment "can be oral, written, 'performative,' as in dance, or visual/artistic" (1995, p. 54). Goh (2004) includes any method of finding out what a given student really knows or can do, such as performances, hands-on activities, and portfolios. Because student problem-solving skills may be documented in different ways, performance-based assessments are less language dependent than are traditional tests, enabling teachers to better distinguish between language proficiency and content proficiency. So although performance-based assessments tax teachers' time, they are more appropriate precisely because they require teachers' attention to the details in students' performance.

Let us reiterate the major caveat about performance assessments: Since their interpretation relies on the judgment of those scoring the tests (Lachat, 1999), it is crucial that individuals knowledgeable about the linguistic and cultural characteristics of emergent bilinguals participate in the development of rubrics for scoring student work. In this way, scorers may be able to disentangle academic performance on the assessment from language proficiency.

Matching the Language of the Test to Language Practices

As we showed in Chapter 4, the language practices of emergent and proficient bilingual students are very different from those of monolingual students. Thus, a test constructed for monolinguals cannot match the language use of individuals who draw from more than one language. Bachman refers to the distinction between the language of the test and actual language practices when he states:

> That there must be a relationship between the language used on tests and that used in "real life" cannot be denied, since if there is no such relationship, our language tests become mere shadows, sterile procedures that may tell us nothing about the very ability we wish to measure. (Bachman, 1990, p. 356)

Valdés and Figueroa point to the difficulties of testing emergent bilingual students with an instrument that has been normed for monolinguals:

> When a bilingual individual confronts a monolingual test, developed by monolingual individuals, and standardized and normed on a monolingual population, both the test taker and the test are asked to do something that they cannot. The bilingual test taker cannot perform like a monolingual. The monolingual test cannot "measure" in the other language. (1994, p. 87)

Clearly, monolingually constructed and administered tests cannot validly measure the complex language practices of bilingual students.

INEQUITABLE ASSESSMENT PRACTICES

We now turn to our central question, Given what we know theoretically and research-wise about assessment of emergent bilinguals, are these students being assessed according to accepted theories and research evidence about language and bilingualism? The answer to this question is an emphatic *no*. Emergent bilinguals continue to be assessed prematurely with high-stakes instruments that confound academic language and content and that do not align with their language practices. In fact, much educational time is taken up with testing with invalid instruments. And despite the fact that theory and research support the use of performance-based assessments, as they are more valid for these students, they are rarely used as high-stakes tests.

Assessing Prematurely and Intensely

Researchers contend that the high-stakes testing of the American school population mandated by NCLB (2001) has had a negative effect on all students (Nichols & Berliner, 2007). NCLB not only mandates that every student be tested annually in Grades 3–8 in English language arts and math, but at present also requires that emergent bilingual students at the very early stages of English development be included in the testing. For these students, assessing academic language development and content development becomes completely entangled.

Ascenzi-Moreno describes this "testing frenzy" in a New York City fourth-grade classroom:

> Fourth graders have at least 14 days of mandatory testing days (4 days of English Language Arts testing, 4 days of Mathematics testing, 2 days of 'predictives'[1] in English Language Arts, 2 days of 'predictives' in Mathematics, 2 days of Science testing). This amounts to 8% of all school days dedicated to testing. Furthermore, this tally does not include additional mandated testing for bilingual students such as the New York State English as a Second Language Achievement Test (NYSESLAT), which would bring the percentage closer to 10% of the school days dedicated to testing for these students. (2009, p. 10)

Ascenzi-Moreno continues describing the New York City–mandated school-based programs of periodic assessment, which are meant to complement standardized data. These periodic assessments are formative in nature and are meant to guide instruction:

> Schools can choose between using a menu of periodic assessments provided by New York City Department of Education (NYCDOE) or develop assessments of their own. The amount of time allocated to periodic assessment varies according to the assessments chosen. Students may be assessed through test

formats such as base-lines, mid-lines, and end-lines;[2] unit tests and test simulations; or through reading records[3] and student conferences. (p. 10)

While much energy is being spent testing, it is not clear how the data are acted upon to improve the teaching of emergent bilinguals. And although teachers are also assessing students with more performance-based assessments, it is the scores on high-stakes tests that count for the schools, and thus also for the teachers.

The intensity of testing means that less time is being spent in challenging and creative teaching or teaching subject matter that is not tested. The phenomenon known as "washback," that is, the process by which testing and formal assessments drive the curriculum has been well documented, especially in the literature on language teaching (Cheng, Watanabe, & Curtis, 2004; Shohamy, Donitsa-Schmidt, & Ferman, 1996). A recent study by the Center on Education Policy (CEP) found that since 2002, 62% of districts had reported that they had increased the time for reading and required schools to spend a specific amount of time teaching reading, while 53% of districts had also done so for math (CEP, 2005). In contrast, less time is being spent teaching science, social studies, and the arts. Crucially, the reading and math curriculum narrowly follows the exigencies of the tests.

This inequitable practice of testing emergent bilinguals with high-stakes tests prematurely and intensely violates what we know about

- The relationship between academic learning proficiency and content proficiency
- The validity of high-stakes tests for this population
- Matching the test to the population

Using Assessments to Establish Arbitrary Proficiencies

Assessment of emergent bilinguals is especially done to determine whether or not they are proficient in English. But different states measure English proficiency differently, using tests that have diverging views of what the construct of proficiency entails. Thus, emergent bilinguals may be deemed to be proficient in one state and not in another.

Establishing these arbitrary proficiencies also stems from a misunderstanding of language development and bilingualism. Attention is paid only to the stage in which English is being learned, as if that process could be completed. Some arbitrary point of proficiency is established, at which time the student is declared to be "proficient in English." Gándara and Contreras note, "One is either proficient or not; one is either an English learner or a fluent English speaker" (2009, p. 124) is a false dichotomy, and they argue that the dichotomy stems from external funding and other pressures to sort students. It is as if a student emerges from one box and enters into another one (as in Fig. 8.1, top). This traditional view of proficiency is that the student is "cured" and he or she has now "learned" English. The box that contains the English language learner is as small as possible and doesn't contain anything else, defined by the absence of English.

In contrast, as we made explicit in Chapter 4, language is never "possessed." Instead, speakers "language"; they use diverse language practices. Emergent bilinguals come into school as users of a home language that dynamically develops (or not) in relationship to the development of English. We have argued that the bilingual continuum is not a straight-arrow process, flowing unevenly as students' languaging adapts to the social and academic contexts that they encounter. The process is never finished, and the dynamic relationship between the two languages they draw on means that, although students can be placed along a bilingual continuum in terms of development of the home language and English, there is no end point by which students leave one category and become another. Emergent bilinguals are somewhere along the starting point of the bilingual continuum, and developmental progress along the continuum is contingent on their opportunities for languaging. Figure 8.1 (bottom) displays this relationship.

Figure 8.1. Traditional versus Dynamic View of Proficiencies

Traditional View of Proficiency Stages

English Learner	English Proficient

Dynamic View of Proficiencies

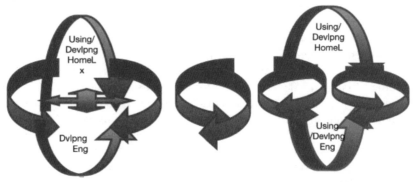

Content proficiency categories that individual states have constructed also have little to do with measuring student learning of subject matter content. Much has been said, for example, about the lack of alignment between state proficiency levels in English reading, writing, math and science and those of the National Assessment of Educational Progress (NAEP). In 2008, 80% of students in New York State were deemed proficient in math according to state assessments. However, that same year, only 34% of New York State students were considered proficient in math according to the NAEP assessment (Medina, 2009).

Despite the enormous amount of time and energy devoted to assessment of proficiency levels, high-stakes tests tell us very little about what emergent bilinguals can or cannot do linguistically or academically.

The requirement that students meet Adequate Yearly Progress (AYP) standards in state exams drives the construction of categories of proficiency that have little to do with students' real learning and development. This inequitable practice of using assessments to categorize arbitrarily, instead of to develop deep understandings and teacher knowledge about students and their learning, violates what we know about (1) the power of tests; and (2) the validity and reliability of high stakes tests.

Ignoring Those Who Need the Most Help

Finally, the emphasis of No Child Left Behind in ensuring that all students are proficient in English means that it has become common for schools to spend enormous time and energy with those who are close to moving up a proficiency level, what many call "the bubble kids" (Booher-Jennings, 2006). As such, students at the bottom are getting very little help. Students at the top are also not being challenged academically and intellectually, for their good scores will not make a difference to the schools' AYP.

ALTERNATIVE ASSESSMENT PRACTICES

Accommodations

One way to improve the validity of monolingual assessments is to provide students with test accommodations. Many educational authorities provide accommodations for emergent bilingual students when they are tested in English. For example, as a result of the new accountability systems associated with NCLB, accommodations have been implemented to test emergent bilinguals in many states. But state accommodation policies vary substantially (Rivera & Collum, 2006). Rivera and Stansfield (1998) organize accommodations in five categories:

1. *Presentation*: permits repetition, explanation, simplification, test translations into students' native languages, or test administration by a bilingual specialist;
2. *Response*: allows a student to dictate his or her answers and to respond in his or her native language or to display knowledge using alternative forms of representation;
3. *Setting*: includes individual or small group administration of the test or administration in a separate location or multiple testing sessions;
4. *Timing/scheduling*: allows for additional time to complete the test or extra breaks during administration;
5. *Reinforcement*: use of dictionaries and glossaries.

Abedi and Lord (2001) show how *linguistic modification*, the paraphrasing of test items so that they are less complex, has resulted in significant differences in math performance among emergent bilinguals in the United States. In fact, additional research has shown that the only accommodation that narrows the gap between emerging bilinguals and other students is linguistic modification of questions that have excessive language demands (Abedi & Lord, 2001; Abedi et al., 2004). Test accommodations are not the ideal solution to the inequitable assessment practices that we have been describing. Nor are all test accommodations equally effective. Nevertheless, accommodations are at least a palliative, which can ameliorate these inequitable assessment practices.

Disentangling Language and Content

Although disentangling language and content for assessment is difficult, some alternatives have been proposed. Shepard (1996) has argued that a fair assessment framework for emergent bilinguals should integrate the two dimensions—*academic language proficiency* and *content proficiency*. Academic performance of bilinguals should be seen as a continuum that is related to a continuum of English acquisition; in this view, the language in the tests of subject matter content is adapted according to the place along the continuum in which the student might be situated.

Duverger (2005) has suggested that another way of disentangling the effects of language proficiency on content proficiency is to have a double scale of criteria; criteria relating to the *content* being delivered and criteria relating to the *language* being used. When content learning takes place through a student's weaker language, which is English in the case of emergent bilinguals, subject matter knowledge should have a higher coefficient and language errors should not mask satisfactory handling of the content.

Assessing Students in Their Home Language

A much more equitable practice would be to assess students in their home languages. In this section we address why this does not happen and the ideological and technical obstacles that stand in the way. The current debate over assessment of emergent bilinguals in the United States largely results from a lack of clarity about the goal of their education, which is whether educating emergent bilinguals should focus only on English language development or on their intellectual, academic, and social development. The education of English language learners—as the name indicates—often focuses narrowly on the acquisition of *English language skills* and not on acquisition of content knowledge. Houser (1995) explains that if content-area knowledge were the primary goal and concern, students would be assessed in their home language. However, assessing students in their home language is generally considered inappropriate because educational policy attends narrowly to the economic advantages associated with fluency in English.

Concerning U.S. Latinos, studies by the National Commission for Employment Policy (NCEP) since the 1980s have generally found that there is an income gap between Latinos who speak only Spanish and Latinos who speak English (see also Bloom & Grenier, 1996). But studies that compare Latino bilinguals with Latinos who speak English only have repeatedly found that Latinos who are bilingual have higher incomes, lower poverty rates, and higher educational attainment than those who are English monolinguals (Boswell, 2000; García, 1995; Linton, 2003). That is, when bilingualism—and not simply Spanish only or English only—is considered, the effects are positive. But because bilingualism in American schools is rarely considered a valuable alternative, assessments continue to bypass the potential and understandings that students might have in their home languages. In addition, teachers would benefit from assessments in their students' home language; they would thereby have a measure demonstrating what students have (or have not) learned in given content areas so that they can efficiently teach them. In spite of these benefits, we know that developing translations and transadaptations of assessments in the home language is complicated, as we explain in the next two subsections.

Test translations. Translating tests is not always feasible or appropriate. Because the testing industry is a market-driven operation, it might be possible to develop translations into Spanish, since the numbers of Spanish-speaking emergent bilinguals would merit it, but developing them into less commonly used languages could be difficult and expensive. Furthermore, assessments conducted in different languages may not be psychometrically equivalent (Anderson, Jenkins, & Miller, 1996). Maintaining construct equivalence is difficult either when the test is translated directly from one language to another or when tests in two languages are constructed. There is the problem of the nonequivalence of vocabulary difficulty between languages, making comparisons for content proficiency between tests given in different languages inappropriate (August & Hakuta, 1998). The Standards for Educational and Psychological Testing put forth by the American Educational Research Association, the American Psychological Association, and the National Council on Measurement in Education state:

> Psychometric properties cannot be assumed to be comparable across languages or dialects. Many words have different frequency rates or difficulty levels in different languages or dialects. Therefore, words in two languages that appear to be close in meaning may differ radically in other ways important for the test use intended. Additionally, test content may be inappropriate in a translated version. (1985, p. 73)

Sometimes, emergent bilinguals are allowed to use both the home language version and the English language version of the test. But developing and validating equivalent versions of a test (two monolingual versions side by side) is difficult and costly (Anderson, Jenkins, & Miller, 1996). Furthermore, research on this issue has repeatedly shown substantial psychometric discrepancies in students' performance on the same test items across languages (August & Hakuta, 1997, p. 122). This means that test items are not measuring the same underlying knowledge.

In addition, translations are viable only when emergent bilinguals have been effectively educated in their home languages. And even then, translations may privilege the standard variety of the language, often having features that differ from contact varieties used in bilingual contexts (Solano-Flores, 2008). If students have limited literacy in that language, the assessment testing content proficiency is also invalid. Furthermore, translations are appropriate only if the students have been taught through the language of the test.

An additional concern is that even an appropriate translation of tests would not obviate the cultural uniqueness and register of high-stakes tests, which might not be familiar to immigrant students—format, layout, bubbling in multiple-choice answers, and discursive styles that are specific to tests (Solano-Flores, 2008). If the language is not used for instruction, then assessment for content proficiency in the students' native language also may be counterproductive. The language of the assessment must match students' primary language of instruction (Abedi & Lord, 2001; Abedi, Lord, & Plummer, 1997).

Transadaption of tests. Transadaptation is a strategy with promise. Transadapted tests are created in the home language from the beginning and are developed and normed for the bilingual population that will be using them. These tests work to eliminate cultural biases, which are prevalent in assessments that refer to cultural experiences or historical backgrounds to which many English language learners have not been exposed (Johnston, 1997). As such, they have more validity than do tests that are translated. This type of testing is now being used in Texas, where transadapted Spanish versions of the Texas Assessment of Knowledge of Skills (TAKS) have begun to be developed. However, even transadapted tests, because they are monolingual, do not fully take into account the full range of challenges and skills of emergent bilingual students, whose full capabilities are enmeshed with their bilingualism.

Assessing Bilingually

The most valid way to assess the content proficiency of emergent bilinguals (and not solely their English proficiency) is to develop large-scale assessments that build on their bilingual abilities. Students could be assessed via a *bilingual mode*, a way of rendering the child's bilingual competence visible. For example, questions can be put in one language and responses requested in another. Or written tests can have the question in English and the responses may be provided in the home language or vice versa. Alternatively, the written text could be produced in English and the oral presentation in the home language or vice versa, thereby providing the teacher with a measure of productive skills across two modes and for all languages, while at the same time giving emergent bilinguals the opportunity to use all their languages. Thus, this bilingual mode of assessment would not only give educators a more accurate picture of what students really know without having language as an intervening variable, but it also would offer a clearer picture of students' English language capacities.

One example of a bilingual mode instrument designed to assess the verbal-cognitive skills of bilingual students is the Bilingual Verbal Ability Test (BVAT). All subtests of the assessment are first administered in English. Any item failed is then readministered in the student's home language and the score added so as to measure the test-taker's knowledge and reasoning ability using both languages (Muñoz-Sandoval, Cummins, Alvarado, & Ruef, 1998).

In cases where school authorities are interested exclusively in students' progress in learning English, students might also be assessed via a *bilingual tap* mode, a way of tapping their home languages in order to produce English. This type of assessment would, for example, give instructions and questions in the students' home languages and ask them to respond solely in English. In this way, the home language would be used to activate knowledge for assessment in much the same way that bilingual children use their home language and culture to make sense of what they know. This bilingual-tap assessment builds on recent work on bilingual language processing by Dufour and Kroll (1995), Kecskes and Martínez Cuenca (2005), and Jessner (2006).

Assessing Dynamically and Bilingually

Dynamic assessment rests on the work of Vygotsky on the interactive nature of cognitive development. Its goal is then to "determine the 'size' of the ZPD [Zone of Proximal Development]" (Gutiérrez-Clellen & Peña, 2001, p. 212) and to transform students' abilities through dialogic collaboration between learners and the assessor-teacher (Poehner, 2007). Dynamic assessment and instruction mutually elaborate on each other.

Garcia and Pearson (1994) support the notion that emergent bilinguals be given performance-based assessments that are dynamic, in the sense that they should find out what the student can do with or without the help of the teacher. In this way, teachers are able to evaluate the kind of support that bilinguals need to complete tasks. For Garcia and Pearson these dynamic assessments can be conducted in English, the home language, or in both languages. Through dynamic assessments that are administered in a bilingual mode, teachers may assess their students' interpretations of material and vocabulary from diverse cultural and linguistic perspectives and then use that knowledge to create further opportunities for students to learn what is appropriate. For example, bilingual students can also demonstrate through these bilingual dynamic assessment their literacy understandings using their home and school language practices, and teachers can then assist them in developing academic literacy in the additional language.

Observing Closely

The best way to assess emergent bilingual students is for teachers to observe and listen to their students and record these observations systematically over long periods of time. Of course to "re-view" emergent bilinguals in the close ways described by Carini (2000a, p. 56), it is important for the observer to be familiar with the language and cultural practices of the student. Carini differentiates between assessing what the child learned, made, or did and "paying close attention to how a child goes about learning or making something" (2000b, p. 9). Carini continues, "It is when a teacher can see this process, *the child in motion*, the child engaged in activities meaningful to her, that it is possible for the teacher to gain the insights needed to adjust her or his own approaches to the child accordingly" (2000b, p. 9, emphasis added). Thus, for Carini, observing closely has to do with understanding the process of learning, and not just assessing a product. These ongoing descriptive reviews of children (Carini, 2000a, 2000b; Traugh, 2000) can develop a multidimensional portrait of bilingual learners. Rather than labeling emergent bilinguals as "limited," "at risk," or "deficient," these kinds of assessments provide avenues for understanding the capacities and strengths of emergent bilinguals. Observing closely allows the teacher/assessor to obtain valid, reliable information about the dynamics of the process of learning that then informs the teaching in a cyclical relationship.

EDUCATING EMERGENT BILINGUALS: ACCOUNTING FOR FAIR ASSESSMENT

The data-driven frenzy of accountability spurred by NCLB (2001) and most recently by Race to the Top,[4] puts assessments rather than teaching at the center of education today. The issue of assessment is particularly important for emergent bilinguals, for whom some of these high-stakes tests are invalid (Menken, 2008). There are, however, ways of improving the construction of valid assessments for this population, and this chapter has considered some of these alternative practices.

Again, we see that misunderstandings about bilingualism in the United States create obstacles to developing assessment mechanisms that are fair and valid for all students. Monolingual high-stakes tests for emergent bilinguals have negative consequences not only for the individual students, but also for the teachers who teach them, the leaders of the schools in which they are educated, the communities in which they live, and the states in which they reside. Scores on assessments are driving not only the kinds of instruction and programmatic opportunities that emergent bilinguals can access, but also the salary that their teachers receive, the funding that their schools and the states in which they reside obtain, and the real estate value of the communities in which they live. This creates a cycle in which the victims will surely be the emergent bilinguals, as teachers, principals, communities, and states will drive these children away, excluding them from all opportunities to learn. Developing fair and valid assessments for emergent bilinguals emerges as the most critical issue in education during this era of increased accountability. Continuing down the path we are on has the potential of not only excluding children from educational opportunities, but of destroying the entire public school system in which our U.S. democracy rests.

STUDY QUESTIONS

1. Why are assessments so powerful?
2. Why are assessments not always valid and reliable for emergent bilinguals?

3. How do the different kinds of tests compare in the way they assess emergent bilinguals' language and content proficiencies?
4. What are some of the complications of establishing categories of proficiencies?
5. Describe some of the test accommodations that can be used with emergent bilinguals. Identify issues to consider and practices that work best.
6. What are the issues that surround translations and transadaptions of tests?
7. Discuss ways of assessing bilingually. In your view, what are the difficulties with implementation of such assessments?
8. What is the difference between observing closely and assessing students? Discuss advantages and disadvantages.

CHAPTER 9

Alternative Paths for Educating Emergent Bilinguals

In this concluding chapter we will:

- Summarize what we have learned about:

    Language theory and research
    Language and classroom practice
    Curriculum and pedagogies
    Family and community engagement
    Assessment

- Put up the signposts for a more equitable education for emergent bilinguals:

    Knowing who they are
    Understanding the shifts in programs and policies
    Building on dynamic bilingualism
    Incorporating multilingual pedagogies
    Embracing challenge and care
    Recreating the school community
    Accounting for fair assessment

- Offer a set of detailed recommendations for advocates, policymakers, educators, and researchers

Throughout this book, we have presented the case for reconceptualizing English language learners in American schools as *emergent bilinguals*. This concept recognizes the value of the students' home languages as resources for learning and as markers of their identity as individuals who have creative ways of knowing, being, and communicating. In repositioning these students as emergent bilinguals, we have been able to expose the dissonance between research findings on best ways to educate them and the current educational policies and practices that have disregarded them.

WHAT HAVE WE LEARNED?

In Chapter 2, we began to address how emergent bilinguals have been iden-tified and demonstrated the discrepancies in the way they have been counted and classified in federal, state, and even school district agencies. We saw that the federal government's allocation of funds to schools has relied on both U.S. census data and state-reported data, each with attendant limita-tions. Despite these problems with counting and sorting, what is clear is that the ethnolinguistic minority population is growing more rapidly than the English-speaking population; the number of emergent bilinguals has in-creased dramatically. What the data also show is that most emergent bilin-guals attend schools in high-poverty urban school districts where classrooms are often crowded, material resources are lacking, and teachers are under-qualified. Students in these schools have high incidences of health problems and absenteeism. Further, in spite of the assumption that these students are speakers of languages other than English, they are not all foreign born; one in four is a native-born U.S. citizen. Finally, we know that the majority of emergent bilinguals in the United States are speakers of Spanish.

In Chapter 3, we charted the types of educational programs that have been available in the United States for emergent bilinguals. These range from programs that require the exclusive use of English in the classroom to those that provide instruction and support in the home language along with English. But over the 50-year history of language education policies, begin-ning with the Bilingual Education Act of 1968 through the NCLB policy, the latter in force since 2002, we have seen a shift away from the bilingual end of the continuum to a largely English-only language policy for ethnolinguis-tic minorities in U.S. schools.

Against this backdrop, in subsequent chapters we explored theories and research that support ways in which emergent bilinguals can learn both English and subject matter content optimally and be assessed equitably. We considered the gaps between the research evidence and language education policies and practices for emergent bilinguals. Most important of all, we put forth alternative policies and practices for an equitable education of these students.

Language Theory and Research

In Chapters 4 and 5, we discussed key theoretical frameworks for under-standing the relationship between bilingualism and academic achievement. These interrelated frameworks have shown the cognitive, academic, and so-cial benefits of drawing on both the home language and English. Because there is a common underlying proficiency in the multilingual brain, as Jim Cummins (1979, 2000) has argued, this linguistic interdependence means that knowledge and proficiency in one language supports knowledge and proficiency in another and that language practices are interdependent. Scholars from an array of academic disciplines—anthropology, education, linguistics, and psychology—have shown that language use varies in different contexts and have provided descriptive analyses of a wide range of language and literacy varieties. The research makes it clear that in educational contexts, learning how to carry on a conversation in an additional language is not the same as learning how to discuss, read, and write about cognitively demanding ideas in that language. We know from extensive research in schools in the United States and around the world that attaining competence in academic literacies requires sustained discussion, reflection, and practice. We also know that these literacies are bound up in relations of power and identity and that literacies entailing two or more languages intensify questions of power and negotiations of identity. Skilled teachers can provide space in the classroom that empowers students to affirm their linguistic and cultural funds of knowledge even as they add to their repertoire of knowledge and communicative practices in an additional language. It is through these linguistic and literacy processes that students engage in identity work: They develop a sense of self through multiple languages in different social situations (Norton, 2000). This is precisely what the notion of pluriliteracies addresses. As we discussed in Chapter 4, the term *pluriliteracies* describes the complex language practices in multilingual communities (see García et al., 2007). It helps us understand young people's diverse and hybrid literacy practices and values in and out of school; it also takes into account the intermingling of multiple languages, scripts, as well as rapidly changing new technologies that further shape their use.

Added to this understanding is the recognition that the path to bilingualism is a dynamic process, and not a linear one, as has been previously argued. So, we introduced the concept of translanguaging, a phenomenon evident in all aspects of bilinguals' communicative practices (García, 2009a). When bilingual students translanguage, they creatively use linguistic features and language modes to make meaning that are socially categorized as belonging to one or another language. By bringing this flexible and subtle language practice into the classroom, teachers open new spaces for optimal meaning-making, identity formation, and eventual academic achievement.

Large-scale evaluations and meta-analyses of studies on bilingual programs beginning in the 1970s and continuing into the present have borne out these theoretical frameworks, showing that judicious use of different language practices in the classroom results in high achievement levels in both content and academic English, sometimes exceeding national norms, provided that teachers and students are given adequate time to develop academic English—5 to 6 years. Bilingual education has been maligned in the United States despite the fact that the most carefully designed reviews of programs for English learners have shown positive educational outcomes. The political climate has overshadowed these empirical findings, and language has been treated as a problem rather than a resource. The problem does not reside in students or their language, but rather in classroom practices that have been shaped by misguided educational policies.

Language and Classroom Practice

We have seen that emergent bilinguals have not generally been in classrooms that apply theory and research findings on the benefits of using the home language to support learning. In addition, in classrooms where both languages are used, the home language and English generally are kept strictly separated (what we called *bracketing* in Chapter 5), despite what we know about the benefits of dynamic bilingualism and translanguaging. Unfortunately, bilingual education programs themselves have decreased dramatically, and most emergent bilinguals today are in English-only programs. Although there are programs that provide pullout ESL classes, these focus mostly on English proficiency without offering specialized instruction in English in the content area. Even ESL support is being curtailed in some states.

Our response to this sad state of affairs is to put forth a strong argument for all students—majority and minority language speakers—to be given the opportunity to reap the benefits of bilingualism in their education. Recent studies of schools where every student receives bilingual instruction have shown positive results. Other studies demonstrate various ways in which teachers use two languages flexibly and extensively for academic development even in program structures that focus primarily on English. Explicit translanguaging pedagogies are also congruent with theory and research on the education of emergent bilinguals and so are pedagogies that develop critical multilingual awareness. Educating for critical multilingual awareness not only foregrounds metalinguistic knowledge for students, that is, understanding the nature of language such as how grammatical and discourse structures vary in different languages and contexts, but also the role of language in social life, that is, the relationship between languages, values, and power relations.

Curriculum and Pedagogies

If we cast the light of social justice and linguistic human rights on typical curricular and pedagogical designs for emergent bilinguals, we see inequities, for the elements of rigor and creativity are missing. Courtney Cazden (1986) has pointed to the fact that two kinds of curricula exist in U.S. schools—one that that has well-designed, challenging content and engages students in creative and collaborative work and another that pays attention only to basic skills. The latter is often the kind of curriculum that emergent bilinguals are-taught. They are subject to deficit models of instruction—"remediation," tracking, mistaken placement into special education, exclusion from gifted programs, and reduced curricular choices because of a narrow focus on English language skills. Moreover, inequities begin early. Ethnolinguistic minorities seldom get an early start through early childhood programs despite the fact that these programs can contribute to later educational achievement.

Challenging and creative curricula can give emergent bilinguals access to rich classroom discourse and literacy experiences across subject matter areas. It is through sustained social interactions that "foster collaborative relations of power" (Cummins, 2000, p. 253) that students' identities are affirmed while learning at the same time.

Teacher preparation is crucial to a high-quality education for emergent bilinguals. We know that effective teachers of these students have a thorough understanding about how language works. They have acquired the knowledge that is necessary to teach these students explicitly about how language is used in different content areas (Wong-Fillmore & Snow, 2000), they have studied child language development and bilingualism, and they have the pedagogical tools to enhance students' translanguaging in social interaction and in literacy events. In addition, effective teachers have been trained to reach out to parents of emergent bilinguals to form a partnership in their education.

Family and Community Engagement

Effective teachers know that they cannot go it alone. As we discussed in Chapter 7, research tells us that parents are emergent bilinguals' primary advocates for an equitable education; their involvement leads to students' improved attitudes about learning and to higher educational achievement. This is true especially for low-income minority students in both primary and secondary school. Moreover, ethnolinguistic minority parents and community members possess distinctive funds of knowledge—ways of knowing that their children learn at home. These too often go unrecognized in the school; worse, these endogenous skills—home language and literacy practices, practical skills and values—are considered inferior and inconsequential to schooling.

Often, parental education programs are designed to "teach" parents how to educate their children; some of these programs betray a deficit model of their parenting skills. Alternative models view family engagement as a shared responsibility between the school, the community, and the family. These models of family and community engagement address learning both inside and outside the school. Teachers and administrators also become learners about the families and communities they serve. In brief, learning becomes bidirectional, and this is to the benefit of emergent bilingual students.

Assessment

Testing is the gatekeeping device that often prevents emergent bilingual students from gaining access to further education and eventually an excellent quality of life. All students, including language minorities, are overtested under current NCLB mandates, but for language minorities, testing is especially burdensome because they are essentially being assessed for their academic language proficiency rather than for their knowledge of subject matter content. Moreover, not only are the tests given in English, they also have been normed on monolingual student populations; they do not take into account English language learners' developing bilingualism. We suggested several alternatives to the way emergent bilinguals are currently tested. They consist of changing the ways that students take the tests or others score them, or taking different assessments altogether, such as tests in the home language or tests that use the students' bilingual practices as a way to tap and assess what they know. The most promising alternatives continue to be close observations of student learning in the classrooms and dynamic bilingual assessments.

So far in this chapter we have provided a synthesis of issues on the education of emergent bilinguals, framing the discussion around the central theme of the growing dissonance between the research and inappropriate educational programs and instruction, limited resources and funding, exclusion of parents and community, and faulty assessment procedures. We now conclude this book by posting a series of hopeful signposts—offering a set of recommendations for a more equitable education of emergent bilinguals.

SIGNPOSTS: POLICY RECOMMENDATIONS

We concluded Chapters 2 through 8 by laying out an essential signpost for educating emergent bilinguals equitably, summarized here:

- know who they are;
- understand the shifts in programs and policies;
- build on their dynamic bilingualism;
- incorporate multilingual pedagogies;
- embrace challenge and care;
- recreate the school community; and
- account for fair assessment.

In this chapter, we detail recommendations that can be carried out by advocacy groups and grassroots organizations; some need the leadership of government at the federal, state, and local levels, and school officials, to move forward; others can be enacted by educators in their schools and classrooms; yet others belong to the realm of researchers. The recommendations that follow for transforming the education of emergent bilinguals take on greater urgency today given the increase in the number of students—citizens and noncitizens alike—coming into classrooms speaking a language other than English.

For Advocates

Educate the American public through the media about the nature of bilingualism.

There are folk theories in the United States that "other" languages and speakers of "other" languages are somehow abnormal and in need of repair. The media and the Internet could play an important role in disseminating essential knowledge about language and bilingualism to the general public. Advocates could post articles online and start blogs with discussions about ways in which bilingualism facilitates learning in school and create work and social opportunities in life. In this way, people would come to an understanding that in acquiring English, linguistic minority students become bilingual; thus English language teaching develops bilingualism. And language majorities would understand the advantages of bilingualism in their own lives and those of their children.

Furthermore, by portraying bilingual Americans in movies and television shows, and representing bilingual language minorities as loyal and hardworking Americans, advocates would help the public come to recognize bilingualism as a characteristic of U.S. society. The mainstream media can play an important role in bringing the sounds of languages other than English and bilingualism to all Americans.

Educate the American public through the media about the benefits of bilingualism as a national resource, especially in the context of a globalized world.

With the help of a wide range of media, the public can come to an understanding about the value of knowing two or more languages. People's use of the Internet is ubiquitous, and they can easily be persuaded about the advantages of multilingual communication for work and education.

Publicize the efforts of good schools and programs for emergent bilinguals, including the role of school leaders, educators, and community in this work.

Advocates can promote stories about schools where emergent bilinguals are learning and where school leaders and educators are making a difference. The media can be convinced that portraits of school success can pique the public's interest perhaps more than stories of failure and conflict. These and similar media presentations can help to dispel folk theories about bilingualism and linguistic diversity.

Urge federal funding for quality schools, educational programs and resources, and teacher education programs for emergent bilinguals.

Advocates can emphasize that fair funding should be given to educate emergent bilinguals. They can also urge that funding not always be tied to test results and that other factors be taken into account so that schools, programs, and teachers serving language minorities can be adequately supported. Quality schools are not always those that have the best test results, but quality schools are safe, clean, and have adequate instructional material and resources. They enjoy teams of teachers generously committed to teaching emergent bilinguals and prepared with knowledge about how students learn and develop academic English proficiency. Equal educational opportunity for emergent bilinguals should be the focus of the advocacy.

Keep the federal government and state and local educational authorities accountable for the education of emergent bilinguals.

Although there has been a major focus on accountability for school leaders and teachers, there are weak accountability measures for federal and state government and educational authorities. Questions can be raised about the irrationality of the federal government imposing unfunded mandates on state governments. Questions can also be raised about the ways in which state governments and local educational authorities report their services to emergent bilinguals, as well as how they assess them and report the test scores.

Urge federal funding for the development of valid and reliable assessment instruments for emergent bilinguals; assessment that takes into account the difference between testing academic knowledge and testing linguistic knowledge, while recognizing the value of multiple indicators of students' academic achievement.

Advocates can insist that the testing industry be made accountable and expose how testing scores are being used to exclude individuals. Advocates can urge that assessment be put back into the hands of educators. To that end, they should call for funding tied to assessment development that is user centered. If test-makers were to spend time in classrooms, they would learn from educators what it is that emergent bilinguals can do and how they learn. Thus, test-makers would be able to develop tests with teachers that can adequately evaluate emergent bilinguals and help teachers understand the students' strengths and weaknesses.

Advocates could urge federal funding for the development and testing of new assessment initiatives that use students' bilingualism. Funding might also support projects that enable schools and teachers to design their own assessments, as well as research on how teachers are using the assessment data to develop understandings about emergent bilinguals, their teaching and student learning.

For Policy Makers

Develop a definition of an English language learner that is stable across federal and state lines. The federal government should require stable and accurate data reporting and classification.

It is imperative that agreement be reached about what constitutes a learner of English. Policy makers could call on scholars of bilingualism to explore how to measure and assess the academic English proficiency needed for success in schools. To be accurate, the measure should include students' home languages and their bilingual abilities. Policy makers could demand that this measure not define a category from which students exit to a "proficient" category, but designate points on a continuum of emergent bilingualism that require different kinds of educational programs and different levels of academic intervention.

Design educational policy based on current theory and research regarding the benefits of an equitable education for emergent bilinguals.

The research evidence supporting the use of emergent bilinguals' home languages in their education is incontrovertible. Policy makers could become well versed in this research and empirical evidence so that this becomes center stage in developing policy.

Support and expand educational programs that have demonstrated success in providing a challenging, high-quality education and that build on the strengths children and youth bring to school, particularly their home languages and cultures.

Policy makers could desist from portraying categories of educational programs as if they were in opposition to each other—ESL or bilingual—for example. Instead, informed policy makers could support the use of children's home language practices in educating emergent bilinguals to a lesser or greater extent, depending on capacity, community, configuration, and desires. They could support and encourage educational programs that follow research findings to the extent the community situation permits.

Support and expand student access to high-quality materials, including new technologies, especially in high-poverty schools, to facilitate access to the changing communication mediascape and give students a better chance to reach academic attainment.

Policy makers need to provide schools with multilingual literacy material—books and digital audio and video resources. Access to technology—computers, translating software, and voice recognition software—are especially important for emergent bilinguals, and policy makers should ensure that this is readily available in all classrooms so that students can read, write, and carry out research using all the languages at their disposal.

Start bilingual educational support early—through meaningful bilingual early childhood programs.

Policy makers could ensure that multilingual early childhood programs are available and that early assessment and intervention, when appropriate, are done in the children's home languages. Language majority children could also benefit from these multilingual early childhood programs, participating in and becoming familiar with different languages and cultural practices early in life.

Pay particular attention to the middle school years.

Emergent bilinguals that are supported in elementary schools—through either ESL or bilingual programs—most often get fewer services when they reach middle school. Policy makers must pay particular attention to the middle school years, for students who continue to be categorized as English language learners after having received 5 to 6 years of education may have serious educational impediments. These students cannot be educated in the same ways as emergent bilinguals who are newcomers; educational programs have to be designed to meet their needs.

Support strong programs for emergent bilinguals at the secondary level.

Especially at the secondary level, emergent bilinguals need challenging educational programs. Policy makers should insist that schools provide these adolescents with the challenging academic content they need, while at the same time developing academic English. A rigorous academic program that can also develop advanced English literacy is essential to make these adolescents college ready.

Support the development of more two-way bilingual education programs and programs that support understandings of bilingualism and linguistic tolerance.

Two-way bilingual education programs hold much promise in developing the bilingualism of both language minorities and majorities. Although much work is needed in supporting the education of language minorities, language majorities also need to develop their bilingualism and further their understandings of bilingualism and bilingual communities, both in the United States and in the world. Policy makers need to support the development of such curricula for all American children.

Require that all school leaders, teachers, and other school personnel be well versed in issues of bilingualism and understand the importance of the home language and culture for the child.

Policy makers could make understandings of bilingualism and emergent bilinguals a requirement for certification and employment. Beyond specialized teachers of English as a second language and bilingual teachers, all teachers should be required by policy makers to demonstrate an ability to work with bilingual children and their families.

Promote strong pre-service/in-service education and professional development that prepares teachers to work with emergent bilinguals.

Given the growing numbers of emergent bilingual children in American schools, policy makers could require that all teacher education programs include coursework on bilingualism and the education of emergent bilinguals. Policy makers could also require that all teachers receive professional development that specifically targets emergent bilinguals and bilingual students as part of their professional commitment.

Provide incentives for the preparation and hiring of additional bilingual staff—from school leaders and teachers to paraprofessionals, school psychologists, school counselors, therapists, and the like.

Because bilingual school staff is more difficult to recruit, prepare, and retain, policy makers should provide financial incentives to those institutions of higher education that prepare bilingual staff and to schools that hire them. Financial incentives should be targeted to members of language minority groups that are particularly needed in the teaching profession. Incentives for community members to become paraprofessionals would be especially important, as are programs in which these paraprofessionals could then extend their preparation and eventually become teachers.

Provide incentives for bilinguals to enter the specialized profession of teaching English to speakers of other languages (TESOL) or to enter the bilingual teaching profession.

Bilingual individuals who can become teachers of English as a second language and bilingual teachers need to be offered incentives to join the profession. Different states and regions may offer incentives to different language groups whose language expertise are sorely needed by school systems.

Require all teachers to develop some experience as emergent bilinguals themselves.

Academic study of an additional language is a worthy aim. However, a richer experience could be considered. Teacher education programs could arrange for prospective teachers to experience a period of time abroad or in a U.S. ethnolinguistic community other than the teacher's own.

Promote the integration of ESL/bilingual education programs so that all ESL teachers would know about bilingualism and all bilingual teachers would be experts in the teaching of academic English.

Policy makers could require that, with the exception of the coursework required of bilingual teachers in teaching content in the home language, the preparation of ESL and bilingual teachers be the same. Being in classes together would ameliorate the divisions between programs that often exist. All should know how to teach content in English to emergent bilinguals, as well as support their development of academic English. Additionally, all should understand how to use the students' home languages as sense-making in educating them.

Require schools to recognize the funds of knowledge that exist in emergent bilingual students' families and communities, to be accountable to them, and to achieve closer mutual engagement for a higher-quality education.

Policy makers could also require that all teachers have coursework on how to work with families of emergent bilinguals who do not speak English and how to provide translation services to parents. This coursework would require that all teachers learn an additional language to maximize the bilingualism of the U.S. teaching force in the 21st century. In addition, the coursework would make teachers aware of what they could learn from the funds of knowledge of the community and parents by developing the prospective teachers' ethnographic skills. This specialized coursework would help teachers develop assignments that build on parents' existing knowledge, whatever that might be, while extending the children's understandings in ways that would not require the parents to be knowledgeable of the same content or linguistic practices.

For Educators

Consider the whole child.

To be effective, teachers would not focus narrowly on the language of the student, but instead "cast [their] inner eye on a particular child," as Carini (2000a, p. 57) would say. Teachers can follow Carini's advice about paying attention to the students' physical presence and gesture, their disposition and temperament, their connection to other people, their strong interests and preferences, and their modes of thinking and learning.

Consider the students in the context of their communities.

Effective teachers become familiar with the community in which the children live and with the histories of the cultural practices in which the children and youth are immersed at home and in the community. If the community has a large immigrant population, educators should understand their histories of (im)migration, their cultural practices, their religion, and their language practices. They could also become familiar with community-based organizations that support the ethnolinguistic groups and with after-school and weekend community bilingual programs that the students might attend.

Observe and listen to language practices closely.

Effective teachers are listeners and observers of their students. Teachers should listen to the students on the playground, in the gym, and in the cafeteria. They might also listen to the mothers as they pick up their children or to the youth as they make their way home when the school day is over. What languages are they speaking? What are they saying? They could pay attention to the signage in the community and around the school. Are they written in other languages? Are they in other scripts? They could inquire about TV programs, computer games, and other forms of media that children and youth engage with, which are in languages other than English.

Learn something about the home languages of students.

Teachers could ask parents to teach them how to say simple phrases such as "Good morning," "Good afternoon," "Thank you," "Please," and "Goodbye." They might experience what it means to write in a nonalphabetic script. Elementary school teachers can try to learn a short song (or obtain a recording) in an additional language to teach the children in the class to sing. Families can be asked to bring in multilingual materials and devise classroom signage in different languages so that the classroom can become a multilingual surround.

Speak, speak, speak. Read, read, read. Write, write, write.

Language is learned through practice in different contexts. Teachers can give students opportunities to use the English language richly—by listening to different discourses on various media, by reading broadly both fiction and nonfiction, and by writing different genres frequently. Whenever possible, teachers should give students opportunities to do the same in their home languages. Finally, teachers should encourage generative dialogue and opportunities to engage in lively, thoughtful, quality interactions.

Encourage students to think about language practices and the power of language.

Emergent bilinguals need to become linguists—comfortable analyzing language, developing metalanguage skills, comparing languages, and thinking aloud about languages. They also need to have practice with subject content and academic language. In addition, emergent bilinguals need to become aware of the power differential between languages in society and in their schools. Teachers can support this development by ensuring that their pedagogy is collaborative and culturally and linguistically relevant. A critical multilingual awareness curriculum would help students develop the ability to analyze social issues of language relevant to their lives.

Encourage the use of translanguaging as a sense-making mechanism.

Instead of bracketing English and excluding the home language practices from instruction, educators should encourage students to translanguage—to render one assignment in the other language, to find research in any language, to use what they have learned in one language in the service of the other, to discuss and think in any language, as they read and write in another. Teachers should empower emergent bilingual students to use translanguaging as sense-making in the service of deeper understandings and more advanced development of academic English.

Provide a challenging and creative curriculum with demanding, imaginative, and relevant material.

Teachers should elaborate the lesson for emergent bilinguals by providing different scaffolds. This does not mean teachers should simplify; they should search for instructional material that is challenging. Whenever possible, they should provide opportunities to read and write in the students' home languages, enabling the development of complex ideas that can be expressed better in a language one knows while the target language is still being developed. Teachers should encourage the use of technology and the Internet, since these can be important resources for students to find challenging material written in their home languages—material that is relevant to students' lives, encourages positive identity development, and engages them in challenging ideas.

Provide differentiated instruction for emergent bilingual students with different educational profiles.

Some emergent bilinguals are new to the school language—because they have come to school from homes in which English is not spoken or from schools in other countries where instruction was in a language other than English. Some of the newcomer students have well-developed literacy in their home language, but others do not. Some have had their education interrupted by war, poverty, and other social conditions. But some emergent bilinguals have been in U.S. classrooms for a long time and yet have failed to develop academic literacy in English. Educators need to be aware of these differences and to provide students with appropriate lessons and pedagogy.

Become an advocate of emergent bilinguals.

Besides parents, effective teachers know what the best academic path is for emergent bilinguals. Teachers should use the data generated from standardized assessments, but supplement it with their own observations and professional judgments. They should resist educational decisions made for emergent bilinguals that are based on one score on a standardized test. They should be advocates for what these students need with other school professionals, other teachers, the school leadership team, and the community.

Develop a strong relationship with the family.

Teachers should learn as much as they can about and from families of emergent bilinguals and the community's funds of knowledge. In case of newcomers to the United States, they need information regarding whether the family or other relatives were separated because of immigration—who the children/youth immigrated with, and who was left behind. They can encourage parents and other community members to participate in classroom activities, inviting them to give presentations about their cultural and linguistic histories and practices.

Inculcate in emergent bilingual students a hunger for excellence, and model dreams of tolerance, equity, and social justice.

Teachers should be particularly focused on high expectations for emergent bilingual students. At the same time, teachers should convey their convictions about the need for tolerance and social justice to build a more inclusive and just world.

For Researchers

Study the cognitive and creative advantages of bilingualism in the United States.

In the United States there has been little neurolinguistic research that focuses on the advantages of bilingualism. This research needs to be advanced.

Develop assessments that tap into children's knowledge construction in English through languages other than English.

This is the most serious gap in research on emergent bilinguals' education. Researchers, and in particular neurolinguists and psycholinguists, need to join with educators and psychometricians in developing these bilingual assessments for bilingual children.

Develop measures of dynamic bilingual proficiency.

As researchers recognize the fallacy of a linear conception of bilingualism, it becomes necessary to develop ways of assessing the complex dynamic nature of language practices and bilingualism. Research in this area needs to be strengthened.

Conduct research on the effects of translanguaging for the teaching and learning of emergent bilinguals.

Past conceptions of bilingualism have been constructed on the basis of monolingual notions of language practices. As a result, English bracketing has been a preferred instructional approach in the United States. But as studies of bilingualism begin to rest on heteroglossic (Bakhtin, 1981) notions of language use, translanguaging has become a more accepted practice. Yet little research has been conducted in the United States on this practice and should be initiated.

Strengthen research on bilingual acquisition and evaluation of education for emergent bilinguals by conducting, for example, more multidisciplinary and mixed-method studies that will help educators and school officials make informed decisions about the fit between children and programs and practices.

Research on the education of emergent bilinguals, focused broadly instead of narrowly on issues of whether bilingual education or ESL programs are more adequate, needs to be encouraged. The focus of the research needs to be the students themselves and the teachers' pedagogies and practices.

EDUCATING EMERGENT BILINGUALS: ALTERNATIVE PATHS

As we have tried to demonstrate in this book, current policies and practices for the education of emergent bilinguals are misguided. They contradict what theory and research have concluded and what scholars and educators have maintained. They also diverge from the realities of engagement in a globalized world with its growing multilingualism. However, despite restrictive educational policies, we see, on the ground, reflective educators who continue to use a commonsense approach in teaching the growing number of these students, building on the strengths of their home languages and cultures. American educators, however, should not be left alone—or even worse, forced to hide what they are doing—when implementing practices that make sense for the students and the communities they are educating. For emergent bilinguals to move forward, and not be left behind, educators need to be supported by policy and resources that bolster their expertise and advance their teaching. Educators need to be given time and space at school to observe students closely and document their work and learning *with and through* language, instead of being required to focus only on their performance through poorly designed tests and assessments. They need the opportunity to teach individual students, instead of seeing teaching as a master plan of scores. With better preparation on the nature of bilingualism, teachers can find ways to work with the good aspects of governmental policy at the federal, state, and local level.

Educators, and all who are concerned about this growing student population, should advocate for changes in aspects of the policy that make no sense for emergent bilinguals. For changes to be effective, the different levels of policy must work in tandem with educators and language minority communities. Only then will we begin to close the gap between levels of abstract policies and local realities through which most disadvantaged students, such as emergent bilinguals, fall. We must start closing the gap of inequity for emergent bilinguals by naming the inequities, as we have done in this book, and then taking action to support their meaningful education.

Notes

Chapter 1

1. According to the NCLB Act of 2001, section 9101, paragraph 25, limited English proficient is defined as an individual
(A) who is aged 3 through 21;
(B) who is enrolled or preparing to enroll in an elementary school or secondary school;
(C) (i) who was not born in the United States or whose native language is a language other than English;
(ii) (I) who is a Native American or Alaska Native, or a native resident of the outlying areas; and
(II) who comes from an environment where a language other than English has had a significant impact on the individual's level of English language proficiency; or
(iii) who is migratory, whose native language is a language other than English, and who comes from an environment where a language other than English is dominant; and
(D) whose difficulties in speaking, reading, writing, or understanding the English language may be sufficient to deny the individual—
(i) the ability to meet the State's proficient level of achievement on State assessments described in section 1111(b)(3);
(ii) the ability to successfully achieve in classrooms where the language of instruction is English; or
(iii) the opportunity to participate fully in society.
2. NAEP data has little validity in the case of these students, since these are by definition unable to reach proficiency on English-language assessments (see Chapter 8 on assessment).
3. Throughout this book we prefer the term *home language* to *mother tongue*. *Mother tongue* is extensively used, especially to refer to the language of minority groups, although it has been called inaccurate (Baker & Prys Jones, 1998; Kaplan & Baldauf, 1997; Skutnabb-Kangas, 1981). Skutnabb-Kangas (1981) reminds us that one can identify a mother tongue based on different criteria—the language one learned first, the language one knows best, the language one uses most, the language one identifies with, and the language others identify one with. Thus, the term is often not useful, so we prefer here to speak of the home languages of students.

4. Even the term *English language learner* can be problematic, as a partici-
pant at a recent conference on the teaching of languages attested to when asking, "You mean these are English students [meaning British] who are learning
languages?"

5. This section is based on García 2009b.

6. We prefer to use *additional language* instead of *second language* because
English may not necessarily be the second language acquired, but a third or fourth.
It is also a more equitable way of expressing the complex acquisition and use of
many languages.

7. Sometimes, building on the home language is accomplished through bilingual education, about which we say more in subsequent chapters. At other times,
this can be accomplished in programs where only English is formally used as a medium of instruction, but where teachers acknowledge and build on the languages
that the students bring to the classroom.

Chapter 2

1. In this chapter, we use primarily three sources of data, supplemented by
other reports, to describe who ELLs are: (1) The *Descriptive Study of Services to
LEP Students and LEP Students with Disabilities* (Zehler et al., 2003), the latest
decennial survey funded by the U.S. Department of Education and conducted by
Development Associates; (2) the *Survey of the States' Limited English Proficient Students and Available Educational Programs and Services Summary* reports known as
the *State Educational Agency Survey* or *SEA Survey*. The SEA is also funded by the
U.S. Department of Education. The latest report available (Kindler, 2002) analyzes
data from 2000–01; (3) The U.S. census, or more specifically the *American Community Survey*. While these are the best data available for analysis, we recognize that
all three of these data sets have limitations, especially in terms of how these students
are identified, counted, and reported. (See García, Kleifgen, & Falchi, 2008, note 5
for these limitations.)

2. The 2004–05 NCELA numbers are distorted by the inclusion of Puerto
Rico, where 99.9% of students are classified as LEPs, and other outlying areas (Mi-
cronesia, American Samoa, Guam, Marshall Islands, North Marianas, Paulau, and
the Virgin Islands). Public schools in these U.S. protectorates are eligible for Title III
NCLB funding to support these students. Excluding these areas outside the 50 states,
the ELL enrollment was 4,459,603 in 2004–05.

3. This is calculated by adding up all those who claim to speak a language
other than English at home, and then who claim to speak English less than very well.

4. The "big states" according to the number of English language learners
have developed their own assessments for English language proficiency, as follows:
California—California English Language Development Test (CELDT); Texas—
Texas English Language Proficiency Assessment (TELPAS); Florida—Comprehensive English Language Learning Assessment (CELLA); New York—New York State
English as a Second Language Achievement Test (NYSESLAT); New Mexico—New
Mexico English Language Proficiency (NMELPA); Arizona—Arizona English Language Learner Assessment (AZELLA). Illinois and New Jersey belong to the WIDA
consortium (see note 5).

5. The WIDA consortium consists of Alabama, Delaware, the District of Columbia, Georgia, Hawaii, Illinois, Kentucky, Maine, Mississippi, New Hampshire, New Jersey, New Mexico, North Carolina, North Dakota, Oklahoma, Pennsylvania, Rhode Island, South Dakota, Vermont, Virginia, and Wisconsin.

6. How academic achievement should be defined has received a great deal of attention in the field of educational measurement. Some argue, as we do here, that language ability should be measured separately from content knowledge; in this view, the language variable in large-scale assessments of academic achievement (such as NAEP) is interpreted as a measurement error. Others contend that knowledge of the content area necessarily includes the specific discourse embedded in it. (See Koenig, 2002, for a discussion of these issues.) We thank Lyle Bachman for calling this to our attention.

7. The numbers reported by Kindler (2002) were 1,511,646 in California, 570,022 in Texas, 254,517 in Florida, 239,097 in New York, 140,528 in Illinois, and 135,248 in Arizona, different from those above.

8. For the period 2001–02, Kindler (2002) reports the percentages as follows: California, 25%; New Mexico, 20%; Arizona, 15%; Alaska, 15%; Texas, 14%; and Nevada, 12%.

9. As we know, it is problematic to count languages. We refer here, however, to figures accounted for in the U.S. census, which enumerates some languages, while ignoring others.

10. We believe that the 75% estimate is more accurate, given the inclusion of Puerto Rico in calculations other than the census.

11. As in all cases where we use U.S. census figures, we calculate emergent bilinguals by adding up all those who claim to speak English less than very well.

12. Scholars point out that categories of race and ethnicity are confounded in the U.S. census as well as in educational policy, where the terms *linguistic minority*, *race*, and *ethnicity* are often ambiguously used (Macias, 1994; Wiley, 2005).

13. High-LEP schools are those that have 25% or more LEP students. Low-LEP schools are those where LEP students represent less than a quarter of all students.

14. Whereas 70% of ELL students were in pre-K to 5th grade in 2001–02, only 40% of students nationwide were at the same grade levels in 2006–07 (U.S. Census Bureau, 2007).

15. *Temporary sojourners* are usually businesspersons who are on a short-term visit.

16. The term *migrant workers* usually refers to persons who work at seasonal jobs and move around, and in the United States it usually describes low-wage laborers in the field of agriculture.

17. This term is contested, since children growing up in English-speaking homes are never referred to as "linguistically isolated."

18. These numbers do not include the 6% of Spanish speaking emergent bilinguals who are said to be from places other than these countries.

Chapter 3

1. Some of the history in this section is taken from García (2009a, chap. 8). A most valuable source for this information is Crawford (2004).

2. The term *dual language* is increasingly used to refer to these two-way bilingual education programs and, in some instances, to what otherwise would be called developmental bilingual education programs. This has to do with the current anti-bilingual climate and avoiding the designation of *bilingual* for any educational program.

3. The original model for international high schools in New York mixed newcomers of different language backgrounds. However, in scaling up the model they were confronted with the reality that some neighborhoods were almost exclusively Spanish speaking. Recently, the international network has opened two schools in New York that are exclusively for Spanish-speaking newcomers, following the same pedagogical principles of collaborative grouping and use of home languages to support English language development.

4. The subgroups of students are racial and ethnic groups (Asian/Pacific Islander, Black, Hispanic, American Indian, White), economically disadvantaged, free/reduced lunch, students with disabilities, and limited English proficient.

5. Title I, Improving the Academic Achievement of the Disadvantaged, provides financial assistance to schools with high numbers or high percentages of poor children to help ensure that all children meet challenging state academic standards.

Chapter 4

1. We use *languaging* to refer to the multiple discursive practices that individuals use, which extend beyond the sociopolitical constructions of a "language" as proposed by states and social groups (García, 2009a; Makoni & Pennycook, 2007; Shohamy, 2006; Yngve, 1996) and used in schools.

2. This term has been considered controversial, since no language, however abstract, can truly be called decontextualized.

3. It is important to understand that the goal of Canadian immersion bilingual education programs was an initiative of the Anglophone majority parents to support their students' acquisition of French in Francophone Canada—that is, to make their children bilingual. Thus, the use of "immersion," or more precisely, "submersion" for English-only programs in the United States has little to do with Canadian immersion programs.

4. It is well known that immigrants to the United States shift to English by the third generation (see, for example, Fishman, 1966).

5. García (2009a) extends the meaning of the term *translanguaging*, coined by Cen Williams (as cited in Baker, 2001) to refer to a pedagogical practice that switches the language mode in bilingual classrooms; for example, reading is done in one language and writing in another. Translanguaging for García (2009a) goes beyond Williams's definition, as well as beyond code-switching and translation to include all hybrid language use that is part of a sense-making process.

6. These included the ITBS, CTBS, Stanford 9, and Terra Nova.

Chapter 5

1. Mini-lessons are short teacher-centered lessons in which teachers model explicit metacognitive strategies used in reading and writing texts (see Calkins, 1994; Velasco & Swinney, in press).

2. García (2005) provides arguments against the use of the term *heritage language*. Nevertheless, scholars and educational administrators often refer to these programs by this term.

Chapter 6

1. According to Zehler et al. (2003), the percentage of ELL students reported to be in special education was smaller than the percentage of all students in special education (9% vs. 13%). This may have to do with an underidentification of ELL students in need of special education services.

2. Eight percent of emergent bilinguals in special education were in multilevel classrooms and thus are not included in this count.

3. Typically state and local tax revenues provide most of the money in the United States for public education, 92% of the total on average, but this is not so for English language learners where the funding mostly comes from federal initiatives, as do other categorical programs to serve "disadvantaged" students.

4. NCLB defines these immigrant children and youth as 3- to 21-year-olds, who were not born in the United States and have not been in school attendance for more than 3 full academic years.

5. The other 15% is for immigrant allocations, and the remaining 5% is for NYSED use.

6. The reader is reminded that Annual Measurable Achievement Objectives (AMAOs) for English language learners include three components:

a. making annual progress;
b. attaining English proficiency; and,
c. meeting Adequate Yearly Progress (AYP) requirements set by their states and measured by state standardized tests.

7. This section owes a great deal to the work done by Lori Falchi for the report written for the Center for Educational Equity. We are grateful to her for this invaluable contribution.

8. These numbers include the cost of the base education plus any additional costs.

9. BCLAD stands for Bilingual, Crosscultural, Language and Academic Development. CLAD is the certification needed to teach English learners in California. BCLAD is the certification to teach English learners in bilingual programs.

Chapter 7

1. Kreider et al. (2007) do not address the advantages of parental leadership in the school and community, an area that we take up in this chapter.

2. For a review of the psychological research on this topic, see Hoover-Dempsey and Sandler (1997).

3. See Johnson (2009) for a critique of the unitary "best practices" approach in parent education programs that do not account for diversity in families' ways of educating their children.

Chapter 8

1. Predictive assessments are developed by Acuity for the NYCDOE in English reading and mathematics. These assessments are given to students Grades 3–5. The content of these exams parallels the state exams that students in these grades will take. They are given twice a year before the official state exam is administered in order to provide timely information predicting how a given student will perform in the subsequent state exam. Teachers are provided with test results in order to develop "interventions" for students.

2. *Baselines, midlines,* and *endlines* refer to assessments that are meant to judge a range of student knowledge and content over a range of time. For example, a baseline is founded on grade-level standards of the previous year. Students are assessed along these standards to determine if they have acquired or if their knowledge exceed the standards to which students were held at the end of the previous grade.

3. Reading records are assessments administered by a teacher to determine a student's reading level and comprehension. Conferences with students can take place during any content area instruction time. Teachers may have a variety of objectives when they have a conference with a student. If conferencing is tied to a school's periodic assessment, it is most likely tied to grade-level content standards.

4. The Race to the Top grant competition announced in 2009 by the Obama administration allows states to compete for federal grants based on how well they do in four tenets of reform. Two of those reforms have to do with assessments and data-driven instruction: (1) adopting standards and assessments that prepare students to succeed and (2) building data systems that measure student growth and success and inform teachers and principals about how they can improve instruction.

References

Abedi, J. (2004). The No Child Left Behind Act and English language learners: Assessment and accountability issues. *Educational Researcher, 33*(1), 4–14.

Abedi, J., Hofstetter, C. H., & Lord, C. (2004). Assessment accommodations for English language learners: Implications for policy-based empirical research. *Review of Educational Research, 74*(1), 1–28.

Abedi, J., & Lord, C. (2001). The language factor in mathematics tests. *Applied Measurement in Education, 14*(3), 219–234.

Abedi, J., Lord, C., & Plummer, J. R. (1997). *Final report of language background as a variable in NAEP mathematics performance* (CSE Tech. Rep. No. 429): University of California at Los Angeles, National Center for Research on Evaluation, Standards, and Student Testing.

Adams, M., Bell, L. A., & Griffin, P. (2007). *Teaching for diversity and social justice* (2nd ed.). New York: Routledge.

Adams, M., Blumenfeld, W., Castañeda, C. (R.), & Hackman, H. (Eds.). (2000). *Readings for diversity and social justice: An anthology on racism, antisemitism, sexism, heterosexism, ableism, and classism.* New York: Routledge.

Al-Azami, S., Kenner, C., Ruby, M., & Gregory, E. (in press). Transliteration as a bridge to learning for bilingual children. *International Journal of Bilingual Education and Bilingualism.*

American Community Survey (ACS). (2004). U.S. Census Bureau. Retrieved February 19, 2010, from http://www.census.gov/acs/www/

American Educational Research Association (AERA), American Psychological Association (APA), & National Council on Measurement in Education (NCME). (1985). *National Council on Measurement in Education standards for educational and psychological testing.* Washington, DC: American Psychological Association.

American Institutes for Research (AIR). (2004). *New York adequacy study: Providing all children with full opportunity to meet the Regents Learning Standards.* Washington, DC, and Davis, CA: American Institutes for Research and Management Analysis and Planning.

Anderson, N. E., Jenkins, F. F., & Miller, K. E. (1996). *NAEP inclusion criteria and testing accommodations: Findings from the NAEP 1995 field test in mathematics.* Washington, DC: National Center for Education Statistics.

Anstrom, K. (1997). *Academic achievement for secondary language minority students: Standards, measures, and promising practices.* Washington DC: National Clearinghouse for Bilingual Education.

Anyon, J. (1997). *Ghetto schooling. A political economy of urban educational reform.* New York: Teachers College Press.

Anyon, J. (2005). *Radical possibilities: Public policy, urban education, and a new social movement.* New York: Routledge.

Artiles, A. (1998). Overrepresentation of minority students: The case for greater specificity or reconsideration of the variables examined. *The Journal of Special Education, 32*(1), 32–36.

Artiles, A. J., & Ortiz, A. A. (Eds.). (2002). *English language learners with special education needs: Identification, assessment, and instruction.* Washington, DC, and McHenry, IL: Center for Applied Linguistics and Delta System.

Artiles, A. J., Rueda, R., Salazar, J., & Higareda, I. (2002). English-language learner representation in special education in California urban school districts. In D. Losen & G. Orfield (Eds.), *Racial inequity in special education* (pp. 117–136). Cambridge, MA: Harvard Education Press.

Ascenzi-Moreno, L. (2009). *Language and assessment.* Unpublished manuscript. Graduate Center, The City University of New York.

Au, K. (1993). *Literacy instruction in multicultural settings.* Orlando, FL: Harcourt Brace.

Auerbach, E. A. (1995). Deconstructing the discourse of strengths in family literacy. *Journal of Reading Behavior, 27*(4), 643–661.

August, D., & Hakuta, K. (1997). *Improving schooling for language-minority children: A research agenda.* Washington, DC: National Research Council, National Academies Press.

August, D., & Hakuta, K. (Eds.). (1998). *Educating language-minority children.* Washington, DC: Committee on Developing a Research Agenda on the Education of Limited-English-Proficient and Bilingual Students, National Research Council, Institute of Medicine, and National Academies Press.

August, D., Hakuta, K., & Pompa, D. (1994). *For all students: Limited English proficient students and Goals 2000. Focus, Vol. 10.* Washington, DC: National Clearinghouse for Bilingual Education.

August, D., & Shanahan, T. (Eds.). (2006). *Developing literacy in second-language learners: Report of the National Literacy Panel on language-minority children and youth.* Mahwah, NJ: Lawrence Erlbaum Associates.

Ayers, W., Hunt, J. A., & Quinn, T. (Eds.). (1998). *Teaching for social justice: A democracy and education reader.* New York: New Press.

Bachman, L. F. (1990). *Fundamental considerations in language testing.* Oxford: Oxford University Press.

Bachman, L. F. (2002). Alternative interpretations of alternative assessments: Some validity issues in educational performance assessments. *Educational Measurement: Issues and Practice, 21*(3), 5–18.

Baker, B. D., Green, P. C., & Markham, P. (2004). *Legal and empirical analysis of state financing of programs for children with English language communication barriers.* Paper presented at the annual meeting of the National Association for Bilingual Education, Albuquerque, NM.

Baker, C. (2001). *Foundations of bilingual education and bilingualism* (3rd ed.). Clevedon, UK: Multilingual Matters.

Baker, C. (2003). Biliteracy and transliteracy in Wales: Language planning and the Welsh National Curriculum. In N. H. Hornberger (Ed.), *Continua of Biliteracy* (pp. 71–90). Clevedon, UK: Multilingual Matters.

Baker, C. (2006). *Foundations of bilingual education and bilingualism* (4th ed.). Clevedon, UK: Multilingual Matters.

Baker, C., & Prys Jones, S. (1998). *Encyclopedia of bilingualism and bilingual education.* Clevedon, UK: Multilingual Matters.

Baker, K., & de Kanter, A. (1981). *Effectiveness of bilingual education: A review of the literature.* Final draft report. Washington, DC: Department of Education, Office of Planning, Budget, and Evaluation.

Bakhtin, M. (1981). *Dialogic imagination: Four essays.* Austin: University of Texas Press.

Barnett, W. S., & Masse, L. N. (2007). Comparative benefit-cost analysis of the Abecedarian program and its policy implications. *Economics of Education Review, 26,* 113–125.

Bartlett, L. (2007). Bilingual literacies, social identification, and educational trajectories. *Linguistics and Education, 18*(3–4), 215–231.

Bartlett, L., & García, O. (in press). *Additive schooling in subtractive times: Dominican immigrant youth in the Heights.* Nashville, TN: Vanderbilt University Press.

Batalova, J. (2006, February). Spotlight on limited English proficient students in the United States. Migration Information Source. Retrieved February 19, 2010, from http://www.migrationinformation.org/usfocus/display.cfm?ID=373 Retrieved February 19, 2010 from http://dq.cde.ca.gov/dataquest/ElP2_State.asp?RptYear=2005-06&RptType=ELPart2_1

Batalova, J., Fix, M., & Murray, J. (2007). *Measures of change: The demography and literacy of adolescent English learners: A Report to Carnegie Corporation of New York.* Washington, DC: Migration Policy Institute.

Ben-Zeev, S. (1977). The effect of bilingualism in children from Spanish-English low-income neighborhoods on cognitive development and cognitive strategy. *Working Papers on Bilingualism, 14.* Toronto: Ontario Institute for Studies in Education, Bilingual Education Project.

BEST (Building Educational Success Together). (2006). *Growth and disparity: A decade of U.S. public school construction.* Washington, DC: Best.

Bialystok, E. (2004). Language and literacy development. In T. K. Bhatia & W. C. Ritchie (Eds.), *The handbook of bilingualism* (pp. 577–601). Malden, MA: Blackwell.

Bialystok, E. (2007). Cognitive effects of bilingualism: How linguistic experience leads to cognitive change. *International Journal of Bilingual Education and Bilingualism, 10*(3), 210–223.

Bilingual Education Act. (1968). Title VII, Bilingual Education, Language Enhancement, and Language Acquisition Programs of Elementary and Secondary Education Act. P.L. 90-247.

Bilingual Education Act. (1974). Title VII of Elementary and Secondary Education Act, 1974 reauthorization, P.L. 93-380.

Bilingual Education Act. (1978). Title VII of Elementary and Secondary Education Act, 1978 reauthorization, P.L. 95-561.

Bilingual Education Act. (1984). Title VII of Elementary and Secondary Education Act, 1984 reauthorization, P.L. 98-511.

Bilingual Education Act. (1988). Title VII of Elementary and Secondary Education Act, 1988 reauthorization, P.L. 100-297

Bilingual Education Act. (1994). Title VII of Improving America's Schools Act of 1994. P.L. 103-382.

Birch, B. M. (2002). *English L2 reading: Getting to the bottom.* Mahwah, NJ: Lawrence Erlbaum.

Blanc, M., & Hamers, J. (Eds.). (1985). *Theoretical and methodological issues in the study of languages/dialects in contact at macro- and micro-logical levels of analysis.* London: Proceedings of the International Conference DALE (University of London)/ICRB (Laval University, Quebec).

Blasé, J., & Blasé, J. (2001). *Empowering teachers: What successful principals do.* (2nd ed.). Thousand Oaks, CA: Corwin Press.

Bloom, D., & Grenier, G. (1996) Language, employment, and earnings in the United States: Spanish-English differentials from 1970 to 1990. *International Journal of the Sociology of Language, 121,* 45–68.

Booher-Jennings, J. (2006). Rationing education in an era of accountability. *Phi Delta Kappan, 87*(10), 756–761.

Borkowski, J., & Sneed, M. (2006). Will NCLB improve or harm public education? *Harvard Educational Review 76*(4), 503–525.

Boswell, T. (2000) Demographic changes in Florida and their importance for effective educational policies and practices. In A. Roca (Ed.), *Research on Spanish in the United States: Linguistic issues and challenges* (pp. 406–431). Somerville, MA: Cascadilla Press.

Bourdieu, P. (1985). The forms of capital. In J. G. Richardson, (Ed.), *Handbook of theory and research for the sociology of education* (pp. 241–258). New York: Greenwood.

Browning-Aiken, A. (2005). Border crossing: Funds of knowledge within an immigrant household. In N. González, L. C. Moll, & C. Amanti (Eds.), *Funds of knowledge: Theorizing practices in households, communities, and classrooms* (pp. 167–181). Mahwah, NJ: Lawrence Erlbaum Associates.

California Department of Education. (2005). *Language census, 2004–05.* Sacramento: Author.

California Department of Education. (2006a). *English learners, instructional settings, and services.* Retrieved February 19, 2010, from http://dq.cde.ca.gov/dataquest/ElP2_State.asp?RptYear=2004-05&RptType=ELPart2_1a

California Department of Education. (2006b). *Number of English learner students enrolled in specific instructional settings.* Retrieved February 19, 2010, from: http://dq.cde.ca.gov/dataquest/ElP2_State.asp?RptYear=2005-06&RptType=ELPart2_1

California Proposition 227 (1998). California Education Code, Sections 300–311.

Calkins, L. (1994). *The art of teaching writing.* (2nd ed.). Portsmouth, NH: Heinemann.

Callahan, R. (2003). *Tracking and English language proficiency: Variable effects on academic achievement of high school ELs.* Unpublished dissertation, University of California, Davis.

Callahan, R. (2005). Tracking and high school English learners: Limiting opportunities to learn. *American Educational Research Journal, 42*(2), 305–328.

Canagarajah, S. (1999). *Resisting linguistic imperialism in English teaching.* Oxford: Oxford University Press.

Canale, M., & Swain, M. (1980). Theoretical bases of communicative approaches to second language teaching and testing. *Journal of Applied Linguistics, 1*(1), 1–47.

Capps, R., Fix, M., Murray, J., Ost, J., Passel, J. S., & Herwantoro, S. (2005). *The new demography of America's schools: Immigration and the No Child Left Behind Act.* Washington, DC: Urban Institute.

Carini, P. (2000a). A letter to parents and teachers on some ways of looking at and reflecting on children. *From another angle: Children's strengths and school standards. The Prospect Center's descriptive review of the child* (pp. 56–64). New York: Teachers College Press.

Carini, P. (2000b). Prospect's descriptive processes. In M. Himley & P. Carini (Eds.), *From another angle: Children's strengths and school standards. The Prospect Center's descriptive review of the child* (pp. 8–20). New York: Teachers College Press.

Carlo, M. S., August, D., McLaughlin, B., Snow, C. E., Dressler, C., & Lippman, D. N. (2004). Closing the gap: Addressing the vocabulary needs of English-language learners in bilingual and mainstream classrooms. *Reading Research Quarterly, 39*(2), 188–215.

Carrasquillo, A., & Rodríguez, V. (2002). *Language minority students in the mainstream classroom* (2nd ed.). Clevedon, UK: Multilingual Matters.

Caspe, M., López, M. E., & Wolos, C. (2007). *Family involvement makes a difference: Family involvement in elementary school children's education.* Cambridge, MA: Harvard Family Research Project. Retrieved February 19, from http://www.hfrp.org/publications-resources/browse-our-publications/family-involvement-in-elementary-school-children-s-education

Castañeda v. Pickard. (1981). 648 F.2d 989 (5th Cir., 1981).

Castro, A. (2005, April 19). Many students in Texas exempt from No Child law; Schools with small enrollments don't have to report the test results for ethnic groups. *Houston Chronicle,* p. B2.

Cazden, C. (1986). ESL teachers as advocates for children. In P. Rigg & D. S. Enright (Eds.), *Children and ESL: Integrating perspectives* (pp. 7–21). Washington, DC: TESOL.

Celic, C. (2009). *English language learners day by day K–6.* Portsmouth, NH: Heinemann.

Center for Applied Linguistics. (2009). *Foreign language teaching in U.S. Schools: Results of a national survey.* Washington, DC: Author.

Center on Educational Policy (CEP). (2005, July). *NCLB: Narrowing the curriculum?* (NCLB Policy Brief 3). Retrieved February 19, 2010, from http://www.cep-dc.org

Center for Equity and Excellence in Education Test Database (2005). Washington, DC: Clearinghouse in Assessment and Evaluation. Retrieved February 19, 2010, from www.ericae.net/eac/

Chamot, A. U., & O'Malley, J. M. (1994). *The CALLA handbook: Implementing the cognitive academic language learning approach.* Reading, MA: Addison-Wesley.

Chatterji, M. (2003). *Designing and using tools for educational assessment.* Allyn & Bacon.

Cheng, L., Watanabe, Y. and Curtis, A. (Eds.). 2004. *Washback in language testing: Research contexts and methods.* Mahwah, NJ: Lawrence Erlbaum.

Chrispeels, J., & Gonz, M. (2004). *Do educational programs increase parents' practices at home? Factors influencing Latino parent involvement.* Retrieved February 19, 2010, from http://www.hfrp.org/family-involvement/publications-resources/do-educational-programs-increase-parents-practices-at-home-factors-influencing-latino-parent-involvement#_ftnref1

Chrispeels, J. H., & Rivero, E. (2001). Engaging Latino families for student success: How parent education can reshape parents' sense of place in the education of their children. *Peabody Journal of Education, 76*(2), 119–169.

Civil Rights Act, Title VI, Section 601 (1964).

Clark, C., & Gorski, P. (2001). Multicultural education and the digital divide: Focus on race, language, socioeconomic class, sex, and disability. *Multicultural Perspectives, 3*(3), 39–44.

Clewell, B., & Campbell, P. (2004). *Highly effective USI schools: An outlier study.* Washington DC: The Urban Institute/Campbell-Kibler Associates.

Clewell, B. C., & Villegas, A. M. (2001). *Absence unexcused: Ending teacher shortages in high-need areas.* Washington, DC: The Urban Institute.

Cloud, N., Genesee, F., & Hamayan, E. (2000). *Dual language instruction: A handbook for enriched education.* Boston: Heinle and Heinle.

Cochran-Smith, M. (Ed.). (2004). *Walking the road: Race, diversity, and social justice in teacher education.* New York: Teachers College Press.

Collier, V. (1995) Acquiring a second language for schools. *Directions in Language and Education, 1*(4), 1–12 (National Clearinghouse for Bilingual Education).

Cook, V. (2002). Background to the L2 user. In V. J. Cook (Ed.), *Portraits of the L2 user* (pp. 1–28). Clevedon: Multilingual Matters.

Cook, V. (2008). *Second language learning and language teaching.* (4th ed.). London: Hodder.

Council of the Great City Schools. (2004, Fall). Title III of No Child Left Behind: A Status Report from the Great City Schools. Washington, DC. Retrieved February 19, 1010, from http://www.cgcs.org/pdfs/Title%20III%20Survey%20Report%202004—Final.pdf

Council of Europe. (2000). *Common European framework of reference for languages: Learning, teaching, assessment.* Language Policy Division, Strasbourg. Retrieved February 20, 2010, from http://www.coe.int/T/DG4/Linguistic/Source/Framework_EN.pdf

Crawford, J. (1993). *Hold your tongue: Bilingualism and the politics of English only.* Reading, MA: Addison Wesley.

Crawford, J. (1997). *Best evidence: Research foundations of the Bilingual Education Act.* Washington, DC: National Educational Clearinghouse for Bilingual Education.

Crawford, J. (2002). *The Bilingual Education Act 1968–2002: An obituary.* [Electronic version]. Retrieved February 20, 2010, from http://www.rethinkingschools.org/archive/16_04/Bil164.shtml

Crawford, J. (2003). *A few things Ron Unz would prefer you didn't know about English learners in California.* [Electronic version]. Retrieved from http://www.humnet.ucla.edu/humnet/linguistics/people/grads/macswan/castats.htm

Crawford, J. (2004). *Educating English learners: Language diversity in the classroom* (5th ed.). Los Angeles: Bilingual Educational Services.

Crawford, J. (2007). The decline of bilingual education in the USA: How to reverse a troubling trend? *International Multilingual Research Journal, 1*(1), 33–37.

Crawford, J., & Krashen. S. (2007). *English learners in American classrooms: 101 questions. 101 answers.* New York: Scholastic.

Creese, A., Baraç, T., Bhatt, A., Blackledge, A., Hamid, S., Wei, L., Lytra, V., Martin, P., Wu, C. J., & Yağcıoğlu-Ali, D. (2008). *Investigating multilingualism in complementary schools in four communities.* Final Report to ESRC RES-000-23-1180.

Creese, A., & Blackledge, A. (2010). Translanguaging in the bilingual classroom: A pedagogy for learning and teaching. *The Modern Language Journal, 94*(1), 103–115.

Cronbach, L. J. (1989). Construct validation after 30 years. In R. L. Linn (Ed.), *Intelligence: Measurement theory and public policy* (pp. 147–171). Urbana, IL: University of Illinois Press.

Cummins, J. (1979). Cognitive/academic language proficiency, linguistic interdependence, the optimum age question, and some other matters. *Working Papers on Bilingualism, 19,* 121–129.

Cummins, J. (1981). *Bilingualism and minority language children.* Toronto: Ontario Institute for Studies in Education.

Cummins, J. (1984). *Bilingualism and special education: Issues in assessment and pedagogy.* Clevedon, UK: Multilingual Matters.

Cummins, J. (2000). *Language, power, and pedagogy: Bilingual children caught in the cross-fire.* Clevedon, UK: Multilingual Matters.

Cummins, J. (2003). Biliteracy, empowerment, and transformative pedagogy. Retrieved February 20, 2010, from http://www.iteachilearn.com/cummins/biliteratempowerment.html

Cummins, J. (2006). Identity texts: The imaginative construction of self through multiliteracies pedagogy. In O. García, T. Skutnabb-Kangas, & M. Torres-Guzman (Eds.), *Imagining multilingual schools: Languages in education and glocalization* (pp. 51–68). Clevedon, UK: Multilingual Matters.

Cummins, J. (2007). Rethinking monolingual instructional strategies in multilingual classrooms. *The Canadian Journal of Applied Linguistics, 10*(2), 221–240.

Cummins, J. (2009). Foreword. In D. Fu (Ed.), *Writing between languages: How English language learners make the transition to fluency, grades 4–12* (pp. ix–xii). Portsmouth, NH: Heinemann.

Cummins, J., Bismilla, V., Chow, P., Giampapa, F., Cohen, S., Leoni, L., Sandhu, P., & Sastri, P. (2005). Affirming identity in multilingual classrooms. *Educational Leadership, 63*(1), 38–43.

Cummins, J., Brown, K., & Sayers, D. (2007). *Literacy, technology, and diversity: Teaching for success in changing times.* Boston: Allyn & Bacon.

Danoff, M. N. (1978). *Evaluation of the impact of ESEA Title VII Spanish/English bilingual education programs: Overview of study and findings.* Palo Alto. CA: American Institutes for Research.

Darling-Hammond, L. (1999). *Teacher quality and student achievement: A review of state policy evidence.* Seattle: Center for the Study of Teaching Policy, University of Washington.

De Cohen, C. C., Deterding, N., & Chu Clewell, B. (2005). *Who's left behind? Immigrant children in high and low LEP schools.* Washington, DC: Program for Evaluation and Equity Research. Urban Institute. Retrieved from http://www.urban.org/UploadedPDF/411231_whos_left_behind.pdf

DeGraff, M. (2005). Linguists' most dangerous myth: The fallacy of Creole exceptionlism. *Language in Society, 34*(4), 533–591.

DeGraff, M. (2009). Creole exceptionalism and the (mis)-education of the Creole speaker. In J. Kleifgen & G. C. Bond (Eds.), *The languages of Africa and the diaspora: Educating for language awareness* (pp. 124–144). Bristol, UK: Multilingual Matters.

Delgado-Gaitán, C. (1990). *Literacy for empowerment: The role of parents in children's education.* London: Falmer Press.

Delgado-Gaitan, C. (1992). School matters in the Mexican-American home: Socializing children to education. *American Educational Research Journal, 29*(3), 495–513.

Delgado-Gaitan, C. (2001). *The power of community: Mobilizing for family and schooling.* Blue Ridge Summit, PA: Rowman & Littlefield.

Delgado-Gaitan, C., & Trueba, H. (1991). *Crossing cultural borders: Education for immigrant families in America.* New York: Falmer Press.

Dewey, J. (1938). *Experience and education.* New York: Macmillan.

Dufour, R., & Kroll, J. F. (1995). Matching words to concepts in two languages: A test of the concept mediation model of bilingual representation. *Memory and Cognition, 23*(2), 166–180.

Dunn, L. (1987). *Bilingual Hispanic children on the U.S. mainland: A review of research on their cognitive, linguistic, and scholastic development.* Circle Pines, MN: American Guidance Service.

Durán, R. P. (1983). *Hispanics' education and background: Predictors of college achievement.* New York: College Entrance Examination Board.

Duverger, J. (2005). *L'enseignment en classe bilingue* [Teaching in a bilingual class]. Paris: Hachette.

Eccles, J. S., & Harold, R. D. (1993). Parent–school involvement during the early adolescent years. *Teachers College Record, 94*(3), 568–587.

Echevarria, J., Vogt, M. E., & Short, D. J. (2004). *Making content comprehensible for English learners: The SIOP model* (2nd ed.). Boston, MA: Allyn & Bacon.

Education Law Center. (2007). Starting at 3: Securing access to preschool education. Retrieved February 20, 2010, from http://www.startingat3.org/news/Sa3news_070323_ECE_HispanicsReport.htm

Eisner, E. (2001). What does it mean to say a school is doing well? *Phi Delta Kappan, (82)*5, 367–372.

Epstein, J. L. (1990). School and family connections: Theory, research, and implications for integrating sociologies of education and family. In D. G. Unger & M. B. Sussman (Eds.), *Families in community settings: Interdisciplinary perspectives* (pp. 99–126). New York: Haworth Press.

Esch, C. E., Chang-Ross, C. M., Guha, R., Humphrey, D. C., Shields, P. M., Tiffany-Morales, J. D., et al. (2005). *The status of the teaching profession 2005.* Santa Cruz, CA: The Center for the Future of Teaching and Learning.

Esch, C. E., & Shields, P. M. (2002). *Who is teaching California's children? Teaching and California's Future.* Santa Cruz, CA: Center for the Future of Teaching and Learning.

Estrin, E. T., & Nelson-Barber, S. (1995). Bringing Native American perspectives to mathematics and science teaching. *Theory into Practice, 34*(3), 174–185.

Fairclough, N. (Ed.). (1992). *Critical language awareness.* London: Longman.

Fairclough, N. (1999). Global capitalism and critical awareness of language. *Language Awareness, 8*(2), 71–83.

Ferguson, G. (2006). *Language planning and education.* Edinburgh: Edinburgh Press.

Figueroa, R., & Hernandez, S. (2000). *Testing Hispanic students in the United States: Technical and policy issues.* Washington, DC: President's Advisory Commission on Educational Excellence for Hispanic Americans.

Fishman, J. A. (1966). *Language loyalty in the United States: The maintenance and perpetuation of non-English mother tongues by American ethnic and religious groups.* The Hague: Mouton.

Fix, M., & Passel, J. (2003). *U.S. immigration: Trends and implications for schools.* Washington, DC: Immigration Studies Program, Urban Institute.

Fleischman, H. F., & Hopstock, P. J. (1993). *Descriptive study of services to limited English proficient students: Volume I. Summary of findings and conclusions. Report submitted to the U.S. Department of Education.* Arlington, VA: Development Associates.

Foucault, M. (1979). *Discipline and punish: The birth of the prison.* New York: Vintage Books.

Freeman, R. D. (1998). *Bilingual education and social change.* Clevedon, UK: Multilingual Matters.

Freeman,Y., & Freeman, D. (2008). *Academic language for English language learners and Struggling Readers*. New York, NY: Heinemann.

Freire, P. (1970). *Pedagogy of the oppressed*. New York: Herder and Herder.

Fry, R. (2003). *Hispanic youth dropping out of U.S. schools: Measuring the challenge*. Washington, DC: Pew Hispanic Center.

Fu, D. (2003). *An island of English: Teaching ESL in Chinatown*. Portsmouth, NH: Heinemann.

Fu, D. (2009). *Writing between languages: How English language learners make the transition to fluency, grades 4–12*. New York: Heinemann.

Gajo, L. (2007). Linguistic knowledge and subject knowledge: How does bilingualism contribute to subject development? *International Journal of Bilingual Education and Bilingualism, 10*(5), 563–581.

Gándara, P. (1999). *Review of research on the instruction of limited English proficient students: A report to the California legislature*. Santa Barbara: University of California at Santa Barbara, Linguistic Minority Research Institute.

Gándara, P., & Contreras, F. (2009). *The Latino education crisis: The consequences of failed social policies*. Cambridge, MA: Harvard University Press.

Gándara, P., Maxwell-Jolly, J., & Driscoll, A. (2005). *Listening to teachers of English language learners*. Santa Cruz, CA: Center for the Future of Teaching and Learning.

Gándara, P., O'Hara, S., & Gutiérrez, D. (2004). The changing shape of aspirations: Peer influence on achievement behavior. In G. Gibson, P. Gándara, & J. Koyama (Eds.), *School connections: U.S. Mexican youth, peers, and achievement* (pp. 39–62). New York: Teachers College Press.

Gándara, P., Rumberger, R., Maxwell-Jolly, J., & Callahan, R. (2003). English learners in California schools: Unequal resources, unequal outcomes. Education Policy Analysis Archives. Retrieved February 20, 2010, from http://epaa.asu.edu/epaa/v11n36/

GAO (United States Government Accountability Office). (1976, May 19). *Bilingual education: An unmet need. Report to the Congress by the Controller General of the United States*. Washington, DC: Author.

GAO (United States Government Accountability Office). (2006, December). *No Child Left Behind: Education's data improvement efforts could strengthen the basis for distributing Title III funds*. Washington, DC: Author

GAO (United States Government Accountability Office). (2009). *Teacher preparation*. Washington, DC: Author. GAO-09-573.

Garcia, E. (2005). *Teaching and learning in two languages: Bilingualism and schooling in the United States*. New York: Teachers College Press.

Garcia, E., & Gonzalez, D. (2006, July). *Pre-K and Latinos: The foundation for America's future*. Washington, DC: Pre-K Now Research Series.

Garcia, E., & Jensen, B. (2009). Early educational opportunities for children of Hispanic origins. *Social Policy Report, 23*(2), 1–19.

Garcia, G., & Pearson, P. (1994). Assessment and diversity. *Review of Research in Education, 20,* 337–391.

García, O. (1995). Spanish language loss as a determinant of income among Latinos in the United States: Implications for language policy in schools. In J. Tollefson (Ed.), *Power and inequality in language education* (pp. 142–160). Cambridge, UK: Cambridge University Press.

García, O. (1999). Educating Latino high school students with little formal schooling. In C. J. Faltis & P. Wolfe (Eds.), *So much to say: Adolescents, bilingualism, and ESL in the secondary school* (pp. 61–82). New York: Teachers College Press.

García, O. (2005). Positioning heritage languages in the United States. *Modern Language Journal, 89*(4), 601–605.

García, O. (2006a, Fall). Equity's elephant in the room. Multilingual children in the U.S. are being penalized by current education policies. *TC Today,* p. 40.

García, O. (2006b). Lost in transculturation: The case of bilingual education in New York City. In M. Putz, J. A. Fishman, & N. V. Aertselaer (Eds.), *Along the routes to power: Exploration of the empowerment through language* (pp. 157–178). Berlin: Mouton de Gruyter.

García, O. (2008). Multilingual language awareness and teacher education. In J. Cenoz & N. Hornberger (Eds.), *Encyclopedia of language and education* (2nd ed., Vol. 6, pp. 385–400). Berlin: Springer.

García, O. (2009a). *Bilingual education in the 21st century: A global perspective.* Malden, MA: Wiley/Blackwell.

García, O. (2009b). Emergent bilinguals and TESOL. What's in a name? *TESOL Quarterly, 43*(2), 322–326.

García, O., & Bartlett, L. (2007). A speech community model of bilingual education: Educating Latino newcomers in the U.S. *International Journal of Bilingual Education and Bilingualism, 10*, 1–25.

García, O., Bartlett, L., & Kleifgen, J. (2007). From biliteracy to pluriliteracies. In P. Auer & L. Wei (Eds.), *Multilingualism and multilingual communication: Handbook of applied linguistics* (Vol. 5, pp. 207–228). Berlin: Mouton de Gruyter.

García, O., Flores, N., & Chu, H. (in press). Extending bilingualism in U.S. secondary education: New variations. *International Multilingual Research Journal.*

García, O., Kleifgen, J., & Falchi. L. (2008). *Equity perspectives: From English language learners to emergent bilinguals.* Campaign for Educational Equity, Teachers College, Columbia University, New York.

García, O., & Traugh, C. (2002). Using descriptive inquiry to transform the education of linguistically diverse U.S. teachers and students. In L. Wei, J. Dewaele, & A. Housen (Eds.), *Opportunities and challenges of (societal) bilingualism* (pp. 311–328). Berlin: Walter de Gruyter.

García, O., Zakharia, Z., & Otcu, B. (Eds.) (in press). *Bilingual community education in the Multilingual Apple.*

Gay, G. (2002). Preparing for culturally responsive teaching. *Journal of Teacher Education, 53*(2), 106–116.

Genesee, F., Lindholm-Leary, K., Saunders, W. M., & Christian, D. (Eds.). (2006). *Educating English language learners.* New York: Cambridge University Press.

Genishi, C., & Borrego Brainard, M. (1995). In E. Garcia & B. McLaughlin (Eds.), *Meeting the challenge of linguistic and cultural diversity in early childhood education* (pp. 49–63). New York: Teachers College Press.

Ghaffar-Kucher, A. (2008). The (mis)education of Pakistani immigrant youth. Unpublished doctoral dissertation, Teachers College, Columbia University, New York.

Gibbons, P. (2002). *Scaffolding language, scaffolding learning: Teaching second languages in the mainstream classroom.* Portsmouth, NH: Heinemann.

Gibbons, P. (2009). *English learners, academic literacy, and thinking: Learning in the challenge zone.* Portsmouth, NH: Heinemann.

Gibson, M. A., Gándara, P., & Koyama, J. P. (2004). The role of peers in the schooling of U.S. Mexican youth. In M. A. Gibson, P. Gándara, & J. P. Koyama (Eds.), *School connections: U.S. Mexican youth, peers, and school achievement* (pp. 1–17). New York: Teachers College Press.

Giroux, H. (1988). *Teachers as intellectuals: Toward a critical pedagogy of learning.* Westport, CT: Bergin & Garvey.

Goh, D. S. (2004). *Assessment accommodations for diverse learners.* Boston: Pearson.

Gold, E., Simon, E., & Brown, C. (2002). *Strong neighborhoods, strong schools: The indicators project on education organizing.* Chicago: Cross City Campaign for Urban School Reform.

Goldenberg, C. (2008). Teaching English language learners. What the research does—and does not—say. *American Educator, 32*(2), 8–23, 42–44.

González, N. (2005) Beyond culture: The hybridity of funds of knowledge. In N. González, L. C. Moll, & C. Amati (Eds.), *Funds of knowledge: Theorizing practices in households, communities, and classrooms* (pp. 29–46). Mahwah, NJ: Lawrence Erlbaum.

González, N., Moll, L. C., & Amanti, C. (2005). *Funds of knowledge: Theorizing practices in households, communities, and classrooms.* Mahwah, NJ: Lawrence Erlbaum.

Gormley, Jr., W. (2008). The effects of Oklahoma's pre-K program on Hispanic children. *Social Science Quarterly, 89*(4), 916–936.

Gottlieb, J., Alter, M., Gottlieb, B. W., & Wishner, J. (1994). Special education in urban American: It's not justifiable for many. *The Journal of Special Education, 27*(4), 453–465.

Gottlieb, M. (2006). *Assessing English language learners: Bridges from language proficiency to academic achievement.* Thousand Oaks, CA: Corwin Press.

Grant, E. A., & Wong, S. D. (2003). Barriers to literacy for language-minority learners: An argument for change in the literacy education profession. *Journal of Adolescent & Adult Literacy, 46,* 386–394.

Graves, M. (2006). *The vocabulary book: Learning and instruction.* New York: Teachers College, Columbia University.

Greenberg, J. (1989, June). *Funds of knowledge: Historical constitution, social distribution, and transmission.* Paper presented at the annual meeting of the Society for Applied Anthropology, Santa Fe, NM.

Greenberg, J. (1990). Funds of knowledge: Historical constitution, social distribution, and transmission. In W. T. Pink, D. S. Ogle, & B. F. Jones. (Eds.), *Restructuring to promote learning in America's schools: Selected readings* (Vol. 2, pp. 317–326), Elmhurst, IL: North Central Regional Educational Laboratory.

Greene, J. (1997). A meta-analysis of the Rossell and Baker review of bilingual education research. *Bilingual Research Journal, 21,* 103–122.

Grosjean, F. (1985). The bilingual as a competent but specific speaker-hearer. *Journal of Multilingual and Multicultural Development, 6,* 467–477.

Grosjean, F. (1989). Neurolinguists, beware! The bilingual is not two monolinguals in one person. *Brain and Language, 36,* 3–15.

Gutiérrez, K. D., Asato, J., Pacheco, M., Moll, L. C., Olson, K., Horng, E., Ruiz, R., et al. (2002). "Sounding American": The consequences of new reforms on English language learners. *Reading Research Quarterly, 37*(3), 328–343.

Gutiérrez-Clellen, V., & Peña, E. (October 2001). Dynamic assessment of diverse children: A tutorial. *Language, Speech, and Hearing Services in Schools, 32,* 212–224.

Hakuta, K. (1986). *Cognitive development of bilingual children.* University of California at Los Angeles, Center for Language, Education, and Research.

Hakuta, K., Goto Butler, Y., & Witt, D. (2000). *How long does it take English learners to attain proficiency?* University of California, Linguistic Minority Research Institute.

Harklau, L. (1994). Tracking and linguistic minority students: Consequences of ability grouping for second language learners. *Linguistics and Education, 6*(3), 217–244.

Harmer, J. (1998). *How to teach English.* Essex, UK: Pearson.

Haskins, R., & Rouse, C. (2005). Closing achievement gaps. *The Future of Children, 15,* 1–7.

Heath, S. B. (1983). *Ways with words.* Cambridge, UK: Cambridge University Press.

Heller, M. (1999). *Linguistic minorities and modernity: A sociolinguistic ethnography.* London: Longman.

Heller, M., & Martin-Jones, M. (Eds.). (2001). *Voices of authority: Education and linguistic differences.* Westport, CT: Ablex.

Hélot, C. (2006). Bridging the gap between prestigious bilingualism and the bilingualism of minorities. Towards an integrated perspective of multilingualism in the French education context. In M. O'Laoire. (Ed.), *Multilingualism in educational settings* (pp. 49–72). Baltmannsweiller, Germany: Schneider Verlag Hohengehren.

Hélot, C., & Young, A. (2006). Imagining multilingual education in France: A language and cultural awareness project at primary school. In O. García, T. Skutnabb-Kangas, & M. E. Torres-Guzmán (Eds.), *Imagining multilingual schools: Languages in education and glocalization* (pp. 69–90). Clevedon, UK: Multilingual Matters.

Henderson, A., & Berla, N. (1994). *A new generation of evidence: The family is critical to student achievement.* Washington, DC: National Committee for Citizens in Education.

Henderson, A. T. (Ed.). (1987). *The evidence continues to grow: Parent involvement improves student achievement.* Columbia, MD: National Committee for Citizens in Education.

Henderson, A. T., & Mapp, K. L. (2002). *A new wave of evidence: The impact of school, family, and community connections on student achievement.* Austin, TX: Southwest Educational Development Laboratory.

Herdina, P., & Jessner, U. (2002). *A dynamic model of multilingualism: Changing the psycholinguistic perspective.* Clevedon, UK: Multilingual Matters.

Hidalgo, N. M., Siu, S. F., & Epstein, J. L. (2004). Research on families, schools, and communities: A multicultural perspective. In J. Banks & C. Banks (Eds.), *Handbook of research on multicultural education* (2nd ed., pp. 631–655). San Francisco: Jossey-Bass.

Hobson v. Hansen. (1967). 269 F. Supp. 401, 490; DDC 1967.

Honig, B. (1996). *Teaching our children to read: The role of skills in a comprehensive reading program.* Thousand Oaks, CA: Corwin Press.

Hoover-Dempsey, K. V., & Sandler, H. M. (1997). Why do parents become involved in their children's education? *Review of Education Research, 67,* 3–42.

Hopstock, P. J., & Stephenson, T. G. (2003a). *Descriptive study of services to LEP students and LEP students with disabilities. Special Topic Report #2: Analysis of Office of Civil Rights Data related to LEP students.* OELA, U.S. Department of Education. Retrieved February 20, 2010, from http:/www.neela.gwu.edu/red/bibliography/BE021197/

Hopstock, P. J., & Stephenson, T. G. (2003b). *Descriptive study of services to LEP students and LEP students with disabilities. Special Topic Report #1: Native languages of LEP students.* OELA, U.S. Department of Education. Retrieved February 20, 2010, from http://www.ncela.gwu.edu/files/rcd/BE021196/BE021196DSSST1_NativeLangsofLE.pdf

Hornberger, N. (Ed.). (2003). *Continua of biliteracy: An ecological framework for educational policy, research, and practices in multilingual settings.* Clevedon, UK: Multilingual Matters.

Hornberger, N. (2005). Opening and filling up implementational and ideological spaces in heritage language education. *Modern Language Journal, 89*(4), 605–609.

Hornberger, N. (2006). Nichols to NCLB: Local and global perspectives on U.S. language education policy. In O. García, T. Skutnabb-Kangas, & M. Torres-Guzmán. (Eds.), *Imagining multilingual schools: Languages in education and glocalization* (pp. 223–237). Clevedon, UK: Multilingual Matters.

Hornberger, N., & Skilton-Sylvester, P. (2003). Revisiting the Continua of biliteracy: International and critical perspectives. In N. Hornberger (Ed.), *Continua of biliteracy: An ecological framework for educational policy, research, and practices in multilingual settings* (pp. 35–70). Clevedon, UK: Multilingual Matters.

Houser, J. (1995). *Assessing students with disabilities and limited English proficiency.* Working Paper Series. Working Paper 95-13. Washington, DC: National Center for Education Statistics.

Jacobson, R., & Faltis, C. (1990). *Language distribution issues in bilingual schooling.* Clevedon, UK: Multilingual Matters.

Jensen, L. (2001). The demographic diversity of immigrants and their children. In R. Rumbaut & A. Portes (Eds.), *Ethnicities: Children of immigrants in America* (pp. 21–56). New York: Russell Sage Foundation.

Jessner, U. (2006). *Linguistic awareness in multilinguals: English as a third language.* Edinburgh: Edinburgh University Press.

Jewitt, C., & Kress, G. (2003). *Multimodal literacy.* New York: Peter Lang.

Jeynes, W. H. (2004/2005). Parental involvement and secondary school student educational outcomes: A meta-analysis. *The Evaluation Exchange, 10*(4), 6.

Jeynes, W. H. (2005b). Effects of parent involvement and family structure on the academic achievement of adolescents. *Marriage and Family Review, 37*(3), 99–116.

Johnson, L. R. (2009). Challenging "best practices" in family literacy and parent education programs: The development and enactment of mothering knowledge among Puerto Rican and Latina mothers in Chicago. *Anthropology and Education Quarterly, 40*(3), 257–276.

Johnston, P. (1997). *Knowing literacy: Constructive literacy assessment.* York, ME: Stenhouse.

Jordan, C., Orozco, E., & Averett, A. (2001). *Emerging issues in school, family, and community connections.* Austin, TX: Southwest Educational Development Laboratory.

Kagan, S. (1986). Cooperative learning and sociocultural factors in schooling. In California State Department of Education (Ed.), *Beyond language: Social and cultural factors in schooling language minority students* (pp. 231–298). Evaluation, Dissemination and Assessment Center, California State University at Los Angeles, Los Angeles.

Kagan, S., & McGroarty, M. (1993). Principles of cooperative learning for language and content gains. In D. D. Holt (Ed.), *Cooperative learning: A response to linguistic and cultural diversity* (pp. 47–66). McHenry, Illinois, and Washington, DC: Delta Systems and Center for Applied Linguistics.

Kaplan, R., and Baldauf, R. (1997). *Language planning: From practice to theory.* Clevedon, UK: Multilingual Matters.

Karoly, L., & Bigelow, J. (2005). *The economics of investing in universal preschool education in California.* Santa Monica, CA: RAND Labor and Population Program.

Katz, A., Low, P., Stack, J., & Tsang, T. (2004). *A study of content area assessment for English language learners.* Prepared for the Office of English Language Acquisition and Academic Achievement for Limited English Proficient Students, U.S. Department of Education. San Francisco, CA: ARC Associates.

Kecskes, I., & Martínez Cuenca, I. (2005). Lexical choice as a reflection of conceptual fluency. *International Journal of Bilingualism, 9*(1), 49–69.

Kenner, C. (2004). Living in simultaneous worlds: Differences and integration in bilingual script learning. *International Journal of Bilingual Education and Bilingualism, 7*, 43–61.

Kenner, C., Mahera, R., Gregory, E., & Al-Azami, S. (2007). How research can link policy and practice: Bilingualism as a learning resource for second and third generation children. *NALDIC Quarterly, 5*(1), 10–13.

Kindler, A. (2002). *Survey of the states' limited English proficient students and available educational programs and services: 2000–2001 summary report.* Report prepared for the U.S. Department of Education, Office of English Language Acquisition, Language Enhancement and Academic Achievement for Limited English proficient Students (OELA). Washington, DC: National Clearinghouse for English Language Acquisition and Language Instruction Educational Programs. Retrieved February 20, 2010, from http://www.ncela.gwu.edu/files/rcd/BE021853/Survey_of_the_States.pdf

Kleifgen, J. (1991). Kreyòl ekri, Kreyòl li: Haitian children and computers. *Educational Horizons, 59*(3), 152–158.

Kleifgen, J. (2009). Discourses of linguistic exceptionalism and linguistic diversity in education. In J. Kleifgen & G. C. Bond. (Eds.), *The languages of Africa and the diaspora: Educating for language awareness* (pp. 1–21). Bristol, UK: Multilingual Matters.

Kleifgen, J. (in press). *Communicative practices at work: Multimodality and learning in a high-tech firm.* Bristol, UK: Multilingual Matters.

Kleifgen, J., & Kinzer, C. (2009). Alternative spaces for education with and through technology. In H. Varenne & E. Gordon (Eds.), *Theoretical perspectives on comprehensive education: The way forward* (pp. 139–186). Lewiston, NY: Mellen Press.

Klein, E., & Martohardjono, G. (2009). *Students with interrupted formal education in New York City.* New York: Report to the New York City Department of Education.

Koelsch, N. (n.d.) Improving literacy outcomes for English language learners in high school: Considerations for states and districts in developing a coherent policy framework. National High School Center. Retrieved from http://www.betterhighschools.org/docs/NHSC_AdolescentS_110806.pdf

Koenig, J. A. (Ed.). (2002). *Reporting test results for students with disabilities and English-language learners.* Washington, DC: National Academy Press.

Kossan, P. (2004, April 4). Arizona easing fed's rules for school standards. *Arizona Republic*, p. B1.

Kramsch, C. (1997). The privilege of the nonnative speaker. *Publications of the Modern Language Association of America, 112*(3), 359–369.

Krashen, S., Rolstad, K., & Mc Swan, J. (2007, October). Review of "Research summary and bibliography for structured English immersion programs" of the Arizona English language learners Task Force. Institute for Language and Education Policy, Tacoma Park, MD.

Kreider, H., Caspe, M., Kennedy, S., & Weiss, H. (2007). *Family involvement makes a difference: Family involvement in middle and high school students' education.* Cambridge, MA: Harvard Family Research Project. Retrieved February 20, 2010, at http://www.hfrp.org/ publications-resources/browse-our-publications/family-involvement-in-middle-and-high-school-students-education

Kress, G. (2003). *Literacy in the new media age.* New York: Routledge.

Lachat, M. (1999). *What policymakers and school administrators need to know about assessment reform for English language learners.* Providence, RI: Brown University, Northeast and Islands Regional Education Laboratory.

Ladson-Billings, G. (1994). *The dreamkeepers: Successful teachers of African-American children.* San Francisco: Jossey-Bass.

Ladson-Billings, G. (1995). Toward a theory of culturally relevant pedagogy. *American Educational Research Journal, 32*(3), 465–491.

Lambert, W. E. (1974). Culture and language as factors in learning and education. In F. E. Aboud & R. D. Meade (Eds.), *Cultural factors in learning and education* (pp. 91–122). Bellingham: Western Washington State College.

Lambert, W. E. (1984). An overview of issues in immersion education. In California State Department of Education (Ed.), *Studies on immersion education: A collection for United States educators* (pp. 8–30). Sacramento: California State Department of Education.

Lanauze, M., & Snow, C. (1989). The relation between first- and second-language writing skills: Evidence from Puerto Rican elementary school children in bilingual programs. *Linguistics and Education 1*(4), 323–329.

Language Instruction for Limited English Proficient and Immigrant Students. (2001). Public Law 107-110. Title III of No Child Left Behind (NCLB), Section 3001.

Lapkin, S., & Swain, M. (1996). Vocabulary teaching in a grade 8 French immersion classroom: A descriptive case study. *The Canadian Modern Language Review, 53*(1), 242–256.

Larsen-Freeman, D., & Cameron, L. (2008). *Complex systems and applied linguistics.* Oxford: Oxford University Press.

Lau Remedies. (1975). *Task-force findings specifying remedies available for eliminating past educational practices ruled unlawful under* Lau v. Nichols. Washington, DC: Office of Civil Rights. Retrieved February 20, 2010, from http://www.stanford.edu/~kenro/LAU/LauRemedies.htm

Lau v. Nichols. (1974). 414 U.S. 563.

Lave, J., & Wenger, E. (1991). *Situated learning: Legitimate peripheral participation.* Cambridge, UK: Cambridge University Press.

Lee, J. S., & Oxelson, E. (2006). "It's not my job": K–12 teacher attitudes toward students' heritage language maintenance. *Bilingual Research Journal, 30*(2), 453–477.

Legislative Analyst Office (LAO) (2006). *Update 2002–2004: The progress of English language learners*. Retrieved February 20, 2010, from http://www.lao.ca.gov/2006/eng_lrnr_updt/eng_lrnr_updt_012606.htm

Lewis, W. G. (2008). Current challenges in bilingual education in Wales. *AILA Review, 21,* 69–86.

Li Wei. 2009. Polite Chinese children revisited: Creativity and use of code-switching in the Chinese complementary school classroom. *International Journal of Bilingual Education and Bilingualism, 12*(2), 193–211.

Liff, S., Steward, F., & Watts, P. (2002). New public places for Internet access: Networks for practice-based learning and social inclusion. In S. Woolgar (Ed.), *Virtual society? Technology, cyberbole, reality* (pp. 78–98). Oxford: Oxford University Press.

Lindholm-Leary, K. J. (2001). *Dual language education*. Clevedon, UK: Multilingual Matters.

Linquanti, R. (2001). *The redesignation dilemma: Challenges and choices in fostering meaningful accountability for English learners*. University of California, Linguistic Minority Research Institute.

Linton, A. (2003). *Is Spanish here to stay? Contexts for bilingualism among U.S.-born Hispanics*. Center for Comparative Immigration Studies Summer Institute, University of California, San Diego.

Lippi-Green, R. (1997). *English with an accent: Language, ideology, and discrimination in the United States*. New York: Routledge.

Littlewood, W. T. (1981). *Communicative language teaching*. Cambridge, UK: Cambridge University Press.

López, G. L. (2001). The value of hard work: Lessons on parent involvement from an (im)migrant household. *Harvard Educational Review, 71*(3), 416–437.

López, M. L., Barrueco, S., & Miles, J. (2006). *Latino infants and their families: A national perspective of protective and risk developmental factors*. Report submitted to National Task Force on Early Childhood Education for Hispanics (Arizona State University) and the Foundation for Child Development (New York, NY).

Lucas, T., & Katz, A. (1994). Reframing the debate: The roles of native languages in English-only programs for language minority students. *TESOL Quarterly, 28,* 537–562.

Lucas, T., & Grinberg, J. (2008). Responding to the linguistic reality of mainstream classroom: Preparing all teachers to teach English language learners. In M. Cochran-Smith, S. Feiman-Nemser, & J. McIntyre (Eds.), *Handbook of research in teacher education: Enduring issues in changing contexts* (3rd ed., pp. 606–636). Mahwah, NJ: Lawrence Erlbaum.

Macias, R. F. (1994). Inheriting sins while seeking absolution: Language diversity and national statistical data sets. In D. Spener (Ed.), *Adult biliteracy in the United States* (pp. 15–45). Washington, DC, and McHenry, IL: Center for Applied Linguistics and Delta Systems.

Makoni, S., & Pennycook, A. (2007). *Disinventing and reconstituting languages*. Clevedon, UK: Multilingual Matters.

Manyak, P. (2001). Participation, hybridity, and carnival: A situated analysis of a dynamic literacy practice in a primary–grade English immersion class. *Journal of Literacy Research, 33*(3), 423–465.

Manyak, P. (2002). Welcome to salon 110: The consequences of hybrid literacy practices in a primary-grade English classroom. *Bilingual Research Journal, 26*(2), 421-442.

Manyak, P. (2004). "What did she say?" Translation in a primary-grade English immersion class. *Multicultural Perspectives, 6*(1), 12–18.

Martin-Jones, M., & Saxena, M. (1996). Turn-taking, power asymmetries, and the positioning of bilingual participants in classroom discourse. *Linguistics and Education, 8*(1), 105–123.

Martiniello, M. (2008). Language and the performance of English language learners in math word problems. *Harvard Educational Review, 98*(2), 333–368.

Massachusetts Question 2 (2002). G.L. C. 71A.

Maxwell-Jolly, J., Gándara, P., & Mendez Benavidez, L. (2006). *Promoting academic literacy among secondary English language learners: A synthesis of research and practice*. University of California, Davis, Linguistic Minority Research Institute, Education Policy Center.

Medina, J. (2009, October 14). No gains by NY students in U.S. math. *New York Times*. Retrieved from: http://www.nytimes.com

Mediratta, K., Fruchter, N., & Lewis, A. (2002). *Organizing for school reform: How communities are finding their voice and reclaiming their public schools*. New York: New York University Institute for Education and Social Policy. Retrieved February 20, 2010 at http://steinhardt.nyu.edu/iesp.olde/publications/pubs/cip/org_schl_reform.pdf

Mehan, H., Datnow, A., Bratton, E., Tellez, C., Friedlander, D., & Ngo, T. (1992). *Untracking and college enrollment* (Cooperative Agreement No. R117G10022). San Diego, CA: University of California, San Diego, National Center for Research on Cultural Diversity and Second Language Learning.

Menken, K. (2008). *English language learners left behind: Standardized testing as language policy*. Clevedon, UK: Multilingual Matters.

Menken, K., & García, O. (Eds.). (2010). *Negotiating language policies in schools. Educators as policymakers*. New York: Routledge.

Menken, K., & Kleyn, T. (2009). The difficult road for long-term English learners. *Educational Leadership*, 66(7). Retrieved February 20, 2010 from http://www.ascd.org/publications/educational_leadership/apr09/vol66/num07/The_Difficult_Road_for_Long-Term_English_Learners.aspx

Menken, K., & Kleyn, T. (in press). The long-term impact of subtractive schooling in the educational experiences of secondary English language learners. *International Journal of Bilingual Education and Bilingualism*.

Mercado, C. (2005a). Reflections on the study of households in New York City and Long Island: A different route, a common destination. In N. González, L. C. Moll, & C. Amanti (Eds.), *Funds of knowledge: Theorizing practices in households, communities, and classrooms* (pp. 233–255). Mahwah, NJ: Lawrence Erlbaum.

Mercado, C. (2005b). Seeing what's there: Language and literacy funds of knowledge in New York Puerto Rican homes. In A. C. Zentella (Ed.), *Building on strength: Language and literacy in Latino families and communities* (pp. 134–147). New York: Teachers College Press.

Mercer, J. R. (1989). Alternative paradigms for assessment in a pluralistic society. In J. A. Banks & C. M. Banks (Eds.), *Multicultural education* (pp. 289–303). Boston: Allyn & Bacon.

Messick, S. (1989). Validity. In R. L. Linn (Ed.), *Educational measurement* (3rd ed., pp. 13–103). New York: Macmillan.

Minicucci, C., & Olsen, L. (1992, Spring). Programs for secondary limited English proficient students: A California study (Occasional Papers in Bilingual Education, No. 5). Washington, DC: National Clearinghouse for Bilingual Education.

Moll, L., Amanti, C., Neff, D., & Gonzalez, N. (1992). Funds of knowledge for teaching: Using a qualitative approach to connect homes and classrooms. *Theory into Practice*, *31*, 132–141.

Moll, L. C., & Greenberg, J. B. (1990). Creating zones of possibilities: Combining social contexts for instruction. In L. C. Moll (Ed.), *Vygotsky and education: Instructional implications and applications of sociohistorical psychology* (pp. 319–348). New York: Cambridge University Press.

Moss, M., & Puma, M. (1995). *Prospects: The congressionally mandated study of educational growth and opportunity*. Cambridge, MA: Abt Associates.

Muñoz-Sandoval, A. F., Cummins, J., Alvarado, C. G., & Ruef, M. L. (1998). *Bilingual verbal abilities test: Comprehensive manual*. Itasca, IL: Riverside.

Murname, R. J., & Phillips, R. R. (1981). Learning by doing, vintage, and selection: Three pieces of the puzzle relating teaching experience and teaching performance. *Economics of Education Review, 1*(4), 453–465.

Nagy, W., & Anderson, R. (1984). How many words are there in printed school English? *Reading Research Quarterly, 19*, 304–330.

National Center for Education Statistics (NCES). (2003). *The condition of education 2003.* NCES 2003–067. Washington, DC: U.S. Department of Education.

National Center for Education Statistics. (2006). U.S. Department of Education, Institute of Education Science. Retrieved February 16, 2010, from http://nces.ed.gov

National Clearinghouse for English Language Acquisition and Language Instruction Educational Programs (NCELA). (2006). Frequently asked questions. Retrieved February 20, 2010, from http://www.ncela.gwu.edu/faqs/

National Task Force on Early Childhood Education for Hispanics. (2007). *Para nuestros niños: Expanding and improving early education for Hispanics.* Washington, DC: Author. Retrieved February 20, 2010 from http://www.ecehispanic.org/work/expand_MainReport.pdf

Navarrete, C., & Gustke, C. (1996). *A guide to performance assessment for linguistically diverse students.* Albuquerque, NM: Evaluation Assistance Center—Western Region, New Mexico Highlands University.

New London Group. (2000). A pedagogy of multiliteracies. Designing social futures. In B. Cope & M. Kalantzis. (Eds.), *Multiliteracies: Literacy learning and the design of social futures* (pp. 9–37). London: Routledge.

Newman, P., & Associates. (1996). *Authentic achievement: Restructuring schools for intellectual quality.* San Francisco: Jossey-Bass.

Nichols, S. L., & Berliner, D. C. (2007). *Collateral damage: How high stakes testing corrupts America's schools.* Cambridge, MA: Harvard University Press.

No Child Left Behind Act. (2001). 20 U.S.C. 6301 et seq. (2002).

Nores, M., Belfield, C., Barnett, W., & Schweinhart, L. (2005). Updating the economic impacts of the High/Scope Perry Preschool Program. *Educational Evaluation and Policy Analysis, 27*(3), 245–261.

Norton, B. (2000). *Identity and language learning: Gender, ethnicity, and educational change.* Harlow, UK: Longman/Pearson Education.

NYCDOE, Office of English Language Learners. (2008, Summer). *New York City English language learners: Demographics.* New York: New York City Department of Education.

Oakes, J. (1985). *Keeping track: How schools structure inequality.* New Haven, CT: Yale University Press.

Oakes, J. (1990). *Multiplying inequalities: The effects of race, social class, and tracking on opportunities to learn mathematics and science.* Santa Monica, CA: Rand.

Oakes, J., & Saunders, M. (2002). *Access to textbooks, instructional materials, equipment, and technology: Inadequacy and inequality in California's public schools, found in the Williams Watch Series (wws-rr001-1002).* Los Angeles, CA: UCLA/IDEA.

Office of English Language Acquisition (OELA). (2006). Biennial Evaluation Report to Congress on the Implementation of Title III, Part A of the ESEA.

Office of English Language Acquisition, Language Enhancement, and Academic Achievement for Limited English Proficient Students (OELA). (2008). *Biennial report to Congress on the implementation of the Title III State Formula Grant Program, school years 2004–06.* Washington, DC. Retrieved February 20, 2010 from http://www2.ed.gov/about/offices/list/oela/title3biennial0406.pdf

Oller, D. K., & Eillers, R. E. (Eds.). (2002). *Language and literacy in bilingual children.* Clevedon, UK: Multilingual Matters.

Olsen, L. (1997). *Made in America.* New York: The Free Press.

Orfield, G. (2001). *Schools more separate: Consequences of a decade of resegregation.* Cambridge, MA: The Civil Rights Project, Harvard University.

Ortiz, A. (2001). *English language learners with special needs: Effective instructional strategies*. Arlington, VA: Center for Applied Linguistics. Retrieved February 20, 2010 from http://www.cal.org/resources/digest/0108ortiz.html

Otheguy, R. (2009, November). *Linguistic considerations for bilingual pedagogies*. Lecture presented at the NALDIC Conference, University of Reading, UK.

Ovando, C., & Collier, V. (1998). *Bilingual and ESL classrooms: Teaching in multicultural contexts* (2nd ed.). Boston: McGraw-Hill.

Padrón, Y. N., & Waxman, H. C. (1999). Classroom observations of the Five Standards for Effective Teaching in urban classrooms with ELLs. *Teaching and Change, 7*, 79–100.

Parrish, T. (1994). A cost analysis of alternative instructional models for limited English proficient students in California, *Journal of Education Finance, 19*, 256–278.

Parrish, T. B., Linquanti, R., Merickel, A., Quick, H. E., Laird, J., & Esra, P. (2002). *Effects of the implementation of Proposition 227 on the education of English learners, K–12: Year Two Report*. Palo Alto. CA: American Institutes for Research. Retrieved February 20, 2010 from http://www.air.org/news/documents/227Report.pdf

Passel, J., Capps, R., & Fix, M. (2004). *Undocumented immigrants: Facts and figures*. Washington, DC: Urban Institute.

Peal, E., & Lambert, W. (1962). The relation of bilingualism to intelligence. *Psychological Monographs, 76*(546), 1–23.

Pennock-Roman, M. (1994). *Background characteristics and future plans of high-scoring GRE general test examinees*. Research report ETS-RR9412 submitted to EXXON Education Foundation, Princeton, NJ: Educational Testing Service.

Pérez Carreón, G., Drake, C., & Calabrese Barton, A. (2005). The importance of presence: Immigrant parents' school engagement experiences. *American Educational Research Journal, 42*(3), 465–498.

Peyton, J. K., Ranard, D. A., & McGinnis, S. (Eds.). (2001). *Heritage languages in America: Preserving a national resource*. Washington, DC: CAL/ERIC/Delta Systems.

Philips, S. (1983). *The invisible culture*. Prospect Heights, IL: Waveland.

Phillipson, R. (1992). *Linguistic imperialism*. Oxford: Oxford University Press.

Poehner, M. E. (2007). Beyond the test: L2 dynamic assessment and the transcendence of mediated learning. *The Modern Language Journal, 91*(iii), 323–340.

Portes, A. (1998). Social capital: Its origins and applications in modern sociology. *Annual Review of Sociology, 24*, 1–24.

Portes, A., & Rumbaut, R. (1996). *Immigrant America: A portrait* (2nd ed.). Berkeley: University of California Press.

Pratt, M. L. (1991). Arts of the contact zone. *Professional Association of Departments of English Bulletin, 91*, 33–40.

Ramirez, A. Y. F. (2003). Dismay and disappointment: Parental involvement of Latino immigrant parents. *The Urban Review, 35*(2): 93–110.

Ramírez, J. D. (1992). Executive summary, final report: Longitudinal study of structured English immersion strategy, early-exit and late-exit transitional bilingual education programs for language-minority children. *Bilingual Research Journal, 16*(1–2), 1–62.

Rawls, J. (1971). *A theory of justice*. Cambridge, MA: Harvard University Press.

Rebell, M. (2007). Professional rigor, public engagement, and judicial review: A proposal for enhancing the validity of education adequacy studies. *Teachers College Record, 109*(4). Retrieved February 20, 2010, from http://www.tcrecord.org/content.asp?contentid=12743

Rebell, M. (2009). *Courts and kids: Pursuing educational equity through the state courts*. Chicago: Chicago University Press.

Reyes, A. (2006). Reculturing principals as leaders for cultural and linguistic diversity. In K. Téllez & H. C. Waxman (Eds.), *Preparing quality educators for English language learners* (pp. 145–56). Mahwah, NJ: Lawrence Erlbaum.

Rice, J. K. (2003). *Teacher quality: Understanding the effectiveness of teacher attitudes.* Washington, DC: Economic Policy Institute.

Riches, C., & Genesee, F. (2006). Cross-linguistic and cross-modal aspects of literacy development. In F. Genesee, K. Lindholm-Leary, W. Saunders & D. Christian, (Eds.), *Educating English language learners: A synthesis of research evidence* (pp. 64–108). New York: Cambridge University Press.

Rivera, C., & Collum, E. (Eds.). (2006). *A national review of state assessment policy and practice for English language learners.* Mahwah, NJ: Lawrence Erlbaum.

Rivera, C., & Stansfield, C. W. (1998). Leveling the playing field for English language learners: Increasing participation in state and local assessments through accommodations. In R. Brandt (Ed.), *Assessing student learning: New rules, new realities* (pp. 65–92). Arlington, VA: Educational Research Service.

Robertson, L. H. (2006). Learning to read properly by moving between parallel literacy classes. *Language and Education, 20,* 44–61.

Rolstad, K., Mahoney, K., & Glass, G. (2005). The big picture: A meta-analysis of program effectiveness research on English language learners. *Educational Policy Review, 19*(4), 572–594.

Rosebery, A., Warren, B., & Conant, F. (1992). Appropriating scientific discourse: Findings from language minority classrooms. *Journal of the Learning Sciences, 2*(1), 61–94.

Rosenberg, H., López, M. E., & Westmoreland, H. (2009). *Family engagement: A shared responsibility.* Cambridge, MA: Harvard Family Research Project. Retrieved February 20, 2010, from http://www.hfrp.org/family-involvement/publications-resources/family-engagement-a-shared-responsibility

Ross, D. S., & Newport, E. L. (1996). The development of language from non-native linguistic input. In A. Stringfellow, D. Cahana-Amitay, E. Hughs, & A. Zukowski (Eds.), *Proceedings of the 20th Annual Boston University Conference on Language Development* (Vol. 2, pp. 634–645). Somerville, MA: Cascadilla Press.

Rumberger, R., & Gándara, P. (2000). The schooling of English learners. In E. Burr, G. Hayward, & M. Kirst (Eds.), *Crucial issues in California education.* Berkeley, CA: Policy Analysis for California Education.

Rumberger, R. W. (2002). Language minority students account for most of California's enrollment growth in past decade. *UC LMRI Newsletter, 12*(1), 1–2.

Sanders, W. L., & Rivers, J. C. (1996). *Cumulative and residual effects of teachers on future student academic achievement.* Knoxville: University of Tennessee Value-Added Research and Assessment Center.

Seeley, D. S. (1993). Why home-school partnership is difficult in bureaucratic schools. In F. Smit, W. van Esch, & H. J. Walberg (Eds.), *Parental involvement in education* (pp. 49–58). Nijmegen: Institute for Applied Social Sciences.

Selinker, L. (1972). Interlanguage. *International Review of Applied Linguistics, 10,* 209–231

Selinker, L., & Han, Z. H. (2001). Fossilization: Moving the concept into empirical longitudinal study. In E. Elder, A. Brown, E. Grove, K. Hill, N. Iwashita, T. Lumpley, T. McNamara & K. O'Loughlin (Eds.), *Studies in language testing: Experimenting with uncertainty* (pp. 276–291). Cambridge, UK: Cambridge University Press.

Serra, C. (2007). Assessing CLIL at primary school: A longitudinal study. *International Journal of Bilingual Education and Bilingualism, 10*(5), 582–602.

Shepard, L. A. (1996). Research framework for investigating accommodations for language minority students. Presentation made at CRESST Assessment Conference, UCLA, 1996.

Shohamy, E. (2001). *The power of tests: A critical perspective on the uses of language tests.* Harlow, UK: Longman.

Shohamy, E. (2006). *Language policy: Hidden agendas and new approaches.* London: Routledge.

Shohamy, E., Donitsa-Schmidt, S., & Ferman, I. (1996). Test impact revisited: Washback effect over time. *Language Testing, 13*(3), 298–317.

Short, D., & Fitzsimmons, S. (2007). *Double the work: Challenges and solutions to acquiring language and academic literacy for adolescent English language learners—a report to Carnegie Corporation of New York.* Washington, DC: Alliance for Excellent Education.

Skutnabb-Kangas, T. (1981). *Bilingualism or not: The education of minorities.* Clevedon, UK: Multilingual Matters.

Skutnabb-Kangas, T. (2000). *Linguistic genocide in education—or worldwide diversity and human rights?* Mahwah, NJ: Erlbaum.

Skutnabb-Kangas, T. (2006). Language policy and linguistic human rights. In T. Ricento (Ed.), *An introduction to language policy: Theory and method* (pp. 273–291). Malden, MA: Blackwell.

Skutnabb-Kangas, T., & Phillipson, R. (1994). *Linguistic human rights: Overcoming linguistic discrimination.* Berlin: Mouton.

Skutnabb-Kangas, T., & Toukomaa, P. (1976). Semilingualism and middle-class bias: A reply to Cora Brent-Palmer. *Working Papers on Bilingualism, 19.* Toronto: Ontario Institute for Studies in Education, Bilingual Education Project.

Slavin, R., & Cheung, A. (2005). A synthesis of research on reading instruction for English language learners. *Review of Educational Research, 75*(7), 247–284.

Solano-Flores, G. (2008). Who is given tests in what language by whom, when, and where? The need for probabilistic views of language in the testing of English language learners. *Educational Researcher, 37*(4), 189–199.

Solórzano, R. W. (2008). High stakes testing: Issues, implications, and remedies for English language learners. *Review of Educational Research, 78*(2), 260–329.

Steinberg, L. (1996). *Beyond the classroom: Why school reform has failed and what parents need to do.* New York: Simon & Schuster.

Street, B. V. (1985). *Literacy in theory and practice.* Cambridge, UK: Cambridge University Press.

Street, B. V. (1996). Academic literacies. In D. Baker, J. Clay, & C. Fox (Eds.), *Alternative ways of knowing: Literacies, numeracies, sciences* (pp. 101–134). London: Falmer Press.

Street, B. V. (Ed.). (2005). *Literacies across educational contexts: Mediating, learning, and teaching.* Philadelphia: Caslon Press.

Suárez-Orozco, C., & Suárez-Orozco, M. (2001). *Children of immigration.* Cambridge, MA: Harvard University Press.

Suárez-Orozco, C., Suárez-Orozco, M., & Todorova, I. (2008). *Learning a new land: Immigrant students in American society.* Cambridge MA: The Belknap Press of Harvard University Press.

Sylvan, C., & Romero, M. (2002). Reversing language loss in a multilingual setting: A native language enhancement program and its impact. In T. Osborn (Ed.), *The future of foreign language education in the United States* (pp. 139–166). New York: Greenwood.

Takanishi, R. (2004). Leveling the playing field: Supporting immigrant children from birth to eight. *The Future of Children, 14*(2), 61–79. Retrieved February 20, 2010 from http://futureofchildren.org/futureofchildren/publications/docs/14_02_04.pdf

Taylor, D. (1997). *Many families, many literacies: An international declaration of principles.* Portsmouth, NH: Heinemann.

Téllez, K., & Waxman, H. C. (Eds.). (2006). *Preparing quality educators for English language learners: Research, policies, and practices.* Mahwah, NJ: Lawrence Erlbaum.

Tenery, M. F. (2005). La visita. In N. González, L. C. Moll, & C. Amanti (Eds.), *Funds of knowledge: Theorizing practices in households, communities, and classrooms* (pp. 119–130). Mahwah, NJ: Lawrence Erlbaum.

Tharp, R. G., Estrada, P. Dalton, S. S., & Yamauchi, L. A. (2000). *Teaching transformed: Achieving excellence, fairness, inclusion, and harmony.* Boulder, CO: Westview Press.

Thomas, M., & Collier, V. (1997). *School effectiveness for language minority students.* Washington, DC: National Clearinghouse for Bilingual Education, George Washington University, Center for the Study of Language and Education.

Thomas, W., & Collier, V. P. (2002) *A national study of school effectiveness for language minority students' long term academic achievement: Final report.* Retrieved February 20, 2010 from http://crede.berkeley.edu/research/llaa/1.1_final.html

Traugh, C. (2000). Whole-school inquiry: Values and practice. In M. Himley & P. Carini (Eds.), *From another angle: Children's strengths and school standards. The Prospect Center's descriptive review of the child* (pp. 182–198). New York: Teachers College Press.

Troike, R. C. (1978). Research evidence for the effectiveness of bilingual education. *NABE Journal, 3*(1), 13–24.

UNESCO. (1960). Convention Against Discrimination in Education. Adopted by General Conference at 11th session. Paris, December 14, 1960. http://portal.unesco.org/en/ev.php-URL_ID=12949tURL-I.=Do_TOPIC&URLSECTION-201.html

U.S. Census Bureau. (1979). *Current population survey 1979.* Washington, DC: U.S. Government Printing Office.

U.S. Census Bureau. (1989). *Current population survey 1989: November supplement.* Washington, DC: U.S. Government Printing Office.

U.S. Census Bureau. (1995). *Current population survey: October supplement.* Washington, DC: U.S. Government Printing Office.

U.S. Census Bureau. (2005). *American Community Survey (ACS), 2000–2004, previously unpublished tabulations (November, 2005).* Washington, DC: U.S. Government Printing Office.

U.S. Census Bureau. (2007). *American Community Survey (ACS), 2007.* Washington, DC: U.S. Government Printing Office.

U.S. Census Bureau. (2008). *American Community Survey (ACS), 2008.* Washington, DC: U.S. Government Printing Office.

U.S. Department of Education, Office of the Secretary. (1991, June 30). *The condition of bilingual education in the nation: A report to Congress and the president.*

Valdés, G. (1996). *Con respeto. Bridging the distances between culturally diverse families and schools. An ethnographic portrait.* New York: Teachers College Press.

Valdés, G. (2000). *Introduction: In Spanish for native speakers. AATSP professional development series handbook for teachers K–16* (Vol. 1, pp. 1–20). New York: Harcourt College.

Valdés, G. (2001). Heritage language students: Profiles and possibilities. In J. Peyton, J. Ranard, & S. McGinnis (Eds.), *Heritage languages in America: Preserving a national resource* (pp. 37–80). McHenry, IL: The Center for Applied Linguistics and Delta Systems.

Valdés, G. (2005). Bilingualism, heritage language learners, and second language acquisition research: Opportunities lost or seized? *Modern Language Journal, 89*(3), 410–416.

Valdés, G., & Figueroa, R. A. (1994). *Bilingualism and testing: A special case of bias.* Westport, CT: Ablex.

Valenzuela, A. (1999). *Subtractive schooling: U.S. Mexican youth and the politics of caring.* Albany: State University of New York Press.

Valenzuela, A. (Ed.). (2005). *Leaving children behind: How "Texas-style" accountability fails Latino youth.* Albany: State University of New York Press.

Van Hook, J., & Fix, M. (2000). A profile of the immigrant student population. In J. Ruiz DeVelasco, M. Fix, & T. Clewell (Eds.), *Overlooked and underserved: Immigrant children in U.S. secondary schools.* Washington, DC: Urban Institute Press.

Van Lier, L. (2000). From input to affordance: Social-interactive learning from an ecological perspective, In J. P. Lantolf (Ed.), *Sociocultural theory and second language learning* (pp. 245–260). Oxford: Oxford University Press.

Varenne, H., & McDermott, R. (1998). *Successful failure: The schools America builds.* Boulder, CO: Westview Press.

Velasco, P., & Swinney, R. (in press). *Integrating content and language goals using balanced literacy structures: Working with low literacy ELLs in the upper elementary grades.* Thousand Oaks, CA: Corwin Press.

Vialpando, J., & Linse, C. (2005). *Educating English language learners: Understanding and using assessment.* Brown University, National Council of La Raza and the Education Alliance.

Villegas, A., & Lucas, T. (2002). *Educating culturally responsive teachers.* Albany: State University of New York Press.

Vygotsky, L. S. (1978). *Mind and society.* Cambridge, MA: Harvard University Press.

Walqui, A. (2006). Scaffolding instruction for English learners. A conceptual framework. *International Journal of Bilingual Education and Bilingualism, 9*(2), 159–180.

Walqui, A., García, O., & Hamburger, L. (2004). Quality teaching for English language learners. In *Classroom observation scoring manual.* San Francisco: WestEd.

Warriner, D. (2009). Continued marginalization: The social cost of exceptionalism for African refugee learners of English. In J. Kleifgen & G. C. Bond (Eds.), *The languages of Africa and the diaspora: Educating for language awareness* (pp. 199–213). Bristol, UK: Multilingual Matters.

Weiss, H., Caspe, M., & Lopez, M. E. (2006). *Family involvement makes a difference: Family involvement in early childhood education.* Cambridge, MA: Harvard Family Research Project. Retrieved February 20, 2010, from http://www.hfrp.org/publications-resources/browse-our-publications/family-involvement-in-early-childhood-education

Weiss, H., & Lopez, M. E. (2009). Redefining family engagement in education. *FINE Newsletter, 1*(3). Cambridge, MA: Harvard Family Research Project. Retrieved February 20, 2010, from http://www.hfrp.org/family-involvement/publications-resources/redefining-family-engagement-in-education

Wenglinsky, H. (2000). *How teaching matters: Bringing the classroom back into discussions of teacher quality.* Princeton, NJ: Educational Testing Service.

Wiley, T. (2005). *Literacy and language diversity in the United States* (2nd ed.). Washington, DC: Center for Applied Linguistics.

Wiley, T. (1996). *Literacy and language diversity in the United States.* Washington, DC: Center for Applied Linguistics.

Wiley, T. G., & Lukes, M. L. (1996). English-only and standard English ideologies in the U.S. *TESOL Quarterly, 30*(3), 511–535.

Wiley, T. G., & Wright, W. (2004). Against the undertow: Language minority education policy and politics in the "Age of Accountability." *Educational Policy, 18*(1), 142–168.

Willig, A. C. (1985). A meta-analysis of selected studies on the effectiveness of bilingual education. *Review of Educational Research, 55*(3), 269–317.

Wong-Fillmore, L., & Snow, C. (2000). *What teachers need to know about language.* Washington, DC: U.S. Department of Education, Office of Educational Research and Improvement.

Wright, W. E. (2006). NCLB: Taking stock, looking forward: A Catch-22. *Language Learners, 64*(3), 22–27.

Yates, J. R., & Ortiz, A. (1998). Issues of culture and diversity affecting educators with disabilities: A change in demography is reshaping America. In R. J. Anderson, C. E. Keller and J. M. Karp, (Eds.), *Enhancing diversity: Educators with disabilities in the education enterprise* (pp. 21–37). Washington, DC: Gallaudet University Press.

Yngve, V. (1996). *From grammar to science: New foundations for general linguistics.* Amsterdam: John Benjamins.

Zehler, A., Fleischman, H., Hopstock, P., Stephenson, T., Pendizick, M., & Sapru, S. (2003). *Descriptive study of services to LEP students and LEP students with disabilities.* Vol. 1. Research Report. [Electronic version]. Retrieved February 20, 2010 from http://onlineresources.wnylc.net/pb/orcdocs/LARC_Resources/LEPTopics/ED/DescriptiveStudyofServicestoLEPStudentsandLEPStudentswithDisabilities.pdf

Zentella, A. C. (1997). *Growing up bilingual*. Maiden, MA: Blackwell.

Zentella, A. C. (2005). Premises, promises, and pitfalls of language socialization research in Latino families and communities. In A. C. Zentella (Ed.), *Building on strength: Language and literacy in Latino families and communities* (pp. 13–30). New York: Teachers College Press.

Index

About the Authors

Ofelia García is professor in the PhD programs in urban education and Hispanic and Luso-Brazilian literatures and languages at the Graduate Center of the City University of New York. She has been professor of bilingual education at Columbia University's Teachers College and codirector of its Center for Multiple Languages and Literacies. She has also been dean of the School of Education at the Brooklyn Campus of Long Island University, professor of education at the City College of New York, and visiting professor at universities in Europe and Latin America. Her research focuses on the education of language minorities, bilingualism and biliteracy, and macrosociolinguistics. Among her recent books are *Bilingual Education in the 21st Century: A Global Perspective* (2009); *Handbook of Language and Ethnic Identity* (2010, with J. A. Fishman); *Negotiating Language Policies in Schools* (2010, with K. Menken); *Imagining Multilingual Schools* (2006, with T. Skutnabb-Kangas and M. Torres-Guzmán); *Bilingual Education: An Introductory Reader* (2007, with C. Baker); and *Language Loyalty, Continuity, and Change* (2006, with R. Peltz and H. Schiffman). She is the associate general editor of *The International Journal of the Sociology of Language*. She has been a Fulbright Scholar and a Spencer Fellow of the U.S. National Academy of Education and is a fellow of the Stellenbosch Institute for Advanced Study (STIAS) in South Africa and a board member of the National Latino Education Research Agenda Project. In 2008 she was the recipient of the NYSABE Gladys Correa Award.

Jo Anne Kleifgen is professor of linguistics and education at Teachers College, Columbia University. She codirects the Center for Multiple Languages and Literacies and is president of the International Linguistic Association. The courses she teaches are in general linguistics, bilingualism, discourse analysis, and new media for language and literacy. Her research has focused on language use in multilingual classrooms and the use of technologies to strengthen bilingualism and biliteracy in Haitian and Latino students and their families. Among her recent scholarly contributions is a forthcoming book titled *Communicative Practices at Work: Multimodality and Learning in a High-Tech Firm*, which describes her multiple-year study of a multilingual workplace in Silicon Valley, and a book edited with George Bond titled *The Languages of Africa and the Diaspora: Educating for Language Awareness* (2009). Her articles have been published in book chapters and in journals such as *Anthropology and Education Quarterly*, *Language in Society*, *Research on Language and Social Interaction*, and *Reading Research Quarterly*. She also serves on editorial boards for a number of scholarly journals. Currently, she is directing a 3-year research project funded by the Institute on Educational Sciences (U.S. Department of Education) on the use of new media to support Latino adolescents' language and literacy development. She serves on a number of editorial boards and has been a visiting scholar at universities in China and the United States.